SEAMANSHIP

The complete illustrated guide for the cruising yachtsman

SEAMANSHIP

The complete illustrated guide for the cruising yachtsman

Peter Kemp

MARTIN DUNITZ

First published in the United Kingdom
by Martin Dunitz Ltd

British Library Cataloguing in Publication Data

Kemp, Peter, 1904–
   Seamanship.
   1. Seamanship   2. Yachts and yachting
   I. Title
   623'.88'223   GV813

   ISBN 0–906348–43–9

Consultant Editor: Tom Cox

Picture Editor: Bill Beavis

Diagrams by Alan Roy

Designed by Rose and Lamb Design Partnership

Typeset in Palatino by Input Typesetting Ltd, London

Printed and bound in Singapore

Contents

CONTENTS

Preface

Seamanship has been defined as 'the art or practice of managing a ship at sea' (Oxford English Dictionary) and 'the art of sailing, manoeuvring, and preserving a ship or boat in all positions and under all reasonable conditions' (Encyclopaedia Britannica). It would be impossible to find fault with either of these general and all-embracing definitions, but there is much more that lies within those bald statements that needs to be known and appreciated before the full art and practice can become evident in its entirety.

Beyond all the actual knowledge and technical skill that is embraced within the art of seamanship, there must lie a personal factor of love and respect for the sea itself. It is not enough to know and practise all the individual skills of seamanship – to tie the right knots, to appreciate individual rigging stresses in freshening winds, to know how to work the tides – unless there is love and respect behind them. Without that personal dedication I hold that no man or woman can be a full and complete seaman. Perhaps an example of what I mean could be Captain MacWhirr, the hero (or villain?) of Conrad's story *Typhoon*, who although fully equipped in all the arts of seamanship, took his ship through the eye of a typhoon because he was too unintelligent and pigheaded to heed the weather signs. Such men do exist in real life. I once sailed with one myself and spent an unnecessarily rough and apprehensive night battling off a lee shore when we might have been lying safe and snug in deeper water offshore. Men like this show a lack of the respect that is always due to the sea.

Good, intelligent seamanship brings its own rewards. There can be few of us who have not at one time or another experienced the quiet delight of a good landfall and a safe haven after a difficult passage. To have read the weather signs correctly, worked out the daily positions with reasonable accuracy, used the tides to best advantage, and perhaps above all to have found sails and rigging accepting every demand made upon them (ever a sign of the good seaman) can bring a sailor as near to his personal heaven as ever he has any right to be. It's a lot more than mere job satisfaction and a lot more than a sudden thought that one has beaten the sea at its own game. There comes in the end the feeling, and sometimes the knowledge, that the sea has accepted your respect and your love and has taken you into the select company of true seamen. It is not, I think, that the sea is necessarily cruel, except perhaps to those who walk unprepared into its immense power or try to challenge its different conditions with inadequate knowledge and expertise.

Seamanship is not an art that cannot be learned. A good manual will take even a complete beginner well along the road to becoming a good seaman. But like every other art or practice, the printed word can never by itself take the place of experience, of the 'feel' of a boat under sail. The two need to go hand in hand. A good seamanship manual can, for example, teach you how to tie a reef knot or a bowline, a clove hitch or a fisherman's bend, but you will not be able to consider yourself fully a seaman until you can tie them by feel in the darkness of night on a pitching foredeck. That part of it comes only from experience and trial; no book alone can teach you how that can be done. What a seamanship manual can do is to provide the basic knowledge of the art, the essential and fundamental groundwork on which expertise can be built as experience leavens and refines the book learning.

This book is designed to provide the groundwork, and perhaps even a smell or two of experience dredged up from a varied career at sea, which has ranged from navigating a submarine in the Mediterranean, racing a 6-metre in British coastal regattas, and spending one summer sailing singlehanded in Norwegian waters. I hope to be forgiven if a few personal anecdotes creep in; they are designed only to make a point of seamanship which I personally have found valuable in the practice of the art. By far the greatest part of the book is directed more

towards the cruising than the racing yachtsman, for racing has these days become a complicated art that demands more of helmsman and crew than the practice of pure seamanship. Moreover, there are probably enough books already written to keep the racing man happy.

Nor have I written this book for the complete beginner; it does not pretend to be an ABC of yachting. I have assumed that a reader has at least the basics of the art; that he knows something about the shape and capability of a boat under sail. There are plenty of seamanship books that explain the meaning of every sea term, or will even show you how to sew your own sails if you want to. I think it would be tedious if I tried to inflict another on the sailing fraternity.

To return to my main preoccupation in writing this book, I pray that no one reads it with a view to 'mastering' the sea. In my sailing philosophy the sea is not to be mastered, and the true art of seamanship lies in respecting its power, understanding its moods and conditions, and using it to the best advantage of the ship or boat being sailed. I read once of some pranksters attempting to sail a floating bedstead across the English Channel. I don't think they made it, and probably rightly so. The sea is not to be fooled, but nor will it fool you if you go adequately prepared.

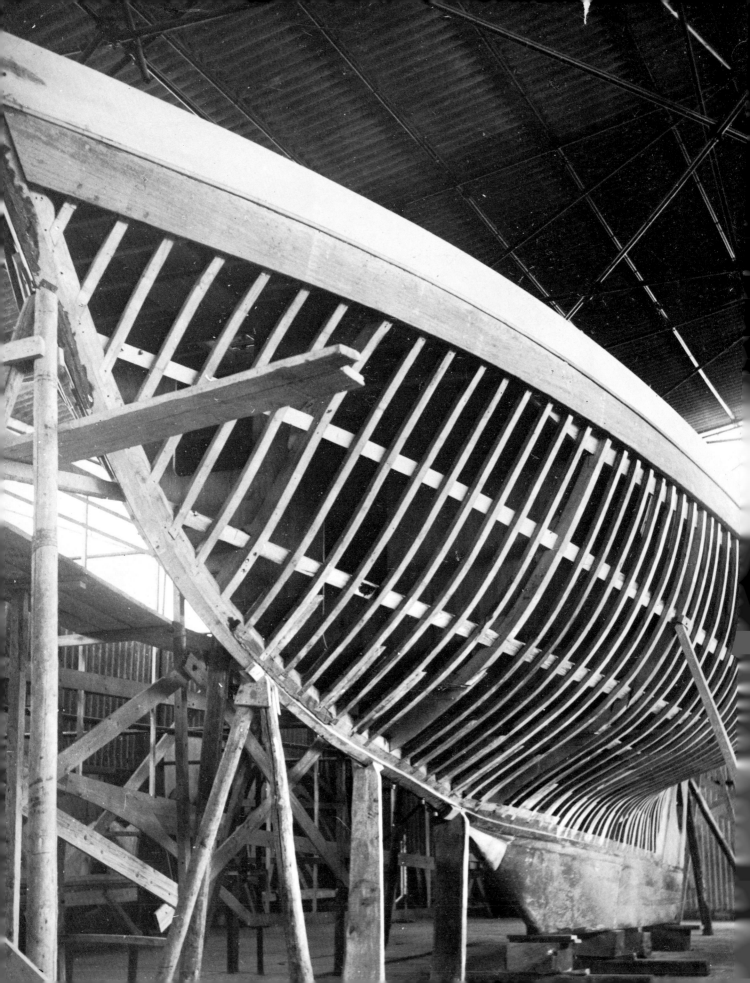

CHAPTER 1

Construction

Any sailor who wants to make the most of his yacht needs, first and foremost, to have a thorough understanding of the innate strength of her construction. It took nearly two thousand years for ship building to develop from the flimsy hull forms of the ancient Egyptians, who built their earliest ships without ribs and deckbeams, into the strong vessels with which Phoenician seamen dominated the ocean trade of a thousand years before Christ. It was the latter who produced the basic hull structure of keel, stem, sternpost, ribs and deckbeams which is still the skeletal form of all ship building, although in a modern, moulded boat some of the principal components are concealed in an integrated whole.

This basic structure (varied only by the introduction of new methods, materials and reinforcing additions) is what gives every ship the strength to stand up to all the strains to which she will be subjected at sea. Your yacht is no exception; she depends just as much for her strength on this time-tried structure as the biggest ship afloat today.

Until surprisingly recently every yacht was built individually either to a lines drawing or to a model made by the builder. It is only within the last thirty years that new materials and methods have made it possible to produce huge numbers of yachts to a single design. The largest proportion of yachts today are built with these new materials, thus allowing the speed of production to keep pace with the ever-expanding popularity of sailing as an absorbing and rewarding sport. There are of course owners who still want something specially built for their own purposes, but their needs can generally be catered for by adapting one of the basic designs.

Design (lines)

The shape of a yacht's hull can be judged in advance from her lines – the designer's plans – to which she is built. The plans show the shape of the hull in various cross- and longitudinal sections, and they need to be studied and compared as a whole in order to appreciate the hull form in all its aspects. They are, of course, essential to an assessment of likely performance if you are having a yacht designed, but if, like the majority of sailors, you are buying a second-hand boat or a standard production design, her lines will be of interest only in helping you to understand how and why she behaves as she does – what she can do, the yacht herself will tell you when you try her out.

The lines normally consist of three separate drawings: the profile or sheer plan, the body plan or sections, and the half-breadth plan.

Profile or sheer plan
It is usual to show the starboard side of the yacht so her bow is towards the right-hand side of the paper. The plan shows the actual profile of the yacht, and further curved lines drawn within this (the bow and buttock lines) show what her shape is at other longitudinal sections. These lines indicate the direction in which the water must flow under the yacht as she moves forward. In order to get the best performance they should be easy and fair with no pronounced change of direction. The straighter they are as they run from amidships aft below the waterline, the faster the yacht will sail since they will give an easier flow to the water.

Body plan or sections
The body plan shows the cross-sections

through the hull seen from the stem and the stern.

Half-breadth plan

The half-breadth plan indicates the shape of the hull at the deck, at the load waterline and at equidistant planes above and below this. Here again, we are shown the direction of the water flow around the hull by the load waterline and the lines below it. Like the bow and buttock lines, they should be fair and easy without any sharp curves or bulges.

Hull construction

The basic skeleton of a boat, which is described later for construction in wood, holds good for building in steel and aluminium alloy. In the case of GRP (glass-reinforced polyester resin), also commonly called fibreglass, the major features are still present and have the same purpose, but the method of construction forms them all into one integrated hull moulding and so dispenses with some components such as ribs, knees and

Profile or sheer plan

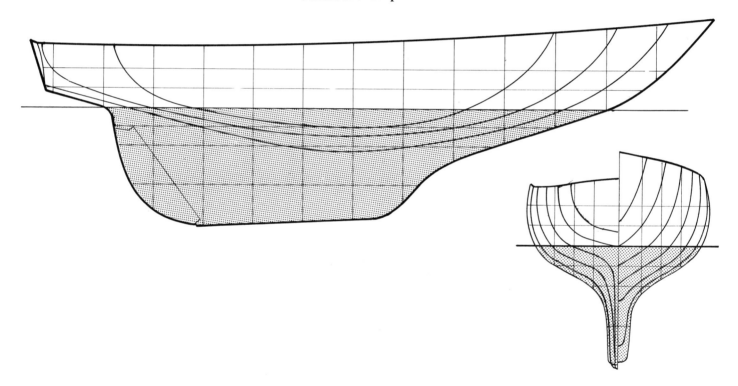

Body plan or sections

Half-breadth plan

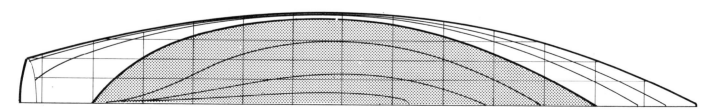

breasthooks which would otherwise be needed to hold the structure together. The construction of a ferrocement boat is fairly similar, but it does have frames or ribs.

Wooden-hulled yachts are not often built in Western countries today, partly because plastic hulls are simpler in construction, may be mass-produced, and need less maintenance, whereas building is far more costly in wood and demands a higher level of craftsmanship. However, I suspect that many experienced yachtsmen would, were the cost not so high, still prefer a well-built wooden hull, and indeed wood is by no means an outdated material. Many yards in the Far East, with their ready access to suitable timber and low labour costs, continue to build and export yachts with the traditional material. The WEST system for sealing wooden boats described on page 21 has also generated renewed interest in wood as a building material.

Since resin for plastics is a petrochemical product it may be that building costs in this material will soon equal those of wood, but meanwhile the GRP vessel remains the typical modern yacht. Since GRP came into general use in the 1950s, techniques have greatly improved and the standard of construction is now high, encouraged in Britain by the recommendations of the Ship and Boat Builders' National Federation (SBBNF) for boats up to 20ft (6m) loa and by Lloyd's rules for vessels above that size. A Lloyd's-ap-

Split mould (right) being pulled away from fibreglass hull.

proved moulder is able to provide the owner with a certificate of standards of construction that is recognized world-wide. Most countries in the West with a boat-building industry now have safety standards for small craft which generally include construction. These are laid down by such authorities as the French Ministry of Transport and in Scandinavia the Det Norske Veritas rules. There are also Italian and EEC regulations. The USA has no special construction safety requirements but some companies use Lloyd's specifications. In Australia the Lloyd's standards are likewise sometimes used, but most of the pleasure-boat industry works to the Standards Association of Australia Small Boat Code of Construction.

GRP laminate
The most popular method of construction with reinforced plastic is by lamination in a

mould. This means that the hull is laid up (laminated) with alternate applications of polyester resin and glass-fibre mat or cloth reinforcement in a mould that exactly matches the pattern of the finished GRP hull. The mould is female and thus its curvature and finish are reproduced on the exterior of the moulded hull.

Lamination starts with the application of a gel coat applied very thinly otherwise it might crack on curing. Apart from being pigmented to give the hull its colour, it has two purposes. It cloaks the glass mat and lay-up resin, which is semi-transparent, and it gives a hard, impervious surface to the moulding. Owners should recognize how important it is to maintain the integrity of the gel coat because exposed ends of glass fibre are hygroscopic, and if damage is not promptly repaired, the lay-up resin will leach out, leaving the mat unsupported and soft.

Laminating a fibreglass boat in two halves. Later the mould will be bolted together and the two parts, plus transom, will be joined.

14

Next, alternating layers of resin and fibre are applied. A moulder may use either mat or cloth or both according to the naval architect's specification. Chopped strand mat (csm) is, as its name suggests, composed of short filaments of glass lying in random directions. To make it easy to handle it is bound together in mats of various weights and thicknesses by a binding agent which is soluble in the lay-up resin. The csm or cloth is laid into the mould and stippled against the surface with stiff brushes. This forces the wet resin up through the mat, which dissolves the binder and enables the glass fibres to 'drape' and conform with the mould shape.

The moulding will go on curing for some time after the initial setting stage but any attachments in the hull, such as stringers and engine bearers, should be put in before this stage as additional applications of resin do not bond well during the curing period.

Alterations or additions to an old hull which has completely cured are best made with epoxy rather than polyester resin in order to get the best bond.

That, briefly, is the moulding procedure for a hull and it applies also to the moulding of other parts of the complete boat structure – deck and coachroof, any moulded internal lay-out and the sub-mouldings which may be fitted in. The hull and deck mouldings are bonded together with wet mat, and reinforcement may also be given by through-bolting the rubbing strake. It is in the integration of deck, coachroof and cockpit into one moulded unit that the method saves the most time, and if the vessel is all GRP, including its interior arrangement, the saving is very great indeed because an internal moulding can incorporate so many things that would otherwise need to be made and fitted separately – the cabin sole, bunk bases, bulkheads

Steel yacht under construction. In this example the plates are rolled and shaped. The rise in oil prices is making steel a more competitive material, while the improvement in paints and coverings means that susceptibility to corrosion is no longer a valid criticism.

and galley space together with landings for subsequent fitments can all be catered for in one moulding. Such liberal use of GRP inside the boat can give a rather sterile effect, however, unless it is adequately trimmed with some homely timber, but it obviously has advantages for a production run of modestly priced yachts.

Spray moulded GRP

This employs a conventional female mould, but instead of the material being laid up by hand, an admixture of chopped glass filaments and resin is sprayed into the mould until the required thickness is obtained and it is then consolidated by rollers as in hand lay-up. Obviously a consistent skin thickness is more difficult to achieve by this method and a skilled operator is required, but one way of removing the risk of unevenness is to alternate layers of spray material and glass cloth. The cloth is sprayed over until it is completely covered and then another cloth is added and the process repeated.

Vacuum press moulded GRP

This process also uses a female mould but otherwise is a complete departure from the customary lay-up of resin and glass reinforcement. The lay-up in the mould is of glass mat or cloth with intervening layers of sisal mat only. This dry lay-up is covered with a polythene sheet which is trapped at the edges of the mould to make it airtight and has a funnel in the centre through which the resin is poured. The funnel is then closed, the air is evacuated from beneath the polythene and the resin flows through the sisal mat to all parts of the moulding.

Atmospheric pressure on the polythene sheet puts a compressive force over the whole mould area which makes the wall very strong in relation to its thickness. Another chief advantage of the process is that it dispenses with the messy business of handling wet resin, brushes, rollers, and so on.

The process described differs somewhat from the standard vacuum press method which uses sheet plastic without reinforcement. The latter, because of the nature of the material and the size of the press required, is normally used only for dinghies and other small craft.

Foam sandwich GRP

Although this process can be used success-fully with a conventional female mould, one of its most advantageous uses is in the building of one-off GRP hulls without the cost of a female mould. Instead, an elementary male mould or framework of wood is built to support the expanded foam sheets which form the core of the sandwich. The framework needs to be accurate to lines but it does not need to be solid or finished.

The PVC foam sheet used is semi-rigid and will bend to the mould shape without sagging; and when the mould has been completely skinned with sheet and faired, glass cloth may be stippled onto it with resin. Once it is set and rigid the mould framework is removed from the inside, making the foam sheet accessible for a similar lay-up of resin and glass on the interior. The result is a sandwich of GRP/foam/GRP and the mechanical strength is determined both by the thickness of the two lay-ups and the thickness of the core – giving it higher strength for weight than a conventional GRP lay-up. Since, however, the outer skin has not had the benefit of a mould, it is necessary to put in a good deal of work on filling and fairing the surface before it is finished with a protective coat of polyurethane paint.

Since the foam core is relatively soft it is necessary to insert compression pieces of wood or harder material in areas of the hull where attachments such as chainplates and winches are to be made, otherwise through-bolting will crush the core material. This is done before the internal GRP lay-up.

It is claimed that sandwich construction of hulls starts to be a cost-saving method with boats over 30ft (9m) loa and that the bigger the boat the better the economy. The greatest advantage of the method is that large hulls can be given the rigidity they need without the use of excessively thick and heavy GRP.

Steel and aluminium alloy

These materials have been used in yacht building for some time but they tend to be expensive. This is due not only to the cost of the metal but also to the advanced machinery and welding equipment which are needed to process it. This is acceptable for building large vessels but for a small yacht, which makes a relatively greater demand for curvature, fairing and finish, it is costly unless you can get a production run of several boats. The Dutch have for many years built small standard yachts in steel, but in Britain, except for super-yachts and power cruisers of the largest kind, metal boats have not been popular.

Current treatment available for steel sheet and plate helps reduce the problem of corrosion. Epoxy paint applied before delivery keeps the metal in good condition and this need only be ground off on the edges to be welded. These are subsequently repainted with epoxy to get an overall protection. Incidentally, metal of $^3/_{16}$in (4.8mm) or less in thickness is known as sheet; above this it becomes plate. Small yachts are generally built of sheet.

Steel can readily be welded by gas or an electric arc, but aluminium is a rather more difficult material to weld, requiring the use of an inert-gas shielded arc. However, despite the many construction difficulties it presents, aluminium alloy, with its high strength for weight and its immunity from corrosion is still a very desirable material for yacht building.

The framing for a metal hull is much the same as that for a wooden boat – keel, stempost, ribs and deckbeams. For steel, the ribs and deckbeams will be rolled sections, given the necessary curves by a bending machine. The hull plating will also be put through bending rolls to get any required curvature. In the case of aluminium the ribs and beams will be extruded sections but otherwise the process is the same.

The aluminium used for boat building is an alloy of magnesium and aluminium, which requires no protection from the elements, so painting is a matter of choice rather than necessity. There are, though, other precautions to be considered. All metals have a different electrical potential and if two different metals are immersed in a conductor, such as salt water, the nobler of the two will erode the other. The yacht builder will take care of this problem by using a suitable barrier paint, or a neoprene gasket to separate different metals, such as steel and aluminium, (or attaching zinc anodes nearby), but the owner would also do well to remember this factor if he makes additions to his boat.

Ferrocement

As the name implies, this is steel-reinforced cement. The first boat to be made from this material was built in France by Jean-Louis Lambot as long ago as the middle of the nineteenth century. But it was nearly a hundred years after his pioneering experiment that the idea was given major impetus by the work of Professor Nervi in Rome. He showed that the elasticity of cement (and of concrete with a high cement content) could be greatly improved by a close-mesh steel reinforcement and that this also produced a much higher resistance to cracking.

In the 1940s Professor Nervi built several vessels with ferrocement, including the yacht *Nenelle*, which is still in use. However, more than a decade elapsed before boat builders showed much interest, although further studies were made in Ireland and in North America. Windboats Marine in Britain took out a patent for 'Seacrete', which enabled them to build vessels that were very strong but were light and thin-shelled. Both professional and amateur builders in many countries have for many years been busy furthering the ferrocement boat, and the process is now universally acceptable for yacht and boat building, although it has not yet gained great popularity in North America.

The basic structure of a ferrocement boat is a set of accurately made frames in steel which are set up with steel pipe and rod longitudinals to make the foundation of a metal armature. The principal connections are welded, but lighter reinforcing rods may be tied with wire. The whole is then covered with several layers of close-mesh wire netting tied at frequent intervals to the framework. The completed armature is covered with cement, which is forced through the mesh and smoothed down on both sides. This part of the work needs to be a continuous operation and requires a degree of professional skill. Major bulkheads and tanks inside the hull can be similarly constructed, or else the interior may be completed by joinery in the usual way. The deck and coachroof may also be either ferrocement or wood.

The completed hull needs to be left for some weeks to dry and cure, after which it can be sanded off, filled and faired to give a smooth, even surface. For normal ocean sailing, the material does not need protection but is painted for the sake of its colour and finish. However, ferrocement hulls have poor impact strength and in areas of coral reefs they need a protective skin of fibreglass.

Ferrocement is a comparatively heavy material and so not ideal for building small craft although it becomes more advantageous with boats of increasing size. Ferrocement vessels

The attraction of ferrocement for the do-it-yourself builder is that materials are cheap, no special skills are needed and construction can take place in the open. Professional help is, however, available – and advisable – especially for plastering, which has to be done in one operation.

Mortar is pushed through the wire armature and vibrated to fill each crevice. The outside will be plastered.

of 40ft (12m) loa and larger bear no greater weight penalty than boats made of other materials. The Australian 73-footer *Helsal* which recently won line honours in the Sydney–Hobart race showed how successfully ferrocement could be used in large, light displacement designs. As it is only for the frames that the work needs any special equipment beyond a welding outfit, the ferrocement yacht has become of particular interest to amateur builders.

Wood

A vessel made of wood is still dear to the hearts of many and its construction can teach us more about the essential structure of all boats and of the names of their component parts than can any of the other building methods so far described.

We start with the main fore and aft structural members – keel, stem and either sternpost or transom. These are always the first to be put in position; and the keel and stem are scarphed together and through-bolted. A stem-to-stern long groove, called a rabbet, is cut along each top corner, port and starboard, of this assembly to lodge the first plank (the garboard strake) against the keel, and to house the forward (hood) ends of higher planking. Incidentally, the keel is the bottom member of the hull proper; any deepening below this, forming a skeg or fairing for the ballast keel, is known as a deadwood.

Moulds, which are rough wooden frames conforming to the shape of the hull sections, are now set up vertically at regular intervals on the keel, and then the first permanent longitudinal members are put on. These are the beam shelves which run from stem to stern. They are recessed into the moulds and conform both to the shape given by these and to the curve of the sheer line (the top edge of the hull). The moulds are also landings to give a perfect fair shape to long strips of wood called ribbands which go from stem to transom and, like the moulds, are only a temporary framework for the final structure.

A longitudinal called a stringer or clamp is now put in at the turn of the bilge. This will tie all of the ribs together and in some boats several stringers are incorporated. The ribs are laminated with resorcenol glue or steamed to make them pliable and bent to fit inside the ribbands so that they extend from the keel up to the sheer line, thus conforming with the drawn sections. The fastening of the

ribs to the keel is reinforced by cross members (floors) of wood or wrought iron or sometimes steel plate which are bolted to the keel. The ballast keel will eventually also be bolted through these floors and through the keel, but this job is left until much later.

Planking up, whether for clinker (overlapping strakes) or carvel (edge to edge strakes) always starts with the garboards (that is, the planks nearest the keel on either side) and it is continued alternately on port and starboard so that the hull is not distorted by the pressure of planks on one side. As the planking progresses, the ribbands are removed, although the moulds are not disassembled and removed until deck beams and bulkheads are installed to replace them. At one time planking was caulked in the seams with cotton and white lead but nowadays a proprietary compound or edge glueing is more often used. With the planking completed, the engine bearers may be put in. These are half-jointed to the floors and if they are of any significant height they are cross-choked for extra stiffness.

The next stage is the laying of the beams: the deckbeams, whose ends are lodged on the beam shelf, the half-beams and the fore and aft beams (carlins). The cabin coaming is screwed to the inside of the carlins and it has a light beam shelf at the top to take the coachroof beams. The deck is laid on the deckbeams starting with the central or king plank and working outwards. Marine plywood makes a stronger deck than laid planks and is also cheaper and less likely to leak. A plywood deck can be finished off by canvassing and deck paint, or by sheathing with glass fibre or teak planking. The coachroof may also be marine plywood.

The deckbeams in way of the mast are often doubled, or 'partnered', and fitted out with supporting chocks to take the side thrust where it goes through the deck, while the heel of the mast is stepped on the keel. A shoal draft centreboard boat may, to be able to clear low bridges, have the mast stepped on deck in a 'tabernacle' with a pillar below deck to take the weight down to the keel. The tabernacle is usually a stout steel base plate with two vertical cheeks that hold the mast upright. A steel pin goes through the cheeks and the heel of the mast so that it is hinged to the deck and may readily be lowered.

That in brief completes the basic structure

of the wooden-hulled boat. She still needs a rudder, rubbing strake, hatches, cockpit arrangement and a host of deck fittings and, not least, furnishing and fitting out below, but none of these (apart perhaps from the bulkheads) are necessary to the basic construction, which gives the boat her strength and her ability to stand up to the seas.

Marine plywood
The production of good-quality marine plywood did for some time prolong the use of wood in building small hard chine or panelled cruisers, but they too have now been largely overtaken by GRP.

Marine plywood (which must conform in Britain with the BS1088, in Australia with the AS2277, and in North America with the equivalent specification) is still used to some extent – particularly for small kit boats that you build at home. Even here, though, the ubiquitous resin plays its part in the tapes for the hull seams and to protect much of the wood. However, the principal use of marine plywood is in fitting out GRP (fibreglass) and other hulls with bulkheads and furniture. You can get wood for this purpose in a variety of wood veneers, such as teak, mahogany, cedar, silver ash, makore, sapele or utile. In more expensive craft the fitting out below deck is usually all solid wood and plywood panelling so as to make the rather clinical GRP less evident. The points where the plywood bulkheads are attached to the GRP

The more common method of building with wood is with marine plywood used in a series of flats or 'chines'. Here the second chine is being glued to its stringer.

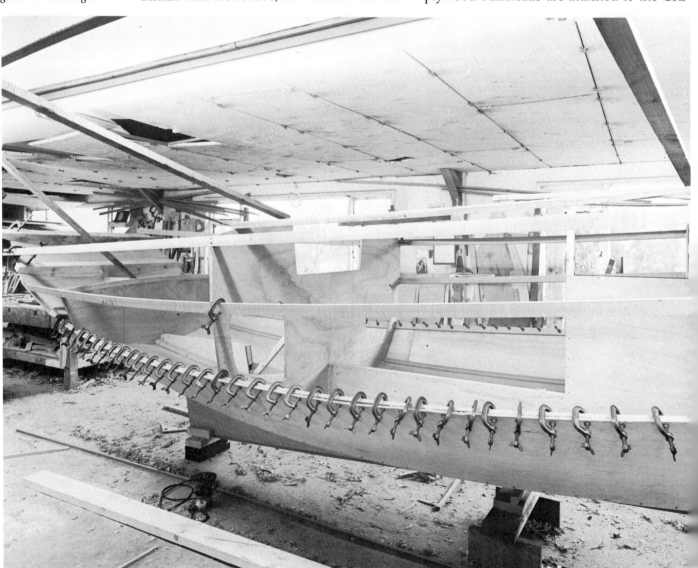

hull are resin-taped and/or matted but these joints should be specially designed to relieve the pressure on the GRP skin.

A GRP boat fitted out in this manner with all its joints concealed achieves the best of both worlds. It has a low-maintenance hull but its interior furnishing may still please the eye and comfort the traditionalist.

The WEST system

Although for some twenty years wood has been increasingly superceded by other boat-building material, within the last half-dozen years it has started to come back into favour as a result of the introduction of the WEST system. The letters stand for Wood Epoxy Saturation Technique, which is a method of sealing wood to prevent the entry of water vapour. Wood normally contains about 10 per cent moisture, and this proportion rises quite quickly during periods of high humidity. Water vapour entering or leaving wood changes the wood's size and shape, and after a while will start to rot it. If, however, an efficient barrier can be erected to stop the water vapour getting in, wood can be made to combine the qualities of a stiff building material with its already valuable properties of tension and compression. It is still relatively cheap and easy to work.

The sealing is done with a special self-levelling resin which is mixed in a five to one ratio with a hardener. The wood is not in fact saturated, as the name of the system implies,

The cold-moulded process is probably the most satisfactory method of building in wood. It is lighter and with a final cover of fibreglass scrim the timber is made waterproof and thus more stable than with the conventional construction. A further advantage is that damage is localized. The boat here under construction was later severely damaged off Tahiti. Yet despite the 12-ft (4-m) gash in her side it was still considered worth while salvaging her and shipping her to New Zealand for repair. A traditionally built wooden boat would have been written off.

The WEST system is an improvement on the cold-moulded process and shows great promise for wood building in the future.

but, rather, encapsulated in the mixture, which is then left to cure for anything from five to nine hours according to the type of hardener used. Every part of a boat that is open to the air needs to be treated, particularly the interior where wet clothes and sails, condensation and poor ventilation are likely to cause a high degree of humidity.

Besides being a sealant, the resin is also a powerful adhesive which is stronger than the wood to which it is applied. This means that all joints become a simple matter of bonding – the perfect fits that the older, highly skilled boat builders had to produce are no longer necessary. Even bulkheads can be fitted with a simple fillet joint with a dense mixture of resin and colloidal silica on one side and a power density mixture of resin and micro-balloon on the other. Since the resin cures quickly, there is no need to clamp the bulkhead during fixing – a few staples are sufficient. The keel and deck fittings can be attached with the same ease and firmness.

The resin also improves the physical properties of wood. The greatest strength of wood is tensile. The resin, however, has greater strength in compression, and it transmits this quality to the wood. The one weak point is that the material can deteriorate as a result of bad weather, but adding aluminium powder to the mix or simply painting and varnishing can help make it more resilient.

This technique is suitable for all methods of wooden boat building, including plywood. It does not necessarily cost more than conventional building in wood as there is no longer any need for exact joints; simplified construction methods reduce the number of man-hours necessary to produce the finished boat.

Durability

Having described the various materials and construction methods available it may be useful to summarize the pros and cons of each, however open to argument such a summary may be! We shall look first at the more obviously degradable material. Both wood and steel demand a fair amount of attention and regular maintenance, but in exchange the first is a kindly and durable material, long proven and readily repaired in any boatyard. Properly looked after it will age with dignity and never lose its appeal. It has one other

great advantage – you get much less condensation in a wooden boat. The value of this will be appreciated by anyone who knows what a bugbear condensation can be.

A steel boat is a tough, go-anywhere vessel, but needs a lot of maintenance if you want it to go on looking good for a long time. Rust is of course the enemy, and although you may shield against it initially with epoxy paint, any knocks or abrasions it suffers will shorten the life of this protection. Unlike wood, but in common with most other boat-building materials, steel has poor insulation qualities and the interior of a steel hull needs to be completely lined above the bilge to make it truly habitable. And here is a point that should not be overlooked. The lining in all boats with condensation problems needs to be extended to lockers and to all stowage spaces below deck if you want a comfortable ship and a damp-free home for your gear.

Among the less demanding materials, aluminium alloy gives high strength for weight, excellent durability and freedom from corrosion. It is not as resistant as steel to knocks and crunches but it is easily strong enough to meet any normal sea-going demands. Aluminium is expensive but does not need much maintenance and you may expect some extra performance from the fact that it is so light.

The GRP boat generally has the advantage of economy, besides which it is easy to maintain, and if built to accepted standards, is durable, though not invulnerable. I have never met anybody who was able to say with any authority what lifespan he would give to a GRP vessel, but we do know that its life can be shortened drastically if you do not quickly repair any damage. Much depends on maintaining the integrity of the outer surface. Det Norske Veritas rules take this a bit further and insist that the bottom of the boat should be protected inside as well as out with gel coat. This might sound like gilding the lily but it reinforces what I have said about the importance of keeping water out of the laminate. Many second-hand prices seem to be based on the theory that GRP boats will last forever but this is not necessarily true. Without reasonable care they will deteriorate like any other boat. In particular, it is known that the ultraviolet spectrum of sunlight causes some eventual breakdown in GRP. Having said that, it is undoubtedly a fact that the advent of GRP hulls and terylene (dacron) sails has made sailing a practical prop-

osition for many people who would not have the time or money to care for boats made in other, more demanding materials.

I suppose the ferrocement boat may still be alien to many people, but the material has proved itself. Although, like steel, it lacks the warmth and appeal of that old charmer wood, much will depend on how comfortably the boat is finished inside. As far as durability is concerned the ferrocement hull scores high. It is not prone to the evil weevils that attack wooden hulls, nor will it rust or go soft if it is damaged. The record to date suggests that it may be the most trouble-free of all hull materials and, of course, it is not difficult to repair.

Performance

We can now turn our attention from the durability of different hull materials to the question of their relative performance. One major factor in this, of course, is weight. For a yacht over 40ft (12.2m) loa, any of the materials can give an acceptable size to weight ratio, but below this length steel and ferrocement need very careful architecture to be comparable with the others. A heavy displacement boat gains in the ability to push her way through the seas but also needs more robust spars and rigging to drive her. Ideas about displacement have changed gradually in favour of making yachts lighter than they used to be – on the theory that they should be designed to go over the water rather than deeply through it.

Another feature of performance related to boat design is that referred to in the old saying: 'Beam never hurt a boat'. The truth of this is now being keenly explored in fast designs. For many years British yachts suffered from the ghost of the old Thames Rating rule which, although it had nothing to do with cruisers, seemed to draw designers towards narrow hulls supporting a fortune in lead. This was in spite of the example being set by North American boats which, with their wider and more practical beams, were succeeding in improving both their sailing ability and their comfort aboard. Slocum's vessel *Spray* had a beam to length ratio that I think even the most adventurous designer has barely approached since, but she handily circumnavigated the globe.

Of course there are some later trends where comfort and sea-going ability do not go so happily hand in hand, and it is difficult in a small cruiser to satisfy both requirements. Small boat profiles are now being made higher than in earlier years in order to get good headroom, but to have the excess windage is far from desirable in adverse weather. I remember an occasion when, having admired the spacious and lofty interior of a friend's new yacht, I later asked him how things had gone on his maiden voyage. He was not jubilant. Not only had the boat heeled excessively (in spite of her good ballast ratio), but her windage caused her to part from her anchor while lying in a reasonably sheltered estuary during a summer blow. Under a bare pole and largely out of control he went up the creek, in two senses. I should add that this was a standard production yacht, not an amateur adventure in design.

Keel and rudder configurations

Perhaps the part of the boat that most typifies her role is the keel. This, in conjunction with the rudder, not only gives the boat ballast but also enables her to get a grip on the water. There are several configurations.

Long keels and fin keels
The long keel has a low aspect ratio in relation to the length of the hull, and the rudder is hung as an extension of the keel. It is a favourite arrangement for a cruiser because it has good directional stability, and assuming the hull is reasonably balanced, it makes less work at the helm. It has, however, a fairly large wetted area and since this induces drag, those looking for high performance have turned to the fin keel with a separately hung rudder. The fin keel is much shorter and deeper in relation to hull length. It gives a good grip on the water and has less wetted area but, as may be expected, is not usually as directionally stable as the long keel, and the helm can therefore become more critical. This is due in part to the shorter length of the keel, but it is also because the rudder, which has become a separate entity, needs to be more carefully designed and positioned since it is no longer dealing with a flow of water conducted to it and straightened out by the keel.

The fin keel and skeg-supported rudder arrangement, or 'fin and skeg' as it is known, gives significant reduction in underwater area and subsequently less drag, but for a cruising man is neither as comfortable nor easy to helm as the long-keel design. The boat in the background would be a good compromise.

A long-keel cruising boat.

Twin or bilge keels

Twin or bilge keels, which have, at least in European water, more or less taken over from the centreboard in shoal-draft boats, first became popular for small marine plywood cruisers and were then taken over by GRP moulders who bond the keels onto the hull without the complexity of fastenings. Twin keels mean that the vessel has less draught and also that she is able to sit upright when she takes the ground. The first recorded yacht to have two keels fitted abreast was the *Iris*, a ketch built in Dublin Bay in 1894. But the advantages of twin keels for shoal-water sailing were not fully recognized until about 1950, when they were introduced by two well-known designers, Maurice Griffiths and Robert Tucker. Twin-keeled boats are still, however, much more common in Europe than in North America or Australia.

There is even a variety of twin-keel arrangements. The boat may have a shallow, ballasted centre keel in association with two plate bilge keels, or, as happens more often now with GRP boats, the centre keel is dispensed with in favour of moulded and ballasted twin keels. The latter arrangement gives less wetted area without sacrificing much of its directional stability. Of course, in the first case the rudder is hung at the end of the centre keel whereas with the twin-keeled boat it is hung separately, either on its own skeg or on the transom.

Most people agree that a fin-keeled boat has every advantage over a twin-keeled one to windward and certainly the performance of twin-keeled vessels does suffer as a result of their pair of shallow but bulky boots. However, given reasonable depth and keel sections of the right thickness, performance can

Performance varies between different bilge keel designs, and criticism of the bad inevitably falls on the good. Later designs have been much improved and compare favourably in performance with deep-keel boats.

still be good. Indeed, the twin-keeled boat can have something in its favour if the angle of the keels to the hull is such that the lee keel is nearly vertical when the boat heels. The fin keel by comparison assumes the same angle as the hull when it heels, so allowing a considerable thwartships flow of water under it and reducing its effectiveness.

Apart from the angle twin keels make with the vertical, there can also be some variation in their thwartships position. The further out they are placed, the greater the depth they achieve on heeling, which is a good thing, but it is possible to take this too far – we still want keels to act as one in ballasting the boat down and not to operate as a pair of counterweights about the centre of buoyancy. I know of one boat which, for reasons of economy in building, had her keels on the waterline beam. She was not, as far as I know,

successful enough to be copied. I expect that the keels proved to be too far out to do their job in improving the self-righting ability of the hull.

Centreboards

Trailable centreboard yachts are becoming increasingly popular among sailors wanting to cruise inshore. A few years ago the trailer-sailer, as it is commonly called, was limited to a few designs under 20ft (6m), now there are a number of bigger and more sophisticated trailer-sailer designs available which can be towed behind a large car or four-wheel-drive vehicle.

Trailer-sailers usually have centreboards that fold up into the hull though some have centreboards that lift vertically while others have a combination of shoal keel and centreboard.

Ballasted centre keel with two plate bilge keels

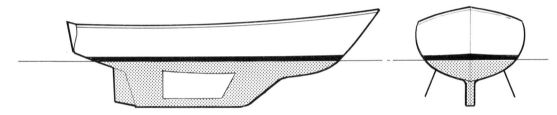

Ballasted bilge keels with no centre keel, and a separate hung rudder

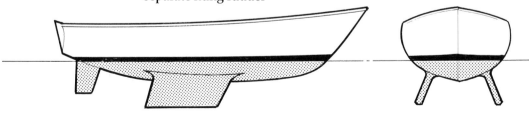

OPPOSITE: The stability and spaceousness of the multihull allow you to move freely around the deck in comparative comfort and safety.

Rudders

The separately hung rudder may be on a full-depth skeg, a part-depth skeg or it may be of the spade type, cantilevered down from the hull. In this last case it will probably be of the semi-balanced variety, which means that a proportion of the rudder's area is forward of its turning centre. Even the narrowest of skegs before the leading edge does a great deal to improve the rudder's ability to retain control of the vessel under all conditions. I believe the balanced spade rudder to be suspect in this respect because, unlike a rudder with a leading edge formed by a keel or skeg, it can sometimes make an angle of attack that is too coarse to maintain a smooth flow of water across it, and, in aeronautical language, it stalls – just as an aircraft wing will do in equivalent conditions. A stalled rudder exerts no control and in adverse conditions when the wind is abaft the beam the boat is liable to broach. A separate, skeg-hung rudder may also be at a disadvantage in this unless the combined area of keel and skeg is sufficiently large. This sort of problem may be acceptable to the racing owner as part of the price he pays for speed, but the lone cruiser in wide waters has different priorities.

Multihulls

So far we have dealt only with the single-hulled boat, but multihulls have recently grown very popular. The catamaran is more common than the trimaran but both are increasing in numbers. They are much faster than monohulls, largely because they have no ballast to drag about and also because they are very stiff and can carry sail well. The twin-hulled catamaran now seen in both racing and cruising roles was developed from Polynesian and Malayan ancestors. The two hulls are bridged by a deck above the water level, which carries the mast, rigging, cockpit and, in a cruiser, part of the cabin accommodation. Their speed is due in part to their very low immersion area, and if they are kept light they will plane readily. The surest way to kill performance is to overload them; this is because weight has a much greater effect on their ability than it does on a monohull.

Multihulls have their own particular handling characteristics. They are spectacularly fast on most points of sailing, but carry little way when going about – which is not, however, a great disadvantage in a cruiser. Their stiffness creates extra strain on hull and rig

Rudder on a full-depth skeg

Rudder on a part-depth skeg

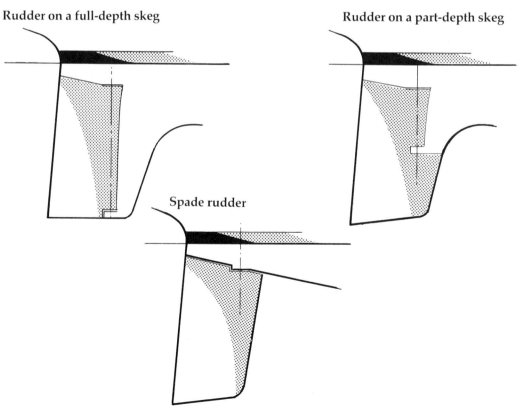

Spade rudder

Multihulls have much to offer: speed, spaciousness, stability and they are at home in shallow water. The buoyant disc at the top of the mast prevents complete capsizing.

The Catamaran

because in heavy weather, when one hull lifts out of the water, there is the danger that, beyond a certain point, the catamaran becomes unstable and may capsize. A special load-released mainsheet arrangement is sometimes used to meet this problem, but this is no mitigation of the danger of a capsize nor the impossibility of such a design's being righted. A large float at the top of the mast will, however, prevent a full capsize.

A trimaran has a central hull with two smaller hulls acting as outriggers, one on either side, but like the catamaran it is completely bridged with an above-water deck. Unlike a catamaran, it will not so readily capsize, but if driven hard in strong winds there

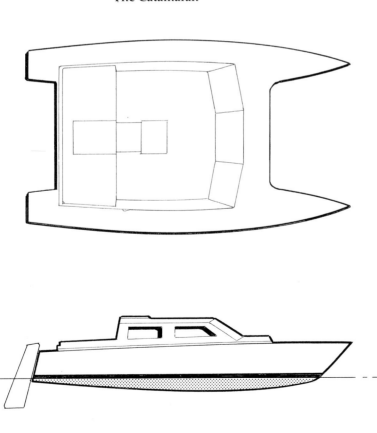

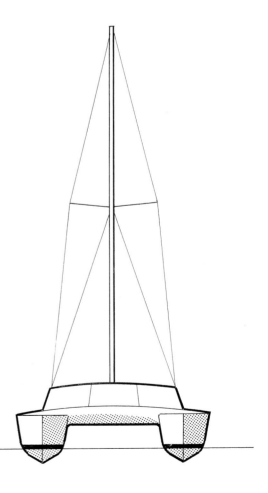

is a tendency for the bows to bury so that the boat pitch-poles, turning stern over bows, and never righting herself. Nonetheless, trimarans have been developed largely for ocean racing and blue-water cruising and have successfully made many long voyages, including circumnavigation.

Apart from greater speed, an attractive feature of multihulls for cruising is the extra accommodation they provide – in a trimaran all three hulls can be used, and in a catamaran the two hulls and a bridge deck. The width that gives so much extra space is a rare blessing for long-distance cruising, and a good many family sailors also appreciate the multihull's space, speed and shoal draught for estuary and coastal sailing.

When out of the water it's easy to see how the trimaran's shallow draught enables it to be moored just about anywhere. It doesn't need deep water and it will sit comfortably on the ground.

The trimaran

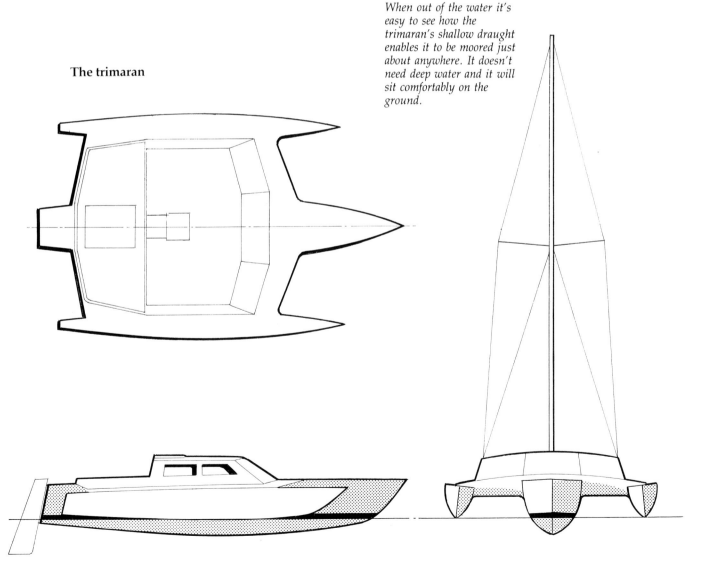

CHAPTER 2

Rigs and rigging

Just as the hull of a yacht can be built to numerous different shapes according to the naval architect's design, so also can her masts and sails be arranged in different combinations to form her rig. The choice of rig for any particular hull is partly one of personal preference, partly one of hull size. It is obvious that the larger the hull the greater the sail area required to drive it through the water. Following on from that – although not always so readily appreciated – the larger the individual sails, the more manpower required on board to handle them.

An approximate figure often quoted is that one man can handle up to 500sq ft (46sq m) of sail by himself. For racing and ocean racing this figure is on the conservative side, both because the period of competitive sailing is limited to the duration of the race and the crew is keyed up to maximum effort, and because the development of modern sail-handling equipment has taken much of the original physical labour out of this task. But for prolonged deep-sea cruising I would myself take that as a maximum figure. It is a very fortunate cruising yacht indeed that does not at some time during a long cruise experience a spell of heavy weather, and those are the occasions – when you have to reef and change sail – that 500sq ft are likely to prove a little over the odds. The actual figure is really immaterial – to a great extent it will depend on the quality and quantity of sail-handling equipment fitted on board. The important thing to remember in this connection is that someone will be needed on the helm when the yacht is at sea, so the crew available for handling sails will be the number on board minus one.

Rigs

Almost all hulls are designed with a particular rig in mind to provide maximum sailing efficiency, and it is usually aerodynamically unwise to try to make changes from an original rig, although I have known a hard-mouthed sloop (one that was heavy on the helm) to be improved by adding a jib on a short bowsprit and turning her into a cutter. This, however, was a remedy for an inherent shortcoming in the original design.

When choosing which boat to buy you have a choice of a number of different rigs, all of which have some advantages and disadvantages. Generally speaking, anyone who is thinking of a yacht in terms of extended cruising is likely to opt for the rig that is easiest to control and handle, even if it is not the fastest possible one (although weather-going ability is of course important to the cruising man). Do not forget that the weather at sea is not always benign and there will inevitably be days of strong winds and high seas when the last thing you will want is a rig designed to give the utmost that the yacht could do in ideal conditions.

In the same context, the owner who uses his boat mainly for day sailing or racing will obviously want the rig that produces the greatest speed even if he does have to work rather harder while he is out. So the choice rests upon the general use for which the yacht is intended.

Gaff rigs and bermudan rigs
Gaff rigs are still a possible choice although much less favoured now that the bermudan rig has proved its convenience and efficiency so universally. The main advantage in a gaff rig for long-distance or world cruising used to be that the shorter mast reduced weight

The gaff rig is the grande dâme of all yacht rigs and nothing comes near to her grace and beauty. But by today's standards her gear is heavy – there is so much of it – and chafe is a constant problem. All this, coupled with the fact that they do not perform so well to windward as a bermudan-rigged yacht, makes it a rig for enthusiasts only.

aloft and added to the boat's stability. It can be seen though that the development of light-weight metal masts has left the older rig little if any advantage on this particular score.

The four-sided mainsail does provide greater driving power than a bermudan sail when sailing off the wind. On the other hand, hoisting the mainsail involves two halyards instead of one, which adds to the windage aloft. Indeed, to get the best out of a gaff rig to windward it is necessary to set a topsail above the main to give a longer leading edge to the sail, and this calls for yet another set of halyards. A further disadvantage is that with a gaff rig it is impossible to have a permanent backstay to the masthead since it would interfere with the swing of the gaff when coming about. Despite a growing num-

ber of gaff sails seen on North American waters, the opinion of most yachtsmen about the relative advantages of these two rigs is reflected in the fact that most new yachts built today around the world are bermudan rigged.

Single-masted rigs (sloops and cutters)
If you are thinking of a boat of more than about 30ft (9m) loa the next consideration may be whether to have a one-masted or two-masted rig. Here again, much will depend upon the intended use of the yacht. Some old 12-metre yachts, originally built purely for racing with a single-masted cutter rig, have (now that their racing days are over) been converted for cruising and given a ketch rig. Of course they have lost some of their high performance by such a conversion, but the two-masted rig effectively reduced the size of the individual sails and made them more manageable for cruising purposes. The radical change of rig does not have the adverse effect on performance that might be expected, because the fine lines of the racing hull make her easily driven. However, the long overhangs at bow and stern are not ideally suited to cruising.

The two types of single-masted rig are the sloop and the cutter. The British and Australian version of a sloop has only two working sails (one mainsail and one headsail), while the cutter has three (one mainsail and two headsails). For aerodynamic reasons (to be explained later) a sloop needs a large headsail which should be either three-quarter or masthead rig and sheeted aft of the mast so that it overlaps the mainsail. If the force of the wind necessitates a smaller headsail which cannot be sheeted so far aft it is much less efficient. This loss is less marked with a cutter because, even when you are using smaller sails in hard winds, the staysail is still sheeted aft of the mast with no gap between its leech and the leading edge or luff of the mainsail.

Both these single-masted rigs carry a considerable advantage over all others in that a permanent backstay can be fitted, as discussed later in this chapter. Moreover, both rigs are simple to use, because the number of sails, and therefore the amount of running rigging to be handled, is less than in any of the two-masted rigs.

Sloop rig with large genoa. The genoa gives excellent light-weather performance but it needs a big and well-trained crew to handle it. A cruising boat must sail within the capability of its crew, which probably means a more modest size sail and certainly one that does not so seriously restrict visibility.

Two-masted rigs (yawls, ketches and schooners)

The two-masted rigs normally found in yachts are yawls, ketches and schooners. The difference between a yawl and a ketch is that in the former the mizzen is stepped aft of the rudder head and in the latter it is stepped forward of it. The main advantage of the yawl and the ketch rigs are that they provide a more flexible mix of sails for differences in weather conditions and at the same time have smaller mainsails, which require less manpower to handle than those on a sloop.

They can also be rigged with a mizzen stay-sail which considerably increases their power when off the wind. A yawl usually sails better to windward than a ketch although a ketch, because of its larger mizzen, has a more adaptable sail plan when the weather starts to get heavy.

The other two-masted rig is the schooner. Occasionally you may see a three-masted schooner but by far the majority have two masts, with the mainmast taller than the foremast. It is not the most efficient of rigs for working to windward, but schooners can be

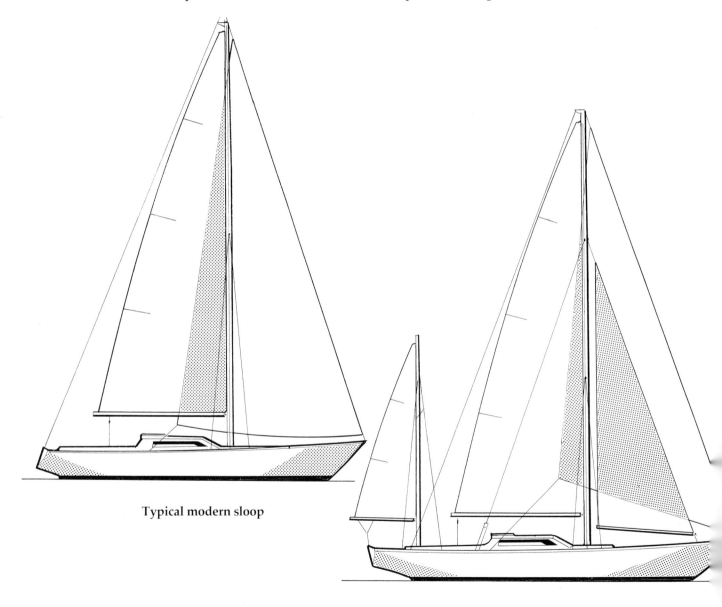

Typical modern sloop

Cutter-rigged yawl

very fast on a reach because of the additional staysails that can be set between the masts. Many people consider the schooner rig particularly lovely – an opinion influenced I expect by the very beautiful Grand Bank fishing schooners that used to work out of Nova Scotia and Gloucester, Massachusetts, and by the growing fleet of converted two- and three-masted coastal merchantmen now providing chartering services on Maine and Caribbean waters.

Ketches and schooners can have their sail area increased by using a wishbone, which is a divided spar pivoted some distance up the mast. Each side of the spar is curved so that the sail, which is held inside it, is allowed to take up its natural parabolic curve when trimmed to the wind. The clew of the triangular sail is set up at the end of the wishbone, leaving a triangular space below it which can be filled with a mizzen staysail in the case of a ketch or a main staysail in the case of a schooner. The wishbone itself is sheeted through a block on the aftermast.

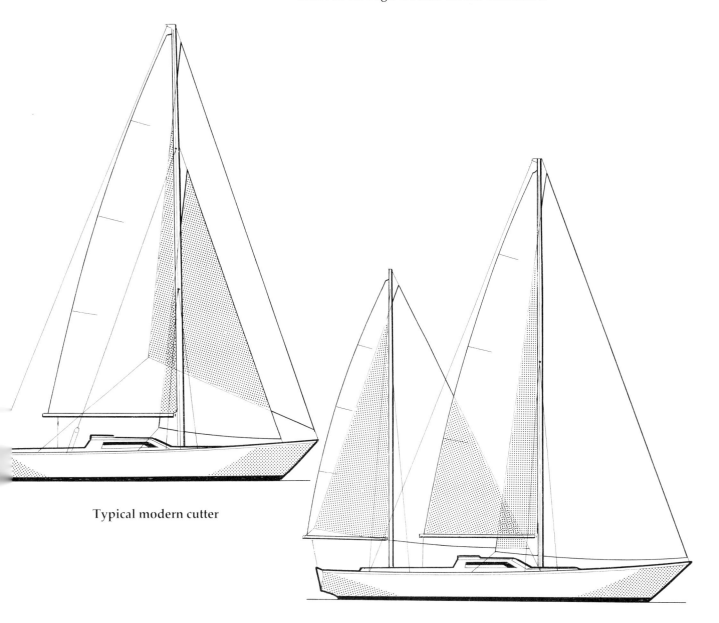

Typical modern cutter

Sloop-rigged ketch, setting mizzen staysail

Choosing a rig

The practical advantages of one rig over another can be discussed only in relation to the size of the yacht. For boats up to 30ft (9.1m) loa the bermudan sloop is ideal, and from 25ft (7.6m) upwards the cutter is also a good choice. For cruiser/racers, sloop and cutter rigs may be suitable for anything up to about 40ft (12.2m) loa, but by this stage you are dealing with very large single sail areas and in general for cruisers over 35ft (10.6m) and up to about 60ft (18.3m) the ketch rig starts to come increasingly into its own. Boats between 30 and 35ft (9–10.6m) have an option of all these rigs and here your choice will probably depend largely on whether you want the boat just for cruising or for cruising and racing.

For a cruiser the ketch is more practical than the yawl because it has a highly versatile sail arrangement and because yachts no longer have counters to provide a base for handling the yawl mizzen. Over 60ft (18.3m) the choice of rigs widens to include every variety of ketch and schooner, as on boats of

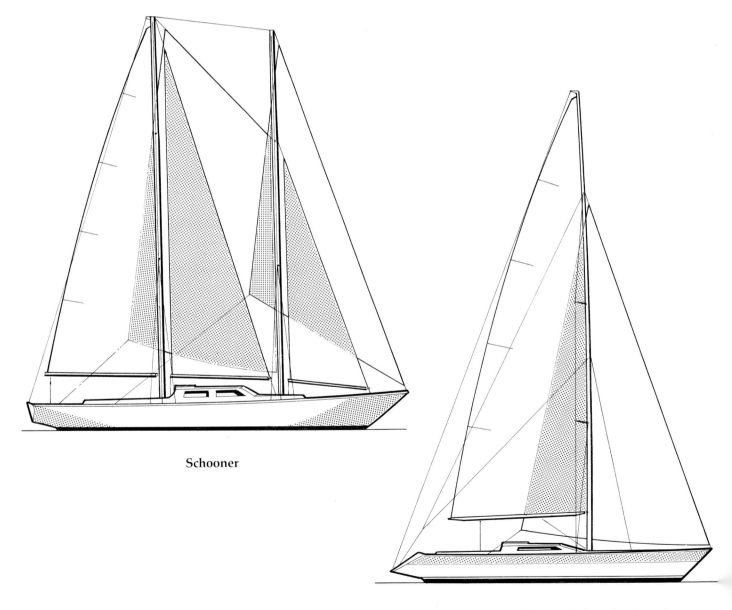

Schooner

Typical modern fractional-rigged racing sloop

The yawl is a two-masted rig which carries a mizzen sail abaft the rudder post. It has all the advantages of a sloop with its large fore-triangle and well-stayed mast, but the mizzen provides better manoeuvring and an advantage off the wind.

The cutter-rigged ketch is not so fast as the sloop but it has advantages for the cruising man. Two headsails give a choice of options. The purpose of the ketch rig is to make the sail area easier to handle by setting it from two masts and bringing down the height. It makes for a comfortable rig and means that even a large boat can be handled by a small crew.

this size it obviously becomes necessary to divide the sail area into a number of small units.

Masthead and fractional rigs both have their adherents. Fractional rigs have the forestay running usually to five-sixths, seven-eighths or as low as three-quarters of the mast height. The masthead rig has up till now been the most popular, and since it enables a yacht to carry very big headsails, it is probably the fastest – but again it depends on how much area you want to handle in one sail, particularly in the case of large sloops. However, the fractional sloop rig is starting to make a comeback in racing yachts, particularly in Australia and New Zealand.

The tendency now – fostered by technicalities in the racing rules – is to have small mainsails and large headsails. A large genoa is employed as the main driving sail, and often almost completely overlaps the foot of the mainsail. In this case the mainsail must be short on the foot, and the boom high on the mast, to lessen backwinding when sailing close-hauled with the genoa sheeted in. Obviously with this rig you sacrifice some of the driving power of a big main when off the wind, but owners who are keen enough to take this sail arrangement to the extreme make up for the problem by getting the maximum use out of their spinnakers for reaching and running.

Standing rigging

So much for rigs – now for the rigging. There are two types of rigging in every sailing vessel – standing rigging and running rigging. The first holds the masts and any other fixed spars such as a bowsprit rigidly in position, the second hoists and lowers the sails and trims them to the wind.

The mast

The mast needs to be supported against the pressure of the wind by stays and shrouds (the standing rigging). In the days of the gaff rig the mast was normally a solid wooden spar, stiff and strong in its own right, and short because the luff of the mainsail that it carried was short. Thus it required only a fairly simple system of stays and shrouds to support it fore and aft and athwartships. But with the bermudan rig, masts need to be much taller because of the great length of the

luff of their mainsails, an essential feature of their efficiency. Solid spars of this length are bound to be heavy and since it is important to save weight aloft, a bermudan-rigged yacht of today will usually have a hollow mast, often made of lightweight aluminium.

A hollow wooden mast is made from selected lengths of spruce which are reversed end for end so that when they are glued up to the required section the wood's natural tendency to warp will cancel itself out. A hollow aluminium alloy mast is an extruded section made by drawing the metal through tube dies that give the required shape – round, oval and so on. Ultralight hollow graphite-fibre masts are making their appearance, but high cost has so far kept them out of widespread use.

OPPOSITE:
A staysail can also be carried from the mizzen mast, which makes a useful addition in off-the-wind light-weather performance.

The advantage of a high-cut headsail is that it gives the helmsman good visibility forward – essential for safe cruising.

A rig with no standing rigging and one which includes a modern adaptation of the wishbone spars. This unstayed rig has proved to be very successful, showing a windward ability that has confounded its critics.

Stays and shrouds

Galvanized wire rope used to be used almost exclusively for the standing rigging and its stainless steel counterpart is still the most popular, but there is some use today of stainless-steel rod rigging. Such rods have many natural advantages, the main ones being their strength in relation to their thickness, the abolition of the terminal thimbles and their longer life in comparison with wire rope. The ends of the steel rods have solid terminal fittings in place of the turnbuckles or rigging screws used with wire standing rigging, but they must have some degree of freedom to move in all directions, otherwise they become liable to metal fatigue. Another drawback is that rod rigging is easily bent and, unlike wire rope, does not spring back into shape. Where this happens it will to some extent unbalance the staying of the mast.

Rod rigging is no doubt excellent for racing yachts and for day and coastal cruisers, but I do not think it is really suitable for yachts that will be engaged in extended cruising except perhaps for the bowsprit if there is one. I feel sure that a large majority of cruising enthusiasts prefer to use wire rope for their standing rigging, partly because any evidence of wear and strain is more immediately visible with wire than with rods, which is very important for the cruising man since a suspect part can then be replaced before any real damage is done.

Wire rope is still made in two kinds, stainless steel and galvanized steel, but you don't see much of the latter about. Although stainless is more expensive than galvanized – up to three times as much – it has a considerably longer life, and unless cost is a vital consideration, it is far better to use it for all the standing rigging, if only because it is trouble-free and you can have complete confidence in it. If wire rope is used for hanking on the luff of a foresail, as in the case of a forestay or foretopmast stay, it must be stainless, as the hanks of the sail, running up and down the stay, will wear off the protective zinc in galvanized steel rope and you will get rusting.

Still, if initial cost is important, it is possible to extend the normal life of galvanized wire rope quite considerably by making sure it is fully protected from contact with seawater. The lower ends of the shrouds are the most vulnerable points since they can be reached easily by spray. The traditional form of protection was by parcelling and serving, but care needs to be taken that the treatment goes high enough up the shrouds, probably 5 or 6ft (1.5–1.8m) at the least, to be quite sure of immunity. Dressing galvanized rigging with boiled linseed oil, well brushed in, also helps to prolong its life. However, it can make a nasty mess of the sails, which are expensive items, so it is best to stick to stainless-steel rigging.

Wire rope size is now given everywhere by its diameter in millimetres or inches. Its make-up is described by two figures, the first indicating the number of strands in the rope, the second the number of wires in each strand: 6 × 19, for example, which is self-explanatory. You can judge the flexibility of the rope by the number of wires in each strand – the larger the number, the more flexible the rope.

Obviously the size of wire rope for standing rigging depends partly on the size of the yacht and her mast and partly on her characteristics under sail – a stiff yacht that stands to the wind requires heavier rigging than does a tender one that heels quickly. A rough and ready rule is that the breaking strain in tons of all the shrouds on one side should be one-third greater than the displacement tonnage of the yacht, but a wise seaman will probably want to exceed this margin to give himself peace of mind when sailing in rough weather. The tensile strength of wire rope will be found in any manual or yachtsman's diary.

Staying the mast

It is generally accepted that a mast needs staying about every 20ft (6m) of its height. The angle the shrouds make with the mast is the important factor in the amount of support provided, and in a normal design a shroud led from the yacht's side to a point on the mast 20ft (6m) above the deck will make an angle of about 15°, which is accepted as satisfactory. If the mast extends to 40ft (12m) above the deck a second set of shrouds is needed to give adequate support, but if these are led straight up from the side of the masthead the angle they make with the mast will be only half that required. The angle has to be increased by fitting spreaders on the mast and leading the second set of shrouds over the ends. In this way the angle between the shroud and mast for the upper bay of the mast is increased to 15° down to the spread-

OPPOSITE: The traditionally well-stayed mast, particularly suitable for offshore cruising. Some modern designers might think it overstayed, but it will certainly give the owner peace of mind.

ers. And of course the process can be repeated if the mast extends above 40ft (12m). At one time spreaders were arranged to bisect the angle made by the shroud as it passed over the end, but it is now usual for them to be horizontal and firmly located in sockets riveted to the mast. The mast cannot bend laterally under pressure from the spreaders because it is held at this point by the lower shrouds.

Fore and aft mast stresses are taken care of by stays. Their angle is always large enough because of the length of the yacht. In the case of a masthead-rigged sloop, the foresail pulls the upper part of the mast forward while the mainsail pulls the lower part aft. The pull of the foresail is corrected by fitting a permanent backstay from the masthead to the stern of the boat and this is balanced by a forestay running from the masthead to the stemhead so that the top of the mast is held in its proper position on the fore and aft line.

Boom vang or kicking strap

A main consideration with a metal mast is to prevent it from bending forward, as this is its weakest stress condition. Forward lower shrouds and the backstay take care of this. The mast can bow aft to some extent without injury and, indeed, with the aid of a kicking strap, boom jack, boom vang or boom downhaul, you can take advantage of the bowing. If the after shrouds are not set up absolutely taut the kicking strap will tend to pull the top of the mast aft. This flattens the mainsail and takes some of the flow out of it which, in hard weather to windward, is an asset. When off the wind with the kicking strap eased, the mainsail regains its fullness and the after lower shrouds take the load.

This practice is of most interest to the racing sailor; cruising yachtsmen often prefer to set everything up taut and sail with a stiff, straight mast. It is however still desirable to keep the boom down when on the wind, and unless the mainsheet will do this for you, a boom vang is the best way to stop the upper part of the mainsail twisting and losing its effectiveness. The vang or kicking strap is a great asset on many points of sailing and experimenting with it can bring rewarding results.

Rigging screws

You can usually expect some slackness to develop in standing rigging so there has to be

The purpose of the kicking strap is to keep the boom down tight and prevent the leach of the mainsail sagging and spilling the wind. This is a mechanical type.

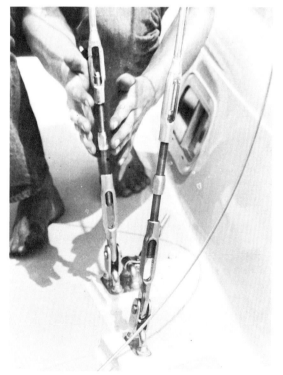

The standing rigging is tightened with rigging screws or turnbuckles, which have locknuts to prevent them from unwinding. Notice also the joining toggle between the end of the turnbuckle and the deck plate. This provides articulation and allows the rigging to twist freely in a rough sea.

a way of taking it up from time to time to restore the proper tension. The normal method is to fit rigging screws (also known as bottlescrews or turnbuckles) to the ends of the rigging where it is secured to the deck. The length can be adjusted by turning the body or barrel of the screw. The upper end takes the thimble spliced into the end of the shroud or stay and the lower end is fixed to the deck. The rigging screws for the shrouds are secured to chainplates, but they must have some latitude for movement otherwise

OPPOSITE: Absence of a kicking strap will cause the mainsail to twist when the mainsheet is eased.

All-wire halyard and mast winch. The advantage is that the halyard remains caged and secure at all times. The disadvantage is that it takes longer to hoist sail because preparatory hand-hauling is impossible. Also if the halyard jams or breaks, you're in trouble.

Hardening the luff of the headsail with a halyard and mast winch. When the boat is on the wind it is important that the luff of each sail is made tight to achieve proper aerodynamic shape.

the screw may be bent. A toggle between the lower eye of the rigging screw and the chainplate overcomes this. The forestay goes to a stemhead fitting, which may also include a bow roller for the anchor cable, and the backstay rigging screw to a fitting bolted to the afterdeck. All of these deck fittings must be very strongly secured to the hull as there is a great strain on them in hard weather.

Running rigging

The running rigging of a sailing vessel hoists and lowers the sails and trims them to the wind. It consists of halyards, topping lift and sheets.

Halyards

In many modern yachts the halyards and topping lift are of thin, flexible steel wire rope, but it is essential to have a fibre rope tail spliced to the end (see technique illustrated on page 60). Wire is difficult to handle and hard on the hands, but its great advantage over fibre rope is that it does not stretch, which is most important in a halyard. Terylene or dacron rope is much easier to handle and simpler to secure and stow on a mast cleat, but it does have some stretch. It is however possible to buy prestretched terylene cordage in which the normal elasticity is considerably reduced, and this is the best rope for halyards if you fight shy of wire.

The main function of a halyard (except for a peak halyard on four-sided sails) is to set up the luff of the sail as taut as it will go. In smaller yachts this is sometimes done by swigging or sweating. This means taking one turn with the halyard round the mast cleat when you have hoisted the sail as high as you can and then pulling the halyard horizontally away from the mast, taking up the slack round the cleat as you release the pull. This is only moderately successful, and at the best of times always results in some slack being left. In larger yachts the simplest, neatest method is to bring the fall of the halyard to a mast winch which will provide all the power needed. Another method for a small yacht is to have the boom gooseneck in a short mast track. The halyard is set up as taut as possible without too much effort and then the boom is brought down with a small tackle between the gooseneck and the foot of the mast.

Hoisting the mainsail

Step 1: Head boat into the wind and free mainsheet. With no wind pressing on sail this can be hoisted by hand. Keep an eye aloft to ensure sail does not foul rigging.

Step 2: To tighten halyard take a few turns around winch or around a cleat and pull hard on the standing part. This will produce a little slack which can be taken in at the winch. Called 'swigging', it is both quick and effective.

Steps 3 and 4: To harden up sail with the winch take at least three turns and use handle.

OPPOSITE: Typical modern sloop with clear deck space, fine entry but wide and generous beam and quarter.

Topping lift

The wire topping lift which is fitted in many yachts to take the weight of the boom when hoisting or lowering sail is shackled to an eye at the end of the boom in the usual way but since it must be slackened off when sailing so that the sail can set properly it is liable to swing about and chafe the sail. Many yachtsmen, and I am one of them, prefer a topping lift of nylon or terylene, which will not damage the sail if it chafes.

Sheets

Main and headsail sheets need some sort of purchase even in the smallest yachts if the sail is to be set easily when the wind blows up. Sheet winches of all sizes are available

for the headsails, but it is important that the fairleads through which the sheets are led to the winches are suitably positioned on either side of the deck. The vital thing is to get the proper flow of the sail when it is sheeted in so that it neither backwinds the mainsail too severely nor cuffs too soon when sailing close-hauled. This positioning of the fairleads in the fore-and-aft line is a trial-and-error job but a first estimate can be made by putting the fairlead at a point where the sheet extended to the deck with the sail drawn aft will make a line at a small angle down from the mitre seam of the sail. The rough rule is that if the leech of the sail shakes before the foot when coming up to the wind, the fairlead is too far aft; if the foot shakes before the leech, the fairlead is too far forward.

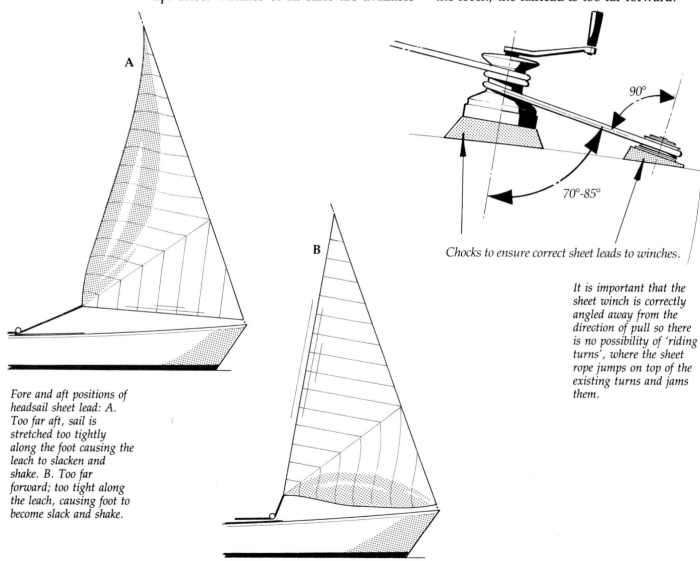

Fore and aft positions of headsail sheet lead: A. Too far aft, sail is stretched too tightly along the foot causing the leech to slacken and shake. B. Too far forward; too tight along the leech, causing foot to become slack and shake.

Chocks to ensure correct sheet leads to winches.

It is important that the sheet winch is correctly angled away from the direction of pull so there is no possibility of 'riding turns', where the sheet rope jumps on top of the existing turns and jams them.

OPPOSITE: *A popular choice: the unstayed Freedom rig.*

Top-action sheet winch used for heaving the headsails tight. It is customary to put three turns around the winch and sometimes a second person is needed to hold the slack that is gained. This is known as 'winch tailing'.

The correct positioning athwartships is equally important and in some ways even more difficult to determine, because the faster a yacht sails, the further inboard the fairlead may be set for efficiency. But this is a counsel of perfection and although many boats have their fairleads in a track for adjustment in the fore-and-aft line, lateral adjustment is generally foregone in favour of an optimum setting. The really important point is that the athwartships position of the fairlead must not cause the leech of the sail to curl in to windward, towards the mainsail. Needless to say, all this careful adjustment is futile unless the luff of the headsail is kept absolutely taut. A sail on a taut stay is more efficient going to windward than a sail on a mast, the reason being that however thin the mast section it still causes some interruption of the air flow over the luff of the sail. Hence the big headsail with the long luff one sees on many cruiser/racers which sometimes have to use a hydraulic backstay tensioner in order to keep the headsail luff taut against the great pressure. This, however, is a tool to be used with caution for it puts an enormous compressive load on the mast and all the stay fittings if used with too much enthusiasm.

In any small or medium-size cruiser the aim should be a power ratio of four to one on the mainsheet. This gives more control for correct trimming and less labour in providing it. It is achieved by using a double block, or two single ones, on the end of the main boom, with a single block and two fairlead blocks on deck. Some mainsheets are rigged using a double block sliding on a horse on the counter in place of the single blocks on deck, but I prefer the other method.

Rope made of terylene or one of its equivalents such as dacron is usually used for sheets as it neither swells nor hardens when wet and does not rot from the action of sea water. Nylon rope has too much elasticity for sheets except possibly on the spinnaker where some stretch can be an advantage. In the days before synthetic fibres, rope made from Egyptian cotton was ideal for sheets but this is now far too expensive to be readily available.

One final point about sheets. They are, of course, in perpetual use while sailing and it is important that you use a rope with a large enough diameter to be comfortable in your hand. Some sailors, worrying I suppose about windage, choose the smallest size of rope that will do the job. But there is very little effect indeed from windage this low down in a yacht, and it is far better to have a comfortable rope to tend, and one on which you can get a good grip, than one that cuts into your hand and may indeed slip through it when the pressure is really on.

Adjustable sheet lead is necessary when different sized headsails are used.

The mainsail is controlled by the main sheet, which is a block and tackle fixed in this case to a slide known as a traveller. It permits better control and improves the shape of the sail.

BELOW LEFT: The slot effect. Volume of air funneling between foresail and mainsail accelerates, which in turn causes a pressure difference on each side of the mainsail. In correcting the difference the mainsail is drawn into the low-pressure area. This action drives the boat along.

BELOW RIGHT: If the slot is too narrow then the air flow is disturbed, the mainsail 'backwinds' and the driving principle collapses.

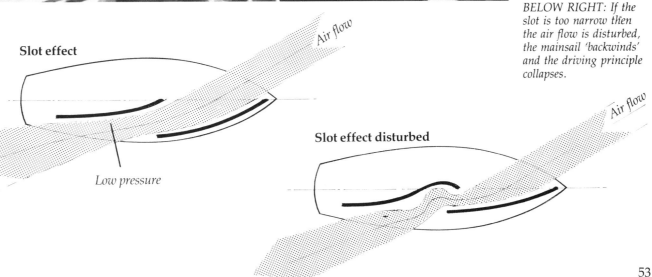

Slot effect

Air flow

Low pressure

Slot effect disturbed

Air flow

CHAPTER 3

Ropes and ropework

Three types of rope construction. Above: the traditional three-stranded rope and still favoured for dock lines and general work. Centre: braided or plaited rope, which is a two-part rope consisting of a central core and an outer covering – very comfortable to handle and used mostly for sheets and halyards. Below: eight-plait rope or Multiplait nylon rope which has a nonkink feature, popularly used for anchor warps and dock lines.

Every yachtsman should be able to make a secure job of a few knots, each suited to the purpose in hand. The important thing to realize when knotting rope is that particular knots have been evolved for particular uses and that they have stood the test of time as the best and simplest for that purpose. Another thing is that you should be able to do more than tie a knot in broad daylight only – you need to be able to do so by feel also. There will be times when a particular knot is needed in a hurry at night and there is no light to tie it by. That is no time to start wondering whether it is right hand over left, or the other way round. However, learning to tie knots without looking is not nearly as difficult as it may sound.

Rope

Before considering in detail the few knots with which you should be familiar, the first thing is to look at the varieties of rope that you might be tying. I imagine that for every fathom of natural fibre rope used in yachts today you will find a hundred fathoms of rope made from synthetic fibres. Synthetics have every advantage over natural rope. They do not absorb water, nor do they swell or stiffen when they are wet – a common failing of all natural fibres. They are not subject to rot, they withstand chafe better, and they retain their strength long after natural rope will have perished and been discarded. Although they are more expensive than natural rope, their long life probably repays their extra cost up to two or three times over.

There is, though, one case when natural fibre cordage seems to have a clear advantage over its synthetic equivalent, and that is for whipping twine. When the synthetic variety is cut into the necessary length the end frays excessively and is difficult to handle. The advice most frequently heard is to burn off the required length with a match or a lighter to seal the fibres and effectively prevent fraying. But how many sailing men have matches or lighters handy when working on deck? And how do you keep the flame burning long enough in a wind? Most people on deck when sailing have – or should have – a knife on a lanyard round their neck, and natural fibre whipping twine does not fray badly when cut.

There is virtually no other function requiring a rope in a yacht for which there is not a suitable man-made fibre. Those in general use are nylon, polyester (terylene or dacron) and polypropylene (ulstron and courlene). Their tensile strength is in the order they have been listed above, but terylene or dacron has less stretch than the others. All of them have a higher tensile strength in braided form than in three-strand rope.

Nylon
Although nylon is the strongest it has great elasticity and so is not suitable for halyards or headsail sheets. Its properties, however, are useful for anchor warps and other purposes where some stretch is an advantage. Three-strand has rather more elasticity than the braided rope.

Polyester (terylene or dacron)
Although it has a slightly lower tensile strength than nylon, polyester rope has good all-round performance and is suitable in either braided or three-strand form for such things as halyards, headsail and mainsail sheets, and indeed for most other purposes aboard.

Polypropylene (ulstron or courlene)
Polypropylene ropes have somewhat less strength and more stretch than terylene or dacron but this can vary with the type and make, and in general they are cheaper than the other synthetic ropes. They have a standard colour according to type (ulstron is green and courlene orange), whereas nylon and terylene are usually white, though terylene rope may now be obtained in a variety of colours to identify its use aboard – a handy idea to stop you grabbing the wrong rope.

Natural fibre
If you want to use a natural rope for halyards and sheets, then white Italian hemp is the best, although manila rope is the classic material and is still occasionally found. Sisal is sometimes used in its place but has a lower breaking strain and swells considerably when wet. The only other natural rope to be considered is coir, also known as grass line, which is made from the fibres of the coconut palm. It is a rough, hairy, dark-brown rope, but it is lighter and more resilient than the other natural ropes and it floats. It does not become as slimy as other natural ropes when

submerged, making it particularly suitable for warps and the buoy ropes on permanent moorings. It is also valuable in really heavy weather, but that will be dealt with in chapter nine.

Small stuff
Cod line or Hambro is the largest of the small cordage needed in a yacht; it is used for lacing sails to spars and for strong lashings. Next in size is marline or spunyarn, according to whether it is dressed with Stockholm tar or not. It is used for splices, seizings and the smaller lashings. Smallest of all is whipping twine, and its name denotes its use on board. All of these can be either natural or synthetic, but in the case of whipping twine I would choose a natural fibre every time, as already mentioned.

Knots

Now for the knots every yachtsman needs to know, and I use the word to include bends and hitches. There are differences, but they all come under the same general heading so far as a yachtsman is concerned. Here I would very briefly like to refer back to the opening paragraph of this chapter to stress the need to learn to tie and untie these knots by feel as well as by eye. It is also worth remembering that tying a knot in any rope always reduces its strength, sometimes by as much as a half.

Figure of eight (stopper)
The first easy knot is the figure of eight or stopper. It is a simple knot which is tied in the end of a rope to prevent it running out through a block or a fairlead. Some people use a simple overhand knot for this purpose, but this can jam so tightly that it becomes very difficult, and on occasions almost impossible, to untie. The figure of eight won't jam, as you can always loosen the top loop by bending back the standing part of the rope.

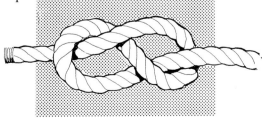

Reef knot
The reef knot is generally useful for other purposes than tying reef points suggested by its name. It is most useful when the ends of a rope have to be secured firmly. Some people use it for joining two ropes temporarily, but such a join loses at least half the strength of the rope, and there are better knots for this purpose, the double sheet bend in particular. It is imperative when tying a reef knot not to tie a granny by getting the second overhand knot the wrong way round. A granny may slip when it takes a strain, a reef knot never will.

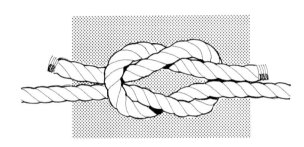

Bowline
The bowline may be single, running, or double. Basically it is used to form a loop in the end of a rope, using a knot that will not slip and it has many everyday uses on board. A running bowline is no more than a bowline tied round the standing part of its own rope so that it forms a noose, being drawn taut as soon as it takes any strain. A double bowline is one tied with the rope doubled on itself so that it forms two loops instead of one. By arranging the amount of rope in each loop, a double bowline can form a temporary bosun's chair if anyone has to be hoisted aloft to clear a jam in the rigging or for any other purpose.

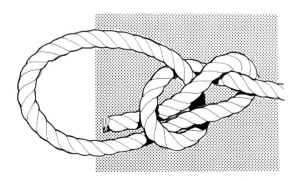

OPPOSITE: Some commonly used ropes.

1. Whipping twine.
2. Nylon.
3. Silver polyester.
4. Polyester.
5. Cod line.
6. Coir.

Round turn and two half-hitches

The round turn and two half-hitches is used when making a rope fast to a post, or to a ring, but it is apt to jam if the pull on it is considerable.

Fisherman's bend

A fisherman's bend is almost the same knot as the one above, except that the first of the two half-hitches is led through the round turn and round the standing part, instead of round the standing part only. It is the traditional knot used for bending a hawser or warp to the ring of an anchor, and when used for this purpose it is wise to seize the end of the warp to its standing part with a short length of marline. This is a worthwhile precaution, since the varying strains on an anchor warp as a yacht swings to the tides can cause the knot to work loose and untie itself if the end is not secured.

Clove hitch

A useful knot for making fast the painter of a dinghy to a post or bollard or where a smaller rope needs to be made fast to the standing part of a larger one. It is a simple knot when making fast to a bollard as it is formed by dropping the two loops of the knot over the bollard and hauling them taut, but here again, if there is much pull on the knot, it will jam itself really tight and be very difficult to untie. In such a case a simple bowline will serve better. It is also the traditional knot with which ratlines are secured to the shrouds, an operation always known as 'rattling down the rigging'.

Sheet bend

A single or double sheet bend is useful for joining two ropes of the same or different sizes. The single sheet bend is used only for a very temporary join, quickly on and off, but the double is a more permanent knot. The point to watch for here is that the first turn is taken round the short end of the rope forming the loop and not round the standing part, as this way round forms the stronger knot.

Rolling hitch

Invaluable for tailing a small line to a rope to hold it taut while it is being made fast or, perhaps, secured to something else. Basically, it is a clove hitch with a second turn. It will not slip when the strain is taken in the same direction as the pull on the rope to which it has been secured.

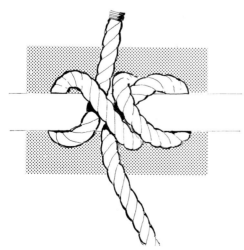

Splicing

So much for knots. The next requirement may be to splice a rope if the need arises.

Eye splice

The eye splice is usually needed to hold a thimble but is also useful for other purposes such as spinnaker guys and mooring ropes. The method for eye splicing is shown in the accompanying diagram sequence.

Splicing rope to wire

Not even the yachtsman who takes pride in doing all his own work on board, including the annual fitting out, is likely to want to splice standing rigging, because the wire is stiff and unyielding. Thank goodness it is no longer necessary. He may, however, if he uses wire halyards, wish to splice a rope tail on the end to make it more comfortable to use (see accompanying photographic sequence overleaf). But in all other cases he will probably resort to the modern alternatives: the Nicopress or Talurit splices.

Nicopress or Talurit splices

All wire ropes used for standing rigging require to have an eye at each end unless they have special terminal fittings. The eye, whether soft or with a thimble, is now made with a Nicopress or Talurit press using swaged sleeves. Most yards have a swaging machine of this kind and, properly used, it makes a neat job with a tight thimble. A soft eye (no thimble) is generally used only on flexible running rigging wire which may have a rope tail and needs to go through a block or perhaps through a hollow mast.

The Talurit system consists of a short sleeve of suitable bore to take both parts of the wire after forming the eye. Under hydraulic pressure the sleeve is compressed around the wire rope and into the gaps, known as contlines, between the strands of the rope. An alloy sleeve is used for galvanized wire and a copper one for stainless steel so as to minimize electrolytic action. Splices made in this way are stronger than tucked eye splices, with a breaking strain as high as 95 per cent of that of the wire rope. Also, incidentally, they use much less rope, which is a worthwhile consideration at today's prices. Old sailors will perhaps say that it is not as pretty as a well-made tucked splice,

Eye-splicing method

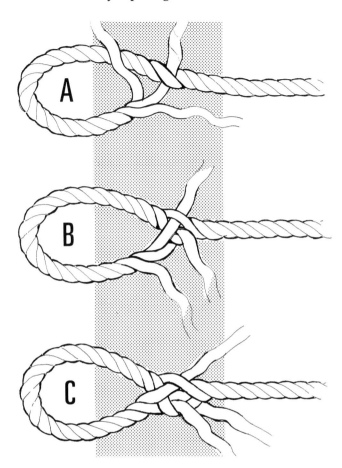

but it is neat and serviceable and a great time-saver.

Swaged terminals

Another method, which dispenses with the splice altogether, is to use a swaged terminal with an integral eye, fork or stud, according to the end fitting you want. The end fitting is bored to fit the wire rope closely. It is threaded on and put into a machine that compresses the metal of the terminal until it flows into the contlines of the wire, in much the same way as the Talurit method. It is as strong as a Talurit splice and neater to the eye but it does limit your choice of terminals to those available from a standard range.

Whipping

Returning to fibre rope, whether natural or synthetic, there is still something the yachts-

Splicing a rope tail to wire running rigging

This technique of splicing braidline to wire is used for putting a rope tail on a wire halyard.

Step 1: Materials needed: 6mm diam 6 × 19 wire, 10mm braidline rope, knife, hollow fid, adhesive tape and a pointed plastic tube available from stockists.

Step 2: Whip the end of the wire with the tape and put a tape mark 16in (40cm) along from this end. This will be the mark to which the wire will be inserted. Lightly whip the end of the rope with tape about 1in (2 or 3cm) from the end and fray the strands. Slide the outer sheath back to expose about 3ft (1m) of the inner core.

Steps 3 and 4: Slide the tube inside the core and then thread the wire up to the tape mark. Remove the tube to leave wire buried inside core. Next tape the core firmly to anchor the wire in a position about 6in (15cm) back from the wire marker. Unlay the strands of the core back to this position, then divide them into three groups.

Step 5: Tape and splice these into the wire.

man needs to know if he wants to keep a tidy ship. Unless the fibres at the end of a rope are held firmly together, the rope will fray – a very unsightly and inefficient state of affairs aboard any yacht. The best way to deal with this is to whip the end of the rope with twine. There are several ways of putting on a whipping, or you can achieve a similarly neat end with plastic sleeve whips, which are shrunk on with low heat.

Common whipping
In this type the end of the twine is held in place along the rope by the turns of the whipping. To make it, lay one end of the twine along the rope and take six or eight turns of the twine over the rope working towards its end against the lay, hauling each turn taut as it is made. Then lay the other end of the twine along the rope in the opposite direction and pass the remaining turns over it, taking the bight of twine over the end of the rope with each turn. When the bight becomes too small to pass over the end of the rope, haul this other end of the twine taut through the turns and cut the ends off.

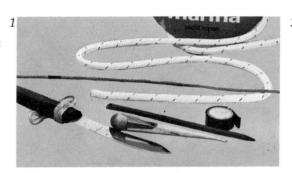

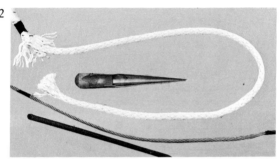

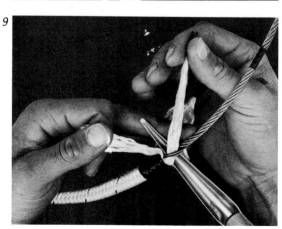

Sailmaker's whipping

The most secure of all. The end of the rope to be whipped is unlaid for about 2in (50mm) and held upright in the left hand with the middle strand furthest away. You make a bight of about 8in (200mm) long with the twine and pass it over the middle strand with both ends towards you. Then, leaving the bight of twine hanging down the back of the rope and the ends in front, lay up the rope with your right hand. Leave the short end of the twine hanging down and pass the whipping turns with the long end, working to- wards the end of the rope against the lay. When you have sufficient turns, take the bight of twine, pass it up outside the whip- ping following the lay of the strand around which it was originally put and pass it over that strand where it comes out at the end of the rope. Haul the short end taut so as to tighten the bight and bring this end up out- side the whipping, again following the lay of the rope. You now have both ends at the top, and the whipping is finished off by securing the ends with a reef knot out of sight in the middle of the rope.

Step 6: Beginning where wire protrudes, pick up two strands and pass the first rope strand under them. Repeat the process with the two adjacent strands, and following this, the next two. This completes the first round of tucks, similar in pattern to a rope splice. Be sure to bed the rope strands down well. Three rounds of tucks are needed to complete the splice.

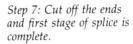

Step 7: Cut off the ends and first stage of splice is complete.

Step 8: Next pull down outer sheath and tape firmly around area of splice. Unlay the strands and tape into three groups.

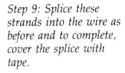

Step 9: Splice these strands into the wire as before and to complete, cover the splice with tape.

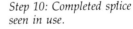

Step 10: Completed splice seen in use.

3

4

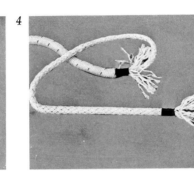

7

8

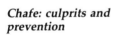

Chafe: culprits and prevention

1. Metal cleats are particularly damaging and can saw through a dock line in a very short while.

2. Plastic hose pipe sleeves can prevent this.

3. Genoa slide track can threaten spring lines.

4. Useful shield again made from hose pipe.

5 and 6. Examples of bad leads.

7, 8 and 9. Boats that winter at a marina or where there is much surge caused by passing vessels need to protect dock line ends.

10. Chafe in sheets caused by shroud plates.

11. Plastic rollers can prevent this.

Blocks, tackles and winches

Blocks

A block is a mechanical means of changing the direction of the lead of a rope, and designed to do so with the minimum of friction and chafe. A fairlead will do so also, of course, but the friction it causes accounts for considerable loss of power and the wear on the rope as it passes under tension backwards and forwards through a fairlead is bound to lead to chafe. Both shells and sheaves of modern blocks are made of laminated plastic, which does not corrode and is also very strong, and their strops and fastenings are of manganese bronze or stainless steel.

Blocks are made in different shapes for different purposes, such as fiddle blocks and sister blocks, but the only variation the yachtsman is likely to need on board is a snatch block.

Tackles

When blocks are used in conjunction they become a tackle, used to multiply the power when lifting or hauling. Disregarding the loss of power through friction, I expect that every yachtsman knows that the power gained is equal to the number of parts of moving rope in the moving block. What some yachtsmen don't always realize is that it depends on the way the tackle is rigged whether you are getting the maximum power available or not. This is what is known as rigging a tackle to advantage or to disadvantage, and the answer is always to rig it with the block that has the most moving parts attached to the object to be moved.

Winches

The wide use of tackles in yachts has today been largely superceded by the use of winches. Basically a winch is a barrel turned by a handle, and the mechanical advantage gained depends on the length of the handle used in relation to the diameter of the barrel. Enough turns of rope are taken round the barrel to prevent it slipping, the barrel is then turned by the handle and is prevented from running back by spring-loaded pawls which engage in teeth at one end of the barrel.

Larger winches, with the power transmitted by the handle to the barrel through gearing are used for windlasses for weighing anchor, and often for hoisting sails and bringing in sheets. Large or small, winches in yachts have a great many advantages. They are easy to operate, simple in construction and provide enough power for all purposes. There are very few cruisers of any size now that do not have sheet winches for the headsails. In many cases these are necessary because of the large headsail area on the modern yacht. They may also be needed in smaller boats when the crew consists of the wife and younger members of the family who may not have the strength to get the jib in smartly without aid before it fills. Their task can be additionally simplified with the self-tailing winch which grips the tail of the sheet while you are winding it in. But in any case, and irrespective of the strength of the crew, the correct setting of the headsail is so critical to performance on the wind that the nicety of adjustment which a winch provides is invaluable even in the smallest yacht.

Leaving aside the geared 'coffee grinder' winches seen on large racing craft, the usual sheet winch, geared or otherwise, may have top or bottom lever operation. The sheet can be brought in more quickly with the top lever type because you can make complete turns with the handle whereas the bottom lever models work with a ratchet movement.

Kicking strap rigged to disadvantage. The hauling part should come off the moving block which is at the top of the picture; this would have given 25 per cent more power. A lead block at the mast base is a better alternative.

CHAPTER 4

Sails

Sailcloth materials

Terylene (or dacron) sails have been a bigger step forward in trouble-free performance for the yachtsman than almost any other development in the sailing scene. Terylene has a little stretch when under load but not enough to affect its efficiency; it is stronger than canvas or cotton; does not absorb water, and therefore does not rot. It is a much smoother cloth than cotton, so reducing friction and giving an easier flow to the wind. It is also less porous so the passage of air through the sail is minimized and the difference in pressure between the windward and leeward sides of the sail is increased. Both of these attributes improve a sail's efficiency. We accept the advantages of terylene and other synthetics now as the norm and tend to be unaware of the trouble we have been saved. In the past sailcloth was mainly woven from cotton or hemp (the word 'canvas' is derived from *kannabis*, the Greek word for hemp), and when made up into sails it required careful handling if the designed shape was not to be permanently distorted. New sails had to be set up without much tension on luff and foot and stretched gently in moderate breezes. They had to be dried before stowing and they were liable to rot.

The other synthetic sailcloth is nylon, which is also stronger than hemp or cotton, but has too much elasticity for working sails. Its main use is for spinnakers and sometimes ghosters, but it will pull out of shape if used for long in a strong wind.

Good sailmaking is today a scientific operation. We have learned so much more about aerodynamics during the last thirty or forty years that the older types of sail, cut rather flat, no longer operate. Modern sails must be cut so that they take up a parabolic curve when filled with wind, and they are given a slight draught, or belly, in the correct place so that they can assume this curve. This is done by varying the amount of overlap at the seams where the individual cloths are joined together, and by giving a curved edge to the luff and foot of the sail. The moral of all this is to employ a first-class sailmaker to make all your sails if you want to get the best out of your boat. Good sails are never cheap, but it is always, without exception, money well spent.

A good sailmaker will know, too, the best thickness of sailcloth (it is measured in terms of weight per area) to use for each sail. This is not judged on the size of the yacht but on the area of each sail, its use on board, and the sort of wind conditions it is likely to encounter. It is difficult to be precise, but a broad general rule with synthetic cloth is to use a rather lighter cloth than for the same sails in natural cloth. Very lightweight terylene is apt to vibrate when the wind blows with any force, especially with smaller sails, and so you should avoid the temptation to use the lightest cloth possible – except for spinnakers and ghosters where lightness is a considerable advantage. Ideally, each sail on board will be made of sailcloth of the right thickness to suit its own criteria.

Chafe

The main danger to sails arises from chafe, but this is only really important for long-distance cruising. A sail that occasionally rubs against a stay during a short sail will not come to very much harm, but where the rubbing is continual it can easily cause damage to the stitching of the seams or to the sailcloth itself. The sail to worry about is the mainsail when the boom lifts on a run or a broad reach. This releases the normal tension in the

Most chafe damage is caused when running before the wind. Notice how the mainsail is pressed against lower mast shroud; a kicking strap could prevent this.

OPPOSITE: Running sails. The yacht has the genoa poled out and mizzen staysail set.

leech of the sail so that it loses its proper shape, and the top half is in danger of rubbing against the rigging. A kicking strap or a boom guy will considerably reduce this particular danger.

The answer to chafe used to be to fit baggywrinkle round those lengths of rigging with which the sail was likely to come into contact. It is easy to make and easy to fit, but unless the lead of the rigging is awkward or wrong (in which case it should be quickly rectified), I do not think that baggywrinkle is really necessary in coastal cruising.

Yachts engaged in deep-water cruising and ocean passages do need some extra protec-

tion, however, because if there is chafe it is likely to be continuous rather than intermittent. I have seen yachts with their standing rigging festooned with baggywrinkle before setting out on a long cruise, but where this occurs I always assume that the skipper is either a confirmed pessimist or has not properly pinpointed the places where chafe is likely to occur.

It is not necessary to use baggywrinkle along the whole length of a wire stay that may endanger the sail. Short lengths at 2ft (0.6m) intervals are quite enough to hold the sail clear. A 3ft (1m) length of baggywrinkle twisted round a stay will give you an opera-

Chafe protection points

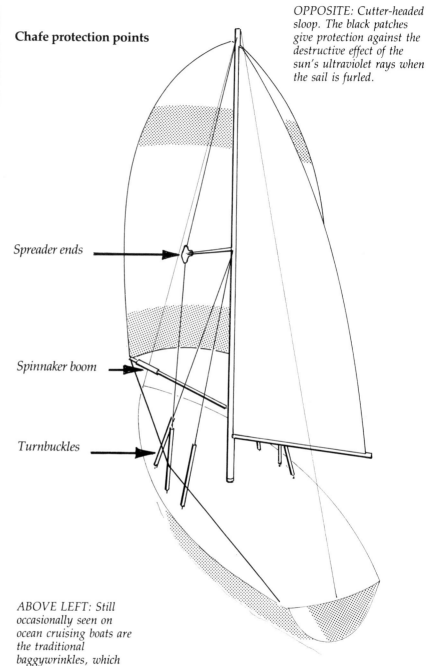

OPPOSITE: Cutter-headed sloop. The black patches give protection against the destructive effect of the sun's ultraviolet rays when the sail is furled.

Spreader ends

Spinnaker boom

Turnbuckles

ional length of about 1ft (0.3m). Where permanent protection is required is usually pretty obvious; any other point where the danger might exist can normally be eliminated by seeing that the rigging is properly set up and that the loose bits – topping lifts are probably the worst offenders – are not allowed to flog about.

As an alternative, many cruiser owners set up their rigging from the beginning with plastic sleeving in the appropriate places and also put plastic spats on the rigging screws to prevent the headsail sheets from snarling up and fraying on the locking wires. These are sensible safeguards.

ABOVE LEFT: Still occasionally seen on ocean cruising boats are the traditional baggywrinkles, which prevent the sail chafing against the shrouds. A close look at this boat reveals plastic piping over the shrouds, which does the same job. Note also the spreader ends have been taped.

Principal chafe prevention points when running: tape or rubber sleeve placed over spreader ends on mast; leather protection pad on spinnaker boom; rollers or 'spats' placed around turnbuckles to protect sheets.

OPPOSITE: On long ocean stretches twin headsails supported by booms are often favoured instead of the mainsail, which would be particularly prone to chafe.

A sure way to destroy sails is to allow them to flap and shake unnecessarily.

Repairs

The second main danger to sails are tears in the cloth. It is always surprising how quickly a small tear will become a large tear if it is not dealt with. One thing is important if you are dealing with a tear in a terylene (dacron) or nylon sail – always use a sailmaker's interlocking stitch when you repair it. When sails were made of cotton or canvas, you could use a simple overhand stitch, known as a round seam, but if you use this on a

Repairing a torn sail

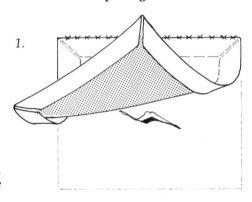

Step 1: Sew a square of similar patching material, with edges folded, outside the damaged area.

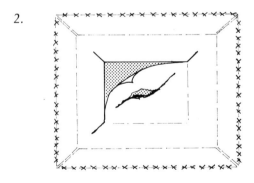

Step 2: Cut away a square around tear.

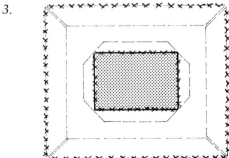

Step 3: Tuck the cut edges under and then sew onto patch.

terylene sail you will get a permanent pucker.

If you are faced with a big repair to a sail that entails patching, there are two points to remember. First, the warp of the patch must run in the same direction as the warp of the sail and, second, the patch should be as near as possible to the same weight of cloth as the sail, and preferably about the same age. In other words, don't patch an old sail with a piece of new sailcloth of a different weight; if you do you may find that in a strong wind the patch may tear the cloth surrounding it. Always turn in the edges of a patch about $^1/_2$–$^3/_4$in (15–20mm) and cut mitres in the corners so that you don't have four thicknesses of cloth at those points. Use a flat seam to sew one side of the patch to the sail, then turn the sail over, cut out the damaged part, make a diagonal cut at each corner so that the edges can be turned under, and sew that edge to the patch, still using a flat seam. Then continue in the same way with the other three edges. Finally, give the seams a good rub to make them lie flat.

For all these jobs you will need to have sail needles, a palm and the appropriate thread, so always make sure that these are on board before you set sail on a long passage. This sounds so obvious that it is hardly worth saying, but it is surprising how many cruising yachts overlook this essential small bit of equipment. Don't use too big a needle just because it is easier to thread; if you do you'll leave a row of tiny holes in the sail which the thread is not thick enough to fill.

Stowage

Terylene (dacron) and nylon sails need little care in comparison with cotton and canvas sails. They can be stowed away when wet without harm, though if they are stowed in a cotton bag they can sometimes be attacked by mildew. So it is always wiser to use terylene bags for this purpose. But if some of the headsails have wire luff ropes, they should be dried before stowing if they are going to remain in their bags for any length of time.

One point to remember with these sails, if you are anchoring or lying to a mooring for any length of time, is that they should not be left exposed to sunlight. Headsails should be stowed in their bags below decks and the mainsail should be protected with a sail cover. There is some controversy as to whether a wet mainsail should be covered or not. If it has been neatly stowed on the boom I doubt whether wetness will do any real harm under a sail cover, though it would probably be wise to dry it at the first opportunity later. Possibly this is no more than a mental throwback to the days of cotton and canvas, when any wetness was a complete bar to the use of a sail cover, but as there is no ventilation under a sail cover and no possibility of the sail drying, I personally tend to sleep a little sounder when I know the sail is dry. Even synthetic sailcloth will collect mould if it is left damp and unattended for a long period.

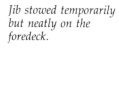

Jib stowed temporarily but neatly on the foredeck.

CHAPTER 5

Below deck

The accommodation in most small yachts is inevitably a compromise between space for comfort in the cabin or saloon and the desire to have all the facilities – galley, heads, chart table and all the rest – within the limited confines available. The boat needs to be of some size before you get adequate elbow room in all the departments, so for most people, choosing which yacht to buy is a matter of deciding priorities. There might be a choice among designs that would all suit your purse and purpose in sailing performance equally well, but that offer different accommodation plans. In that case my top priority would certainly be a comfortable main cabin where you can be dry, warm and rested after a day's sailing when you will sometimes be wet, sometimes cold, but always tired. A cabin where you can relax and really be at ease is a blessing for which I would forego some space in other areas.

Heating

Unless you sail only in a warm climate such as the east coast of Australia or the Caribbean, heating can be of some importance. Even in summer there will be occasions when wet clothes need to be dried out; and in autumn, winter and spring, warmth is essential when cruising. There are small solid-fuel stoves designed for yachts, and these – if you have room for them and the chimney – are most efficient, but it is wise to have an elbow on the chimney to prevent down-draughts. Avoid paraffin (kerosene) space heaters of the usual stove type as they encourage too much condensation. Heaters that blow warm air and use paraffin can however be obtained, and if the intake is outside the cabin that would appear to solve the problem.

All cruisers carry fuel of one sort or another for cooking and for the auxiliary engine, and while I am not suggesting a petrol stove, it is sensible to consider a form of heating that will utilize a fuel you are already carrying. One of the most popular and readily available fuels for the galley is bottled gas, which, being stored as a liquid that vaporizes on release, takes up little space. Besides supplying the cooker, the same fuel will provide accommodation heating using either portable or fixed stoves, which can be of either the flame or the catalytic type. The portable ones are designed so that they are safe if knocked over.

A diesel auxiliary engine uses a fuel that can give a rather more sophisticated method of heating by ducted warm air. There are various systems of this kind which use only a small amount of fuel and from which warm-air ducts can be installed to provide heat in any part of the boat. The duct vents can be opened or closed individually so that you can choose your climate; another advantage is that the area is getting ventilation as well as warmth.

Ventilation

For a comfortable cabin, ventilation is as important as heating. Air can obviously circulate through the forehatch and the cabin doors if the weather is fine, but you should not depend upon this alone as plainly there will be times when they need to be kept shut against rain and spray. There are many types of coachroof and deck ventilators that will take care of the problem but the kind that have a water trap are preferable. As a general specification, have one at either end of the main cabin in the coachroof and one in each

Dorade-type ventilator. The air trunk to the cabin is remote from the cowl and stands several inches high from the deck. This means that any water entering the cowl cannot find its way into the trunk, but drains out of the holes in the bottom. An unbeatable arrangement, but looks better in wood.

Heating and ventilation

Heating and ventilation system using hot air ducted from diesel-run fan heater unit.

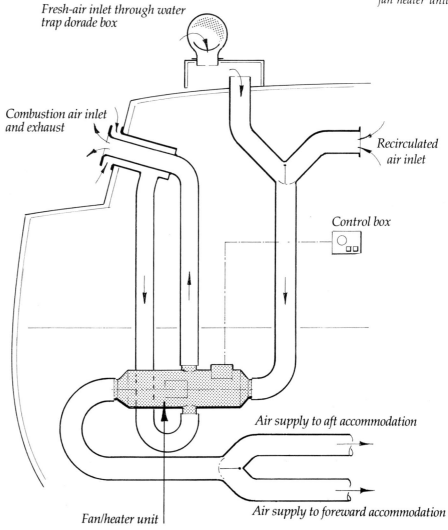

Fresh-air inlet through water trap dorade box

Combustion air inlet and exhaust

Recirculated air inlet

Control box

Air supply to aft accommodation

Fan/heater unit

Air supply to foreward accommodation

of the other separate areas – forecabin, heads, engine and, of course, the galley if it has its own compartment. If it is in the cabin you should arrange for one of the ventilators to be over it. Low-powered, fan extractor vents are an alternative for use in the galley and the heads. A ventilator in the afterdeck in conjunction with a forecabin vent will give a flow of air right through the boat and on moorings all the other vents can be closed. Through-ventilation is the best way of preventing condensation, and in wooden boats particularly it is most important in order to keep them free of rot. Yachts designed to sail in warmer climates such as the South Pacific will usually have several opening ports in the cabin trunk as well as skylight hatches designed to act as ventilators when at sea.

Berths

A full-length sleeping berth is a priority for every member of the crew, and preferably a spare one also. Deep, firm canvas leeboards on each bunk ensure that you can sleep well and avoid that nagging fear of falling. However, the quick-release method of lowering the leeboards should be studied carefully because the ability to get out of your bunk quickly and up on deck in a real emergency could be a lifesaver.

Yacht designers frequently tend to jam in the maximum possible number of berths, and to my mind the boat can be overcrowded if every one is filled. Stowage space is often not over-generous due to this berth hunger and any bunk that is left spare comes in handy. The quarter berth, much in vogue and pushed a long way under the cockpit seats in many small yachts, is a great space-saver but it can be uncomfortable unless there is adequate room over it. For a single berth it needs to be at least as high as it is wide. In the old days a seaman in one of the wooden warships was allowed 14in (0.4m) of lateral space in which to sling his hammock. Few sailors would consider that satisfactory today and fortunately most yacht architects are more generous than this.

Typical accommodation layout of a small cruiser

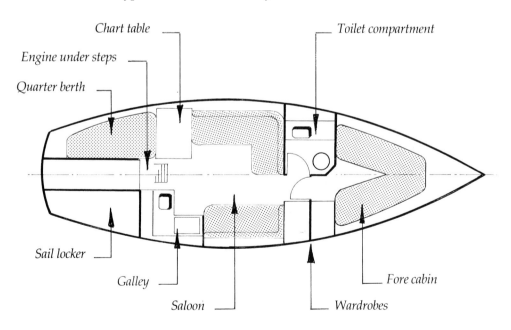

Chart table — Engine under steps — Quarter berth — Sail locker — Galley — Saloon — Toilet compartment — Fore cabin — Wardrobes

There is, I sometimes think, a sort of unwritten law of the sea for cruising yachts which relates the number of crew who can handle the boat comfortably to the degree of comfort available to them. My estimate used to be that a 4-ton yacht, which a crew of two could easily handle, had room enough for two comfortable berths but not for three; a 7-tonner, needing three to handle her, had room for three berths, and so on. If there was a moral in this it was that if you thought you needed an extra hand it was better to go for a bigger boat. To be overcrowded on board is one of the worst discomforts.

This basic moral still applies although the ideal I used to preach needs some adjusting in view of the current cost of yachts, and modern design and methods of construction. Size in relation to weight has changed rapidly in recent years. If you look at old yacht specifications and displacements and compare these with the figures for GRP vessels you find that, size for size loa, the modern boat is considerably lighter. A traditionally built wooden boat of 26ft (8m) loa might displace 5 tons, but the 26ft GRP yacht may weigh less than 3 tons and it will have more room

in it than the earlier example. Modern construction has almost halved the weight, and lines have also changed to give shorter overhangs, more beam and a somewhat higher profile. This, coupled with rather more ingenuity in accommodation plans, gives a great deal of extra space.

I see no reason why a cabin should be Spartan in its fittings. No matter how tough a sailor you like to think you are, it does not mean that you need a 'no nonsense' cabin to prove the point. Pleasant cushion covers, curtains for the scuttles or windows, a book rack and some pictures on the bulkheads as well as the clock and barometer, all these things help to create a welcoming atmosphere much appreciated when you come down from a cold cockpit, and I think most owners will already be on my side in this.

Galley

Next in my list of priorities are cooking facilities. They used to be most difficult to organize satisfactorily in a small yacht but modern design gives much more scope, which is just

Gas bottle stowage. Leaking gas can drain safely over the side via the self-draining cockpit.

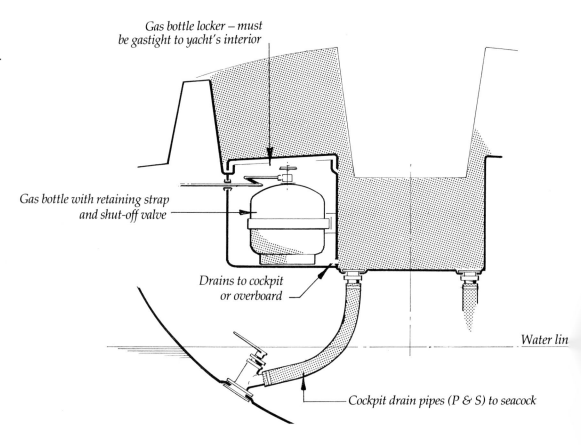

Gas bottle locker – must be gastight to yacht's interior

Gas bottle with retaining strap and shut-off valve

Drains to cockpit or overboard

Water lin

Cockpit drain pipes (P & S) to seacock

as well because owners (and cooks) are much more critical now of their facilities. The old pressure stove and a basin in a corner of the cabin is no longer acceptable, and rightly so. For most yachts the cooking alternatives are either one of the more sophisticated pressure stoves burning vaporized paraffin, which can have more than one burner and an oven if required, or a stove which uses bottled gas. Of the two I rather prefer the gas cooker because it can be lit immediately and most people find it is easier to use. For bigger boats

there are other, more elaborate choices such as anthracite stoves, oil stoves, electric cookers, microwave ovens and so on. I know that in Scandinavia and North America alcohol stoves burning methylated spirits are popular in day cruisers, but although these are clean and handy they are more suitable for short passages and I would not care to ship enough methylated to last for a month or so – it is very volatile and burns rapidly.

One thing to remember about bottled gas is that it is heavier than air and if it leaks

Busy but well-ordered galley. Note secure stowage for mugs and plates, fiddles to prevent pots and pans flying off, the gimballed stove, the central placing of the sink so that it will drain, no matter what tack the boat is on, plus an oil lamp for emergency lighting.

Neat crockery stowage.

pots. So have the cooker in gimbals to ensure it will remain more or less level at all angles of heel, and also fit a fiddle round the top. If the latter is adjustable so that it grips the saucepans then you have done the best you can. If you let the boat heel far enough to thwart these precautions then the cook has every right to complain.

The position of the galley is an important consideration when choosing a boat. A point to bear in mind here is the position of the cook in relation to the movements of the remainder of the crew. From this point of view I prefer not to see the galley fitted in at the after end of the cabin, particularly in small yachts. It is fine for the cook, of course. There's plenty of light and fresh air, and conversation with the rest of the crew in cockpit and cabin is easy. But the drawback is that almost all crew movement below deck when sailing is from the cabin to the cockpit and vice versa, and a cook in the companionway is likely to be sent spinning if there is a sudden call for all hands on deck. One is tempted to think that the answer is to have the galley in the forecastle or sacrifice the forecabin, if there is one, but in a small boat this would not be feasible and even in a larger yacht with the required headroom it would be impractical for a variety of reasons.

That leaves the forward end of the main cabin and, supposing there is sufficient headroom, I think that is probably the best place for it. There is usually enough room there for the cook to work in comfort, and he or she is not cut off from the rest of the crew. Also there is less crew movement at that end of the cabin. Nevertheless, many yachts are designed with the galley at the after end of the cabin, so perhaps the advantages of that position for the cook outweigh the disadvantages of possible obstruction. When it comes round to mealtimes the cook is the most important member of the crew anyway! I do know from experience that there is at least one advantage in having the galley near the cockpit. Cold and hunger quickly take the stuffing out of the crew and in hard weather, when most needed, operations in the galley are necessarily restricted. The situation can often be relieved and cheer given to the crew if you have a rack close to the stove which will hold mugs or beakers, right way up, fairly closely so that they can't jump about. A saucepan of soup (held onto the stove by the cook if necessary with one hand, while he holds

through any connection it will build up in the bilges and stay there. This can have dire results if by chance it is ignited, so watch all connections and test them occasionally. In addition, there are certain basic requirements which, if you observe them, will ensure that gas need offer no more threat in a boat than any other fuel. First, the cylinder should be in a locker above the waterline which is airtight in the bottom and sides except for a drain hole in the bottom which leads directly overside. Second, all the piping should be copper and suitably secured by clips so that it cannot shake about. If you have a gimballed stove it will be necessary to have a short flexible connection and this should be made from the heavy-gauge material specified for the purpose. Finally, make a habit of turning off the gas at the cylinder at all times after use. It should be noted that while cylinder valves are not prone to leakage there is less likelihood of it if the valve is only opened about half a turn. This will generally be adequate and you will not be over-exercising the gland in the valve.

There are other cooking problems, especially in sailing yachts, quite apart from the selection of a stove. When a yacht is going really well on the wind her skipper will certainly look askance if the cook demands less angle of heel because he or she cannot keep the pots on the stove, or even the food in the

A typical yacht interior. Note the folding saloon table which allows access while providing ample room for eating, and the pilot berths behind the saloon seats which maximize sleeping space.

Swordmatting makes the perfect safety strap for the cook to lean against.

onto the ship with the other) can be poured directly into the mugs and these can be passed up one at a time to the crew to warm both their hands and their tummies.

The greatest danger to the cook at sea is being scalded by boiling liquid if it gets thrown off the stove. For this reason it is not a bad idea for the cook to wear waterproof trousers when working in the galley during heavy weather. The worst possible thing to wear is seaboots with the trousers tucked into them – I have heard of a cook getting hot soup into a boot which he then could not remove. The crew even refused the soup!

One of the enemies of the efficient conduct of a vessel at sea is exhaustion, and the most one can do to guard against it is to help support the human frame. If a small boat is rolling and pitching in a lively sea, the crew has to expend a lot of energy just hanging on so that they are not banged and bruised. Clip-

on belts or bars on which cook (and navigator) can take the strain as they work are tremendous energy conservers.

Heads

Modern marine water closets or heads are mostly efficient and reliable. The sea water used for flushing is not only abundant but is also a first-class disinfectant. You may still meet diehards who swear by a bucket but there are not many of them left. There are many compact and easily operated marine heads from which to choose, including hand or electric pump and vacuum types. However, authorities and conservationists are becoming more concerned about the degree of pollution created by an ever-growing number of small boats in rivers, estuaries and inland waters. So if you wish to be able to go anywhere with your boat without problems and you are installing a new WC you might well look to the future and choose an installation that has an integral or separate holding tank. The models that have an integral tank use only a small amount of flushing water in conjunction with a chemical to break down the contents. Others are of the recirculating type. They can be pumped out at sea, or if you are in controlled waters inland, at specially provided pumping-out stations. I do not consider the bucket type, non-flushing, chemical WC suitable for marine use. The US Environmental Protection Agency has come out with strict regulations on this subject. Anyone cruising in North America should find out about the different categories of head (Types I, II and III) and about how the regulations will affect them.

Siting the heads does not call for quite so much consideration as the galley but privacy is obviously desirable and a separate compartment is expected in all but the very smallest cruisers. Full standing headroom is not essential but is an advantage, particularly if there is also a washing facility. Boats that are able to cater for a separate toilet compartment generally manage to find room for a washbasin and sometimes a shower as well. It is often surprising how many amenities designers can incorporate in a minimum of space.

The most usual position for the toilet com-

All the requirements of a functional toilet: privacy, ventilation, and the all-important 'wedgeability'.

partment is between the main and the fore cabin. It is only in old boats that one tends to see the forecastle devoted to the heads. They often have lots of room around them but not much headroom, and it is really wasting space that can be more usefully employed by putting in a couple of berths.

Lighting

Cruisers are generally wired throughout on a circuit powered by the auxiliary engine's battery, and interior lighting is run off this. Charging the battery used to be virtually impossible if you were lying alongside other boats because of the noise it made, but the

An adjustable angled lamp is invaluable for working on charts at night. A well-positioned navigator's den will be adequately illuminated by natural light during the day.

Navigator's den: table should be as large as possible, instruments or repeaters at eye-level, and safe stowage given to books, instruments and pencils.

alternator now fitted to most marine engines, with its high charging rate and ability to deliver current at little more than tick-over speed, means that the battery is kept fully charged with only a short running period at sea. Should you draw on it excessively when at anchor it can be topped up by running the engine at very low speed and with the minimum of noise. Most marinas, of course, have charging facilities either ashore or via a power connection which you can plug into a battery charger on board. Fluorescent light fitments are a good means of saving current, and with tinted tubes, the light need not be at all harsh.

My own preference is also to have sufficient kerosene lamps slung in gimbals to provide lighting throughout the boat. They give a softer light, can't go wrong, and cleaning is not much of a chore. Officially I carry them as a standby; in practice I prefer them and use them almost all the time, but I admit that electricity is a boon for a quick visit below deck at night and many other occasions when you need light promptly without playing around with matches and wicks.

Chart table

Any long passage calls for navigation, so somewhere below deck there must be a place for stowing charts and laying them out. In smaller boats this will have to be the cabin table; larger yachts will have a navigator's table, often alongside the companionway, but preferably with enough room for the navigator to do his work without blocking the gangway. The table should ideally be large enough to take a chart laid flat, which for most of them means 38in × 25in (1m × 0.6m), but there are other sizes and so the drawer in which you keep them should be big enough to take the largest size folded once. In most yachts, this, plus a little extra, will also define the size of the chart table. Admittedly this is not wholly satisfactory, but only in a very big boat is it possible to accommodate a table for the largest charts laid flat. The main thing is to fold the charts rather than be tempted to roll them for storage. It is extremely difficult to work properly on a chart that has been rolled up. Charts of national waterways and coastal areas (available from marine publishers in most coun-

tries) are smaller.

Alongside the table there should be a rack for the secure storage of nautical almanacs, tide tables, a tidal atlas and all the other tools of the navigator's trade. It should be remembered that good navigation requires some concentration so if you have the room it is worth while giving the navigator an area to himself.

Water tanks

So much for the principal facilities in the boat. There are many other fitments needing consideration, and one with priority is fresh-water storage. In the older, wooden boat the tank will be stainless steel or galvanized iron, but a GRP yacht will probably have a tank moulded into the hull either at the fore end or below the cabin sole. In any case, all fixed tanks should have an inspection hole or holes big enough to permit cleaning out periodically and these should have covers that will seal the tank against contamination when they are closed. An alternative for any boat is a heavy-duty rubber tank. These can be obtained in shapes that will conform roughly with their intended position in the hull; in the bow section or below the cabin sole, for example.

For the smallest yachts, large-capacity plastic jerricans are quite suitable. The supply can be piped from these as with any other tank, and since they are portable you don't need to be near a hose for filling and they are easily cleaned. Some water-purifying pills should be kept on board in case you have to fill your tanks from a questionable source.

It is essential to keep a jealous eye on the fresh-water tanks throughout a cruise. I can testify to the misery of being short of fresh water at sea having myself once found that a fresh-water tank had been inadvertently filled with sea water. The filling hose had probably broken while the tank was being topped up so that the end dropped into the sea and salt water was siphoned into the tank as a result. Perhaps no one noticed it; perhaps the chap responsible ashore was too bored or too lazy to do anything about it; but we on board did not discover what had happened until we were well out to sea. It was my own fault, of course, for not checking before we set sail and it was a lesson I have never forgotten.

CHAPTER 6

On deck

Cockpit

Up on deck (if you can call the cockpit part of the deck), the most controversial point is whether or not to have a self-draining cockpit. However, you can only really have a self-draining cockpit in boats with plenty of freeboard. As the outlets of the drainpipes on such a cockpit must be comfortably above sea level it stands to reason that the cockpit floors must also be above sea level. If the cockpit is too shallow, though, it is not only very uncomfortable but can also be highly dangerous in a seaway. In boats with enough freeboard to give you a good, deep cockpit with the floor above sea level, self-draining certainly saves trouble. It can also provide occasional protection to the auxiliary engine, which is usually installed beneath the cockpit floor, by preventing water from swilling around it in rough weather. But if you have not got that amount of freeboard it is better to let water drain into the bilges and pump it out later than to sacrifice the comfort and safety of a deep cockpit.

Topping lifts, crutches and gallows

On most yachts the boom can be supported by the topping lift alone. On some older designs it may be a good idea to provide additional support and in this case the problem is whether to fit a crutch or a gallows. It is a small matter of no great importance but, having sailed with both, my own preference is for gallows. With a gallows you have at least two, and probably three, positions for the main boom, and a wider space for which to aim when lowering the mainsail. A crutch,

however, has an advantage in that it can be unshipped and stowed away when not in use. Another kind of crutch is the folding scissors type, whose feet fit into slots when in use, but I have never found them steady enough to secure the boom if there is a swell or a bit of a blow when anchored.

If you are supporting the boom with the topping lift alone, the mainsheet cleated hard to one side or the other will prevent any vicious swinging.

Dinghy

A bigger problem on the deck is the stowage of the dinghy. They come in many shapes and sizes and in many different materials, from plywood to GRP and, of course, inflatables, which are universally popular and highly practical. The main point about the dinghy is that it should be light in weight and big enough for the job it has to do, which is to run a safe service between ship and shore with room for all the crew. Most important is the possibility of stowing it on deck while at sea, for a dinghy towed astern is a great drag on a sailing yacht, and I suspect that more dinghies are lost through breaking adrift than through any other cause.

If your yacht is large enough, there is, I am sure, no better place to stow a dinghy on deck than amidships abaft the mast. This is the space least used while sailing, except perhaps when rolling down a reef, and although it might obstruct a skylight, that is a small penalty. The only other deck stowage space is forward of the mast, where it will be a nuisance when changing headsails or when the anchor has to be worked. And unless it is a pretty sizable yacht, it will also probably

Lowering a dinghy

Using main sheet and boom to lower dinghy. If dinghy is heavy then back up topping lift with main halyard. Keep boom as high as possible to lessen strain on gear.

Step 1: Arrange the lifting strops.

Step 2: Manoeuvre dinghy into lifting position.

Step 3: With guys rigged to swing boom into correct position, lead lifting rope to winch and hoist dinghy.

Step 4: Swing dinghy outboard. . . .

Step 5: Then lower into water.

block off the forehatch.

It goes without saying that any dinghy carried on deck should be stowed bottom up, otherwise it will catch whatever rain or spray comes aboard. On short passages it is a temptation sometimes to stow it right side up and use it as a convenient hold-all for spare warps, fenders and other gear, but it is something to be resisted if possible. It is not really hard work to capsize even a rigid dinghy once it has been hoisted on deck, and it always pays to do it.

If the dinghy is light, it can be manhandled bows first over the side. If it is too heavy for this, one of the masthead halyards will hoist it out of the water and one of the crew can bear it out away from the side until it has been hoisted high enough to be swung in over the rail.

It is possible to buy dinghies made of wood and canvas which fold flat when on deck, but these are not very stable or suited to hard use. If you are pushed for space the inflatable will serve better. I have never found them as easy to handle under oars as the solid type but that is a small price to pay for the easy solution of the stowage problem.

Reefing gear

Another area of controversy is over the best way of tying or rolling down a reef. If you use the traditional way of tying down a reef with reef points, the method with a heavy boom is to ease the halyard and lower the boom until it is held up by the topping lift or resting in the leeward space in the gallows. Then haul down the first reef cringle on the luff of the sail to the boom and secure it there with a snap shackle or a lashing. The corresponding cringle on the leech is then hauled down and secured as far aft on the boom as you can manage. The only way of doing this efficiently is with a pendant from the reef cringle and a reef tackle rigged along the under side of the boom. The pendant is rove through a bee-block on the side of the boom and then brought to the hook of the tackle. The foot of the sail is then bunched up and secured with the reef points, passing them between the sail and the boom, and not round the boom itself. Some people prefer a lacing, using a row of eyelet holes instead of reef points. A lacing takes longer to reeve than reef points to tie, but as the pressure

The smaller the sail area, the more efficient it has to be!

comes on the sail it does distribute the load more evenly along the whole length of the foot. Finally, having tied or laced the reef down, the halyard is set up and if the topping lift has been used to take the weight of the boom it is eased off.

Roller reefing is quick and simple, and nowadays most cruising yachts are equipped for it. Roller reefing is operated by worm gearing at the gooseneck. The important thing is to wind in the reef against the pull of the halyard so that the luff of the sail is kept taut. Sails with a big roach sometimes cause the boom to droop at the after end when roller-reefed and some owners overcome this by putting battens on the boom at the sheet end so that it has a larger effective diameter when reefed.

It is becoming quite common to reef the jib also in this way by furling it around the headstay. The arrangement is often designed to shorten sail as well as simply to furl it away. A track that will take the luff of the biggest headsail has its own halyard of thin, flexible wire rope, the tail of which goes down to the tack so that the sail may be set up taut. The track has steel fittings at either end – a swivel at the head and a drum with a furling line round it at the tack – and by hauling on the furling line and easing the sheets, the luff can be made to revolve and wind the sail up. It has obvious advantages for coastal cruising and could prove a real boon if you are entering or leaving a crowded anchorage and need to down the jib quickly.

Slab or jiffy reefing

The old slab-reefing method has made a comeback in a new guise popularly known as jiffy reefing. This presents a much improved shape over the roller method, and the use of reefing pendants left permanently rigged means that a reef can be put in very quickly and sometimes without leaving the safety of the cockpit.

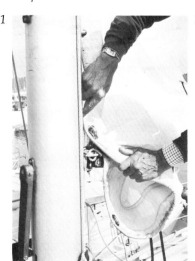

Step 1: Ease halyard and pull down luff of sail until the fixed hook on the gooseneck locates reefing cringle.

Step 2: Pull down the leach of the sail with reefing pendant.

Step 3: In this boat the reefing pendant is permanently rigged with the option of a small or large reef.

Step 4: Sail is now reefed and the boat could be sailed with the excess lying in a bag – frequently the practice when racing.

Step 5: However, it is more seamanlike, and customary in cruising boats, to secure the excess with a line laced through the reefing cringles.

Roller reefing

Step 1: Remove kicking strap.

Step 2: Put on topping lift.

Step 3: Take weight of boom on topping lift.

Step 4: Commence rolling while halyard is eased.

Step 5: Carefully remove sail slides from sail track.

Step 6: Pull leach aft to prevent creases forming as sail is rolled.

Step 7: Completed reef.

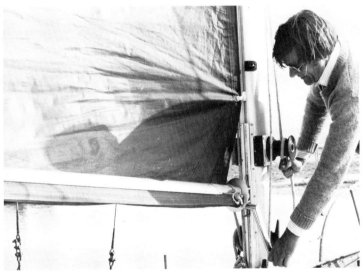

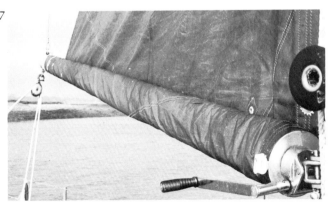

*A better idea is to have a
furling headsail which
can roll up the sail in an
instant.*

*Changing down to a
smaller headsail can be a
hazardous business
especially with a small or
family crew.*

Anchors

Finally, the ground tackle. It is not enough
to think of a yacht lying in a sheltered anchorage and just to equip her with an anchor
and chain sufficient to hold her in those calm
circumstances. You ought to think of your
yacht having to ride out a gale on her anchors
and fit her out accordingly, even if it does
mean a bit of extra weight forward. It is
always a mistake to try to save weight by
using an anchor and cable that may let you
down in an emergency. Furthermore, an anchor must have enough weight on its own
account to get through any bottom obstruction and reach the ground below so that it
can bury its flukes. A light anchor can easily
be held up by heavy weed – unable to dig
itself in, it will not hold a yacht. Like dinghies, anchors come in numerous shapes and
sizes, and their selection is largely a matter
of what will hold best on the bottoms over
which you will be cruising. Whichever kind
you choose you will have to compromise a
bit, either in its ease of stowage aboard or in
its holding capacity.

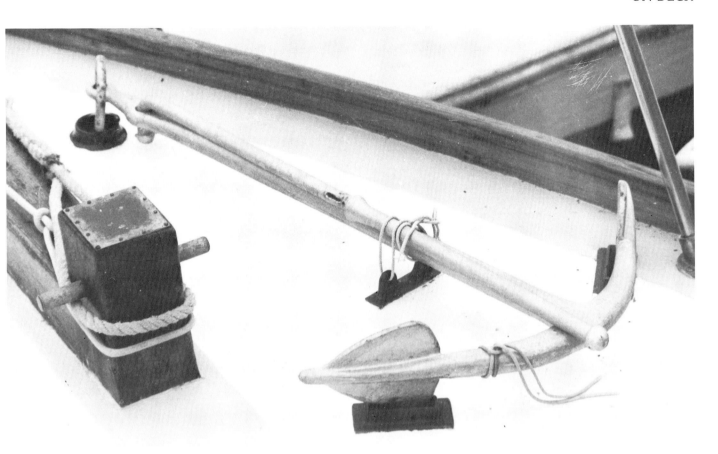

Fisherman's anchor

Up to about fifty years ago, the only anchors used in yachts were either of the fisherman type, which had a stock at right angles to the arms, or of the stockless type, with tripping palms to force the flukes into the ground. I never found either of these unduly difficult to stow on deck. The stockless type lies flat automatically (though the deck may need some protection where the tripping palms lie), and the fisherman's anchor will also do so if you have one with a sliding stock that can be drawn through a hole in the shank and laid parallel alongside it. But neither of these are particularly good holders of the ground compared with more modern varieties, which means that weight for weight you will need heavier anchors if these types are your choice. And you also run the risk of getting a foul anchor, with the cable round a fluke in the stockless anchor and round the stock or the unburied fluke in the fisherman's anchor. Once, having anchored with a fisherman's anchor in reasonably good ground, I could not understand why I was drifting out on the tide until I discovered that the

Fisherman's anchor fold-away type. This old-style anchor is still favoured in areas where rocks or seaweed abound.

Fisherman's anchor ready for use.

93

The CQR anchor stows easily and is good in mud or sand.

The Danforth is a lightweight anchor and a good alternative to the CQR.

stock of the anchor had hooked up on the bobstay and had never even reached below the keel. This can happen, and more easily than might be supposed. However, even if you avoid this stupidity, any anchor fouled by a cable round its fluke will never hold the ground.

CQR and Mesh (Danforth) anchors

It is better to go for one of the modern designs which cannot be fouled by their cables. The two types most commonly used are the CQR Plough and the Mesh, also known as the Danforth. The CQR has a single fluke in the form of two ploughshares back to back which are free to pivot at the bottom of the shank. Being unstable in any other position, whichever way up it lands on the bottom it turns onto its side as soon as a horizontal pull from the cable begins, and the fluke automatically begins to dig in. This digging-in turns the anchor over until it lies level, and eventually it will bury itself. The Mesh (Danforth) anchor is rather like the old stockless type with oversize flukes close together, except that it has a stock across the crown of the anchor instead of at the top of the shank as on the fisherman's anchor. On reaching the ground the stock turns the anchor so that it lies flat, and extensions at the base of the flukes act as tripping palms and force the flukes to dig in.

Both these anchors give an excellent grip of the ground and have proved to have more holding power, weight for weight, than any other type of anchor. The CQR is marginally better than the Mesh in this respect on some ground, but it is a difficult anchor to stow on deck, while the Mesh lies flat and has good penetration on a variety of ground.

No cruising yacht should go to sea without two anchors – a main anchor, or bower, and a smaller one known as a kedge. Large yachts usually carry two bowers, each on its own cable, but it is only in extreme circumstances that a single bower and a kedge are not enough. While I never believe in putting to sea without preparing to meet whatever circumstances are likely to arise, I don't think it is necessary to be permanently armed to the teeth to meet every possible remote occurrence. Much of the delight in cruising is to be found in overcoming the exceptional challenges of the sea by using only the normal tools of the trade.

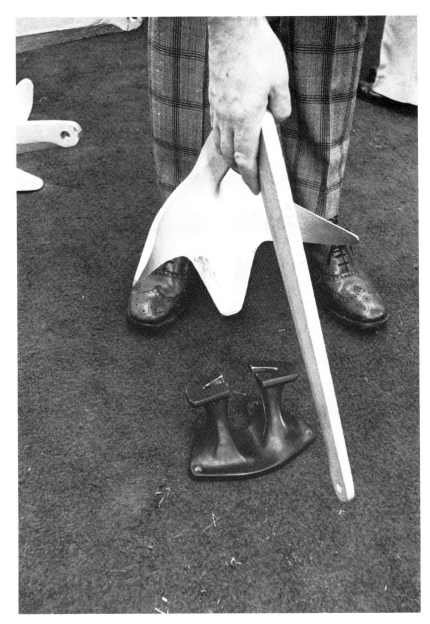

The Bruce anchor has good holding power. It's the most modern of the group, having originally been developed for securing oil rigs.

Black ball hoisted on forestay signals boat is at anchor.

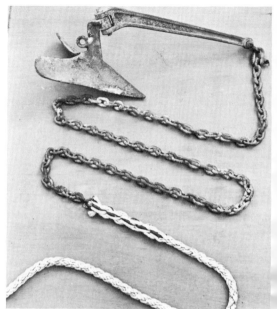

Anchor chains

Those who select chain for their anchor ropes have the comforting knowledge that for all its inconvenience it does provide the strongest hold. This is because the greater weight of chain gives a better catenary to improve the anchor's bite on the seabed. Chain with long links is very apt to kink, which weakens it. Studded links, although stronger and kink-proof, make the chain so much heavier to stow that many yachtsmen fight shy of it. It sounds an obvious thing to do, but make sure that the links of the cable fit comfortably into the recesses of the gypsy if you have one attached to the windlass, and particularly the joining shackles between the lengths of chain (which of course are also known as shackles) if you have not used connecting links to join them. And when joining two shackles of cable, always remember to join them with the bow of the shackle forward and the lugs aft.

TOP RIGHT: If nylon warp is used then a short length of chain will be needed to prevent rope chafing on the sea bed (anchor is the CQR).

The size of chain required, which is measured by the diameter of the metal of which the links are made, depends naturally on the size of the yacht it has to hold. The smallest size of chain is generally $\frac{1}{4}$in (7mm) which should hold a yacht of up to 5 tons Thames Measurement (TM). Chain increases in size in steps of $\frac{1}{16}$in (1.5mm) and a rough guide would be $\frac{5}{16}$in (8mm) chain for yachts up to 8 tons, $\frac{3}{8}$in (9mm) chain up to 15 tons, $\frac{7}{16}$in (10mm) chain up to 20 tons and $\frac{1}{2}$in (13mm) chain up to 30 tons.

You will normally need enough chain for three times the depth (3–1 scope) at high water where you anchor, with a minimum of 30 fathoms (55m) or two shackles of chain. Three shackles, or 45 fathoms (82m), is better. If you have to anchor in water that needs a greater length of chain than you carry, it is not uncommon to use a length of nylon rope bent to the end of the cable. But if this is necessary, remember to protect it against chafe where it comes inboard over the stemhead roller. Kedge anchors are best used with fibre rope as a warp, but the holding power is better if a length of chain is incorporated between the anchor and the warp, a length of chain also prevents the rope being chafed on the sea bed.

Windlasses

In anything but a small yacht, a windlass (with or without a gypsy) is an essential when weighing an anchor. In a small yacht

– up to, say, 6 or 7 tons TM – the weight of cable and anchor is rarely more than the crew can handle comfortably without mechanized assistance, but a modern anchor winch does not take up a lot of room on the foredeck. With no winch a chain pawl fitted on the stemhead roller will prevent the cable from running out again if you need to stop hauling for a short breather. In larger cruisers the weight of cable and anchor is generally too heavy to be manhandled, particularly when it comes to breaking the anchor out. Weighing can be done with a purchase clapped onto the cable, but this will make it a very slow business as a stopper will have to be put on the cable every time the purchase is shifted. Much better, therefore, to have a windlass to do the heavy work, and it should be positioned on the foredeck as nearly directly above the chain locker as possible so that the cable does not have to be led across the deck to reach the navel pipe. In some smaller cruisers, where the weight of the cable is too heavy to be stowed forward, the chain locker is placed just forward of the mast step to give a better distribution of weight.

Some large yachts have powered windlasses, either hydraulic, which means having an engine to drive the hydraulic pump, or electric, which means using quite a lot of amps out of the battery. They are great labour-savers if the boat is big enough to accommodate them and their additional weight, but the smaller yacht makes do with the hand-worked variety. There are two kinds, one of which is operated by turning a crank handle that revolves the drum and the gypsy through gearing, the other by a vertical lever with a fore-and-aft movement that turns the drum with a pawl and ratchet gear. Though it is slower, I prefer the lever variety as it means that you can work it from an upright position; to operate the crank handle of the other, you have to bend down nearly to deck level.

Anchor buoys

While on the subject of ground tackle, an anchor buoy and buoy rope should not be forgotten. It will be needed in crowded anchorages, where there is always a possibility of hooking up someone else's cable or mooring chain with the anchor flukes, or in places where the bottom has rocky outcrops and where the anchor can wedge itself under the top of a rock. Much of the Adriatic coastline

has this sort of bottom, and after the first occasion on which I got hooked to a rock there, I am now a natural convert to buoying the anchor unless I am absolutely sure that the bottom is either sand, shingle or mud.

Buoying an anchor is a very simple operation, needing a length of rope twice the depth of water at high tide, and something to act as a small buoy, which could be anything from a small baulk of timber to a watertight can painted in a distinctive colour to make it immediately recognizable. One end of the buoy rope is bent to the crown of the anchor, the other secured to the buoy, and if the anchor does get fouled on the bottom, it can be weighed on the buoy rope, which being bent to the crown of the anchor, will of course lift the flukes clear of the obstruction. The only point to remember about this is that, when coming to an anchor, the buoy and buoy rope must always be streamed first, and the buoy rope seen to be running clear before you let go.

Anchor buoy. A short length of light chain ensures that at low water the slack does not get tangled with other boats' propellers.

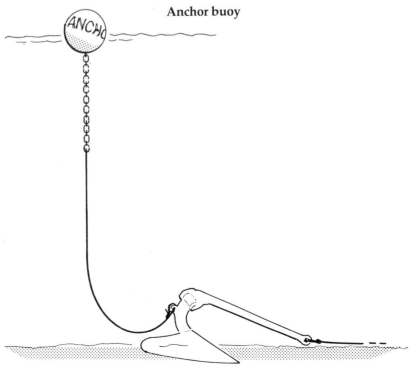

Anchor buoy

CHAPTER 7

Auxiliary engines

Even the most dedicated sailing man appreciates the usefulness of an auxiliary engine. Like the construction and rig it is one of the basic features to bear in mind when choosing your boat and considering its intended use. There are, as you might say, horses for courses, and it is impossible to be dogmatic or to say that any one type has an overall advantage over every other.

Engine power

The first point to consider is how much power is needed to give the optimum speed and economy in a given size of boat. For this the same principles will apply whether the auxiliary uses petrol or diesel fuel. All displacement boats (that is, boats that do not plane – which of course includes all sailing cruisers) have an optimum top speed. This is defined by the ratio of speed to length, and the formula for calculating it is the square root of the waterline length multiplied by a constant defined by the nature of the hull. In the case of a sailing cruiser this constant is 1.34.

The mathematics are simple. For example, if you have a yacht that is 25ft (7.6m) on the waterline you take the square root of this, which is 5, and multiply it by the constant quoted above. The calculation is therefore 5 × 1.34 which comes out at 6.7. And there you have the optimum speed in knots, above which you are going to pay heavily in horsepower for every fraction of a knot you gain.

To find out what power we need to get 6.7 knots we have to use another formula that includes the displacement (weight) of the boat, but fortunately there are tables to help us on this one and from these it transpires

that, supposing our 25ft WL boat displaces 3 tons, we will get 6.7 knots with about 10hp, but if we wanted 7 knots, which would be exceeding the optimum, we would need 13hp. So it would take 3hp more to get an extra 0.3 of a knot. If the boat displaces 4 tons the relevant figures are 13hp and 17hp. The situation gets worse if our ambitions are even higher and obviously the cost in horsepower becomes too high to make the pursuit worth while. Taking into account that we need some reserve power occasionally to maintain speed in adverse conditions, a realistic assessment for the 3-ton boat would be an engine giving 12hp and for the 4-tonner, 16hp.

Engine ratings

The next thing is, what power can you actually get from an engine of given output? A marine engine may be quoted with two horsepower ratings, one of which gives the power it will develop at a stated revolutions per minute (rpm) if run continuously, and the other of which gives the power available at higher or maximum rpm for intermittent operation. Obviously the continuous rating is of more interest to the cruising yachtsman and if only one figure is quoted for power output you should establish whether this is continuous or intermittent.

Another point to note is that engine power ratings vary according to the test conditions laid down by different national authorities. Manufacturers normally state which standard has been used with the quoted horsepower. There are three rating standards that may be used. Generally only one is given but sometimes two may be quoted. DIN, the German rating, is used universally in Australia, New Zealand and Europe, including Britain, and BS, the British rating, is very similar. SAE, the American rating, is different in its requirements. Under DIN conditions the engine must be equipped with its auxiliary units such as a generator. SAE rating permits the engine to be run without these. It will be appreciated that DIN is the more informative because it tells you what power is available from the engine when it is run with all its auxiliary equipment, and the power required to drive these units is by no means neglible. For instance, an engine quoted as 40bhp (brake horsepower) SAE may produce no more power to drive the boat than one given as 30bhp DIN. Further, if the power figure given is shp (shaft horsepower), which includes the gearbox, the divergence will be even greater because this indicates the actual power at the propeller shaft.

For the non-technical it should be mentioned that the power quoted for all marine engines is the developed horsepower or brake horsepower and has nothing to do with the capacity or size of the engine. Unlike a car engine, which may be defined by its capacity (1,500cc, for example), the marine engine will not be described as 15hp. The figure given will always be the brake horsepower, developed at the designed engine speed. To know that an engine is 30bhp tells you nothing about its capacity (that is, bore and stroke × the number of cylinders). But bhp or shp are much more informative because, again unlike a car engine, a boat engine will be run mostly at a steady speed near the top end of its range and the gearing and the propellor will be chosen to match the output in terms of bhp and torque.

Torque and fuel economy

Torque is of particular interest in powering a boat. It refers to the turning effort of the engine and, once again, the requirements for car and marine engines are quite different. In a car we want a high torque for starting a laden vehicle under load, and after an initial rise this can be allowed to drop off at higher engine revolutions when the vehicle will be moving more easily. With a boat the situation is different because the vessel will move easily from rest but will want as much torque as possible later in the range to meet the resistance of the water, which increases with speed.

In general, though it is not always so, fuel economy may be related quite favourably to an engine speed associated with high torque but never to maximum brake horsepower. This is why some car engines converted for marine use tend to be heavy on petrol when required to run at their maximum speed or at the top end of their range. But whether or not he is using a car engine the cruising man will be well advised to choose his gearing and propeller to suit the maximum torque available rather than try to achieve maximum speed by means of the highest continuous

Typical engine power and fuel-consumption curve

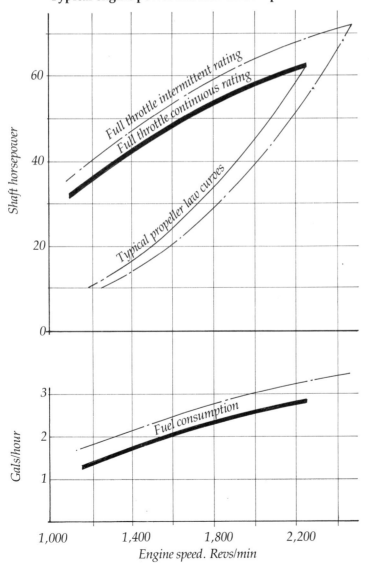

brake horsepower.

All of this might seem rather technical but if you can obtain a useful fuel economy it is well worth knowing. The engine manufacturer will always be helpful in this and in advising you over your transmission requirements.

Inboard and outboard engines

Cruisers come in many varieties, and the range of engines suited to different sizes and purposes is correspondingly wide. Many of the smallest cruisers whose intended scope is estuary and coastal manage very well with an outboard engine on a lifting bracket which keeps it clear when sailing. This saves space aboard and means that the engine is easily accessible. It will rarely be run for extended periods and will generally be reliable. However, I would maintain that manoeuvring is easier with inboard controls, and unless the savings on space or expenditure are your top priorities, a lightweight inboard engine might serve rather better and be more economical on fuel.

Petrol or diesel?

In a small vessel the best choice is almost inevitably a petrol engine. Small and relatively lightweight diesel engines are now available but they are still heavier than petrol ones, and the extra weight is a definite disadvantage in a yacht under about 22ft (6.7m) loa, especially as it will probably be installed under the cockpit where crew weight often gives trim problems anyway. The question of vibration is not particularly acute nowadays but even so the small diesel, which may have only one cylinder and has a much higher compression ratio, is bound to produce more noticeable vibration in a small yacht than does its petrol counterpart. GRP vessels will

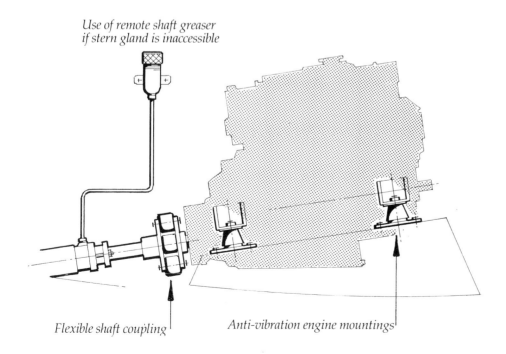

Use of remote shaft greaser if stern gland is inaccessible

Flexible shaft coupling

Anti-vibration engine mountings

Engine installation with flexible mountings and coupling. Also shown is the remote shaft-greasing assembly.

*Outboard engine
mounted on a bracket.*

stand more of this than those built of wood, but to put a single-cylinder diesel in a small wooden yacht with light scantlings can be a bit cruel. I know of one Folkboat which, as a result of just this, ended up with all its ribs in way of the engine cracked and feathered.

The engine's presence may be made rather less noticeable if it is installed on anti-vibration mountings, but if you do this you must make sure there is some flexibility in the shaft line by incorporating flexible couplings or a self-aligning stern gland, otherwise both the shaft and the stern gland will take a terrible caning, and you will need to replace them rather sooner than you expected.

Many yachtsmen opt for a diesel engine because of the lower fire potential but, provided that it can be accommodated, it has many virtues beyond that. Its thermal efficiency is nearly 50 per cent higher than a petrol engine's and that means much better fuel economy. It breathes only air, not an air/fuel mixture; the fuel is precisely metered and injected into each cylinder. Ignition is brought about by high compression and the fact that it needs no electricity while running makes it simple and reliable. Larger engines may be made even more efficient with an exhaust turbo-blower. All in all the diesel has a lot more going for it than just the reduced fire risk.

Cooling for the low-power diesel motors is mostly direct, either by air or, more often, by raw sea water. Medium and larger power units from about 30bhp upwards will generally have indirect cooling, the fresh water circulating in the engine being cooled by sea water via a heat exchanger. You can get a bonus from an indirectly cooled engine by fitting a second heat exchanger which will supply free hot water to the galley and the toilet compartment. It will go on giving you hot water not only when the engine is running but for some time after it has been shut down because of the heat retention in the motor and the temperature rise discussed below.

The relative merits of petrol and diesel engines can be summed up as follows. The petrol engine may well suit the smaller yacht if range is not important; it is cheaper, quieter, lighter and easier to service. It has a certain fire risk but not such as to deter anyone ready to treat it with care and common sense. The diesel engine is more expensive, produces rather more noise and vibration and requires specialized maintenance, but it is economical on fuel and its simplicity makes it more reliable than a petrol engine. It reduces, although it does not eliminate, the fire risk.

Many of the relatively lightweight, high-speed diesel engines available for boats are marinized versions of those used for trucks or for stationary units. Most of these are rather large for sailing cruiser requirements but it may well be that the world oil situation will spur the more rapid development of smaller, lighter, multi-cylinder units for use in automobiles and later for boats as well.

Fire precautions

If a petrol engine is properly installed and maintained there should be no more risk of disaster than there is with a car engine. The operative words are 'properly installed', and the other essential is that it should be a purpose-built or a professionally marinized unit with a flame trap and flame-trapped drip tray; piping, if copper, should be annealed and secured against vibration. Any flexible fuel line must be of suitable petrol-resistant tubing terminating in either screwed connections or recognizably efficient hose clips, and since the engine will be in an enclosed space without the benefit of a continuous stream of fresh air, allowance must be made for adequate ventilation. In many vessels the engine installation is such that the air has to find its way in wherever it can.

Engines of every type need air – not only to breathe but also to keep down the ambient temperature. It should be remembered that this can rise significantly even after the engine has been switched off because there will be no cooling water going through it. With the rise in temperature any petrol in the carburetor will evaporate more readily and if it is in an unventilated compartment you have a potentially dangerous atmosphere. So either turn off the fuel and let the engine run itself down, then switch off; or fit a small flame-proof blower which you can switch on for a few minutes to clear the engine compartment of fumes. Needless to say the switch should be outside the compartment.

With precautions such as these it should be possible to use a petrol engine with minimal risk in even the warmest climate. The necessity to have the tank filler on deck is generally observed and if the engine and the tank are occupying mutual air space the vent pipe should be similarly treated.

Preparation and sensible precaution are essential parts of seamanship and it is usually

Indirect engine-cooling system

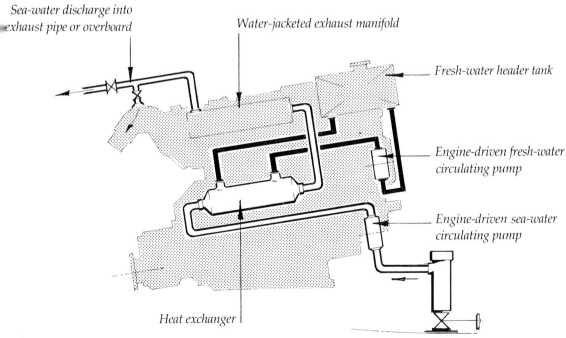

Sea-water discharge into exhaust pipe or overboard

Water-jacketed exhaust manifold

Fresh-water header tank

Engine-driven fresh-water circulating pump

Engine-driven sea-water circulating pump

Heat exchanger

Sea-water inlet with seacock and strainer

Engine fuel system

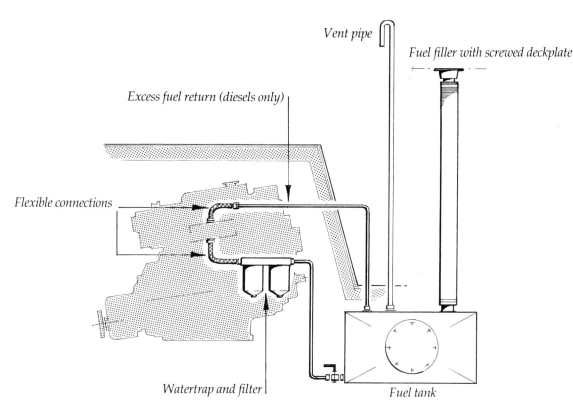

Vent pipe

Fuel filler with screwed deckplate

Excess fuel return (diesels only)

Flexible connections

Watertrap and filter

Fuel tank

the man who is at fault rather than the machine. I know an owner who stopped to pour more fuel into his tank on a hot summer day while on passage between southern Ireland and Cornwall. The fumes from the filling pipe, which was inside the cockpit, must have been excessive and volatile in the heat. No one can remember a spark or any other reason why the ensuing fire should have started, but to their amazement the crew suddenly found their feet enveloped in flames. None of them had socks or any sort of protective clothing and they all leapt into the sea to alleviate the pain. In a moment the entire CRP hull was ablaze and it burned to the waterline before sinking. By the grace of God a passing ship saw the smoke and they were all picked up.

Another yacht was motoring in hot weather in the Mediterranean until the crew decided to stop for lunch and switched off the engine. There must have been either petrol fumes or calor gas in the bilge because when the time came to get under way and the starter button was pressed, an enormous explosion blew the entire deck off the yacht. Fortunately no one suffered worse injury

than concussion and they managed to motor into harbour.

Both these incidents illustrate what can happen if you do not properly appreciate the potential for trouble in an engine that has been badly installed.

Transmission

Transmission – that is, any gears or shafting taking the drive to the propeller – offers rather more options nowadays than the conventional in-line gearbox and shaft. There are V drives and U drives for those who want to tuck the engine out of the way under the after deck; and through-the-hull units known as S drives or saildrives where the engine, gearbox, shaft and propeller are built into a simple, integrated assembly. The advantage of the latter is that installation is simplified as the engine and propeller shaft do not need lining up and there is no stern gland and so on. Outdrives – that is, the engine coupled to a retractable Z drive on the transom – are not normally seen in sailing cruisers although their use has been mooted.

V-drive engine installation

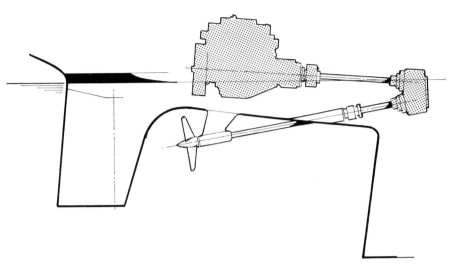

Sail drive engine installation

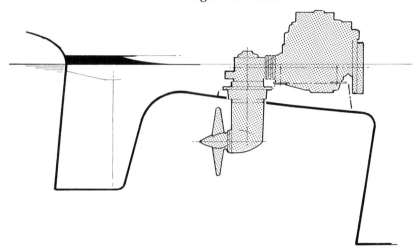

The sailboat drive is particularly applicable to yachts with a fin keel and separate rudder because it can be positioned on the centreline between these, but it could also be installed in a long-keel GRP boat. In this case, though, it might be better to have it off the centreline on the side that will balance the athwartships thrust of the propeller rather than to cut large, drag-promoting apertures in the skeg and rudder. The drive has a streamlined underwater shape and although comparative efficiencies for different installations are not available it is probably preferable to have it off centre rather than make major alterations to a long keel boat.

Propeller

Whatever the nature of the transmission, the final and critical point in the power line is the propeller, and selection of the right one will determine whether or not you get the best out of the engine in performance and fuel economy. As there are many variables such as available power and shaft speed, the shape of the boat and its weight and other considerations which need to be defined before the propeller manufacturer is able to advise you on type, diameter and pitch, the only recommendation I can make here is that you should seek professional advice if you

Feathering propeller shown (1) . . . folds automatically under sail (2) and reduces drag to minimum.

want the best results. Of course, if you acquire a standard production boat all of this will have been taken care of, but otherwise, make sure you get it right.

Alternators

With regard to auxiliary equipment, there is one area that has been improved immensely in recent years and that is the generation of electrical current. Alternators are now fitted as standard or as an option on most engines and their ability to generate at low speeds and at higher outputs makes them much more efficient than a dynamo or generator. In fact only sizable auxiliary yachts with a plenitude of electrical equipment now need to have some additional source of supply. The alternator will supply all the usual needs of engine starting, lighting and navigational aids since the battery may be kept charged so much more easily. However, if you are a lavish user of current it is useful to have two batteries, one supplying the needs of the ship and the other reserved for engine starting. The alternator will charge both and a change-over switch makes them available for either purpose, but at least the arrangement will ensure that you can't be caught out by finding that, after an all-night party when you had every light in the yacht burning bright, your engine refuses to start.

Engine installation

Finally, something more about the installation of an engine. If you are buying a standard boat you will not have much say in the matter but if you are having an engine put in make sure that the builder or boatyard does not enclose it in such a way that some parts are inaccessible. It can and does happen. You will need to do jobs such as cleaning filters, changing oil and so on from time to time. Also, a fault may need attention, and to have to stand practically on your head and grope around is frustrating, to say the least. In addition, if the stern gland is not easily accessible, have an extension tube put on it so that the greaser is well within reach. It is more likely to get the needed occasional turn in good time if you don't have to excavate to get at it.

So far we have had a look at the construction of a yacht, her rig, the standing and running rigging, ropes and ropework, sails, accommodation, deck arrangements and ground tackle, and the auxiliary engine. It is now time to move on and take her out to sea.

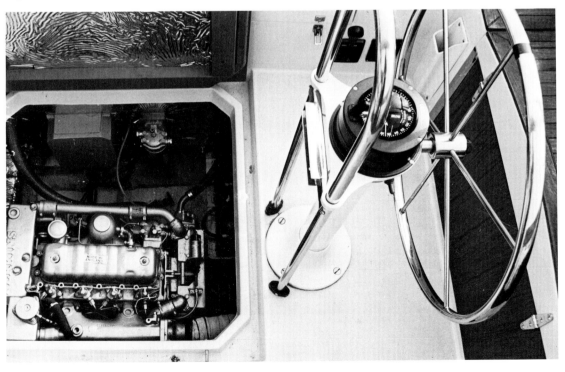

Better engine access provided by a hatch opening in the cockpit sole.

CHAPTER 8

Manoeuvring under sail

There is an old saying that anyone who can sail a dinghy can sail anything. There is little doubt that this is true – for several reasons. You have to go some to capsize a cruiser, while a moment's inattention can capsize a dinghy. If a yacht is decked, any water that comes on board runs off through the scuppers whereas in a dinghy it collects in the bottom. Since a keel provides much greater stability, it is easier to sail a yacht with a fixed keel than a dinghy with a plate or centre-board. And, best of all, a heavy yacht carries her way under sail much better than a centre-boarded dinghy so that she is easier to tack and wear.

Fortunately, the opposite of the old saying, that if you can't sail a dinghy you can't sail anything, is certainly not true. What all this comes down to is that, for the young, the best introduction to cruising is dinghy sailing, as it needs above all quickness of decision, agility, and an appreciation of what the boat can do in the various strengths of wind it meets. Any mistakes that are made – and there will always be some – are not normally very severe on the pocket. But there is no reason why the not so young who want to omit that introduction should not still develop into experienced helmsmen. It is surprising how much can be learned about handling a yacht under sail in even a week or two of practice, particularly if there is an experienced sailor on board for the first few occasions when you take a yacht to sea. Knowledge of the rule of the road (see chapter fourteen) will avoid collisions, and the rudiments of coastal navigation will prevent a beginner finishing up with his yacht on the mud or a sandbank. Once those basics are reasonably established, the rest will come naturally with experience.

Aerodynamics

When you take a boat out under sail, it is helpful to understand what forces are making the boat move through the water and how they operate. I do not just mean the forces of the wind blowing on the sail, which of course are the forces we are concerned with, but the way they are resolved to give the boat forward motion. Every sailing man or woman knows, I am sure, that in order to distinguish the actual amount of wind striking a sail at an angle, which provides forward motion, you resolve the component which is striking the sail at right angles in relation to the fore-and-aft line of the boat. You are then left with a small component pushing the boat in the direction you want to go. This is known as the parallelogram of forces (illustrated in the diagram on page 110). The fact that the larger final component, acting at right angles to the fore-and-aft line does not drive the boat direct down to leeward is because the keel resists direct movement in this direction.

But there is a bit more to it than this, and it is this bit more that is important. When we resolved the wind into its two component forces we assumed that the sail was a flat surface trimmed at an angle to the fore-and-aft line. But the sail is not a flat surface; a well-cut sail filled with wind adopts a parabolic curve in which the steepest part of the curve is at the luff of the sail. Aerodynamic research, directed initially on aircraft wings, has indicated that air flowing over the leading edge of a wing that has a parabolic curve creates a partial vacuum which has a lifting effect; a wind flowing over the parabolic curve at the luff of a sail creates a partial vacuum in exactly the same way. But this partial vacuum does not lift in this instance, but pulls.

The faster the air flows over an aircraft wing, the greater the partial vacuum, and therefore the lifting force, created. And of course the same is equally true for a yacht's sail. So how can we increase this wind speed over a mainsail's luff? The answer is by creating a funnel effect by setting a headsail forward of the mast and sheeting it aft to overlap the luff of the mainsail. A moderate overlap is enough to create a funnel effect, and if the mainsail is larger than the headsail, a general guide is to sheet the headsail so that it overlaps the mainsail by about one-sixth of the length of the mainsail's foot. If however the genoa is the principal driving sail and the mainsail is smaller and set high, the desired overlap will clearly be much greater than this.

So, to sum up the practical results of this knowledge of forces, *don't* flatten in your mainsail when close-hauled so hard that you tend to destroy its natural curve; and *do* sheet the headsail so that its clew overlaps the luff of the mainsail. If you follow these guidelines, you will get the maximum forward drive that the wind is capable of giving you. Taking this a little bit further, the longer the luff of the sail, the greater the vacuum effect produced. This is, of course, why the bermudan rig is always more efficient to windward than the gaff rig. Indeed we can take it a little further still by using a high-aspect-ratio mainsail, though the efficiency of this particular sail depends more on the fact that it has only a negligible amount of twist from head to foot in comparison with a more normally proportioned sail; a kicking strap assists in getting the desired effect. A high-aspect-ratio sail allows you to point a little nearer the wind, but will not materially affect the parabolic curvature, which is where the vacuum is created. But it is certainly a racing sail, a bit out of place, I think, in a cruising yacht where the overriding desirability is the robustness of the rig and its ability to take even the heaviest of weather.

The parallelogram of forces

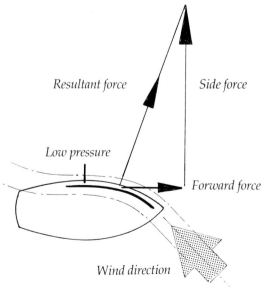

Side force

Forward force

The resultant force of a quarterly wind acting on a flat plate sail can be broken down into two separate components. The effect of the keel will largely overcome the sideways component, leaving the forward force to drive the boat.

Wind direction

Forward drive of bow wind

Resultant force   *Side force*

Low pressure

Forward force

The forward drive of a bow wind – which the boat experiences when beating – comes from the lifting or pulling effect of the aerodynamically shaped sail. The resultant force at approximately right-angles to the sail can again be broken down into two separate components.

Wind direction

Casting off

Let us start by taking a yacht out to sea without relying on an auxiliary engine. First of all, you assemble the basic information required for this – it will be there quite unconsciously after a little experience. The time of day tells you what the tide is doing, and you know that, except at slack water, a sailing yacht lies to the tide, not to the wind. There are the occasional exceptions to this general rule.

A strong wind and a slack tide will make the yacht wind-rode or, in other words, lie facing the wind, and with the wind against the tide she is apt to sheer about, but in

*Moving off under sail:
with the wind blowing off
the berth there's no
problem.*

Getting under way from anchorage (opposite)

Step 1: Hoist mainsail and shorten anchor chain.

Step 2: Set mainsail.

Step 3: Hoist headsail.

Step 4: Allow boat to move slowly forward under mainsail to take weight off anchor chain and assist lifting.

Step 5: Anchor chain still just holding ground.

Step 6: Sail boat over anchor to 'break it out'.

Step 7: With anchor up, back headsail to bring boat's head around.

Step 8: Come through the wind and prepare to sail off on starboard tack.

general it is the tide that holds her, not the wind.

A look round the anchorage will show you how much room you've got to manoeuvre in, and whether it is going to be better to get away on the port or starboard tack, or cast to port or starboard as the proper phraseology has it. Then take into consideration how you do this if you are lying on a mooring or to your own anchor. The first is simple; the other not quite so easy. Look at the direction of the wind and its effect on your sails as you hoist them, and with this basic knowledge assembled, you should be able to recognize the best way of getting your yacht out to sea without undue trouble. With a little practice it becomes automatic, but for the first few times you have to do it, and getting all the relevant facts in place has to be a conscious process.

Lying to an anchor
Let us assume as an example that a yacht is lying to her own anchor, that the wind is coming from forward of the beam, and that your decision is to cast to port. With the wind in this direction you can hoist the mainsail as, with the sheet eased away, it will flap in the wind and not hold any of it. With the mainsail hoisted, you can then shorten in the cable until the anchor is not quite up and down, in other words is still just holding the ground. Then you hoist the jib and back it to the wind by sheeting it to windward, put the helm over to starboard (rudder to port) so that the pressure of the tide will act on the rudder to help the bows round. Then you can weigh the anchor, bringing it inboard as quickly as you can. You now have the rudder turning the yacht's bows to port, the backed jib doing the same, and the mainsail still flapping and empty of wind. As the yacht 'pays off' – as its sails fill and it begins to cover ground – you let go the windward jib sheet, set up the lee one, and sheet in the mainsail. The yacht is now sailing normally, and if you have a staysail in addition to a jib, now is the time to set it.

It is not quite as easy as this if the wind is abaft the beam as you are lying to the anchor. If you start by hoisting the mainsail you will not be able to ease it far enough forward to spill all the wind out of it since the after shrouds will prevent the boom taking up an angle directly away from the wind. This is a case where you need to weigh the anchor

before hoisting any sail, for if either is hoisted the yacht will drive forward over her anchor, making weighing difficult. So have the mainsail and jib ready for hoisting with the halyards shackled on, or hoist the jib stopped to its luff with twine, and then break out the anchor. You will have to rely on the rudder to give you the initial cast of the bows in the desired direction. As soon as the anchor is out of the ground, get the jib up or break it out if you have hoisted it in stops and, as the bows begin to come round, sheet it in backed to the wind to help the swing. On occasions you may find that the jib alone will be all you need to bring the yacht into clear water where the mainsail can be hoisted, but there is no need to delay with the mainsail unless it is easier to do so. The sooner all the sails are set and drawing, the sooner you have complete control of the yacht.

If your yacht is lying with her bow pointing in completely the opposite direction to the course you need to steer to reach the open sea, you may have to take other steps to get her away. It will depend on how much room you have in which to turn her. It may be better to sail the anchor out instead of shortening it in before hoisting the sails, as this will give you way on the boat as the anchor leaves the ground and will therefore make your yacht more responsive to the rudder. It is quite a simple operation, involving setting the sails before weighing and sailing up to the anchor, rounding in the cable smartly as the boat does so. As there is no weight on the anchor while this is being done, it requires very little physical effort to get the cable in. It should be hauled in so that the anchor is up and down as your yacht reaches the position directly above it, and the boat's way will break it out of the ground, ready for lifting quickly inboard.

There will no doubt be times when you are lying to an anchor, pointing in the wrong direction, and without enough room to turn her under sail, perhaps because of other yachts in the anchorage, perhaps because of the closeness of the shore. There may still be ways of solving this dilemma if you are determined not to use the auxiliary engine. Most yacht owners are only too happy to let you take a line over to them when you are in this sort of difficulty, and you may be able to get out this way. Or you can always lay out your kedge anchor and secure the warp to the stern before weighing your bower anchor

so that, as you do so, the tide will swing your yacht round until she points in the direction you want. This is, of course, advice for the purist; most of us, I think, would use the auxiliary engine to take her clear where there is really no room to turn under sail alone. However, it is nice to know that if for any reason you find yourself unable to use your auxiliary engine, there is almost always a way of overcoming this.

Casting off from a mooring

If you are lying to a mooring, it is a simple matter to turn the yacht in the other direction by bringing the mooring warp aft and securing it to the yacht's stern. She will then be pointing in the direction you want her, and all that is necessary is to cast loose the warp as soon as you are ready to proceed.

Sailing in open sea

There are three main points of sailing – running, reaching and sailing close-hauled. If you are running or reaching, you will be sailing either by compass or towards some visible mark; if you are sailing close-hauled, you

are sailing by the wind, or in other words as near to your desired course as the direction of the wind will let you. And the wind you are sailing on is not the true wind but the apparent wind. The apparent wind is the effect that a yacht's speed through the water has on what seems to be the direction from which the wind is blowing, making it appear that you are sailing closer to the wind than you really are. The diagram shows how you can determine the difference between the true and the apparent wind. It is all, perhaps, a little exotic, but if you go into the differences it shows fairly clearly why, if your yacht is sailing fast on a wind, you need to harden in your sheets a bit more than if she is sailing slowly. After a little experience, this sort of knowledge becomes automatic, and you can forget about true and apparent winds in the sheer pleasure of pushing your boat along at the best speed she is capable of in the prevailing conditions.

Sailing close-hauled

Where, I think, some beginners are apt to come to grief when sailing close-hauled is that they are too greedy. This is my own word for anyone who 'pinches' a yacht in order to try to gain a little extra to windward.

Apparent wind effect

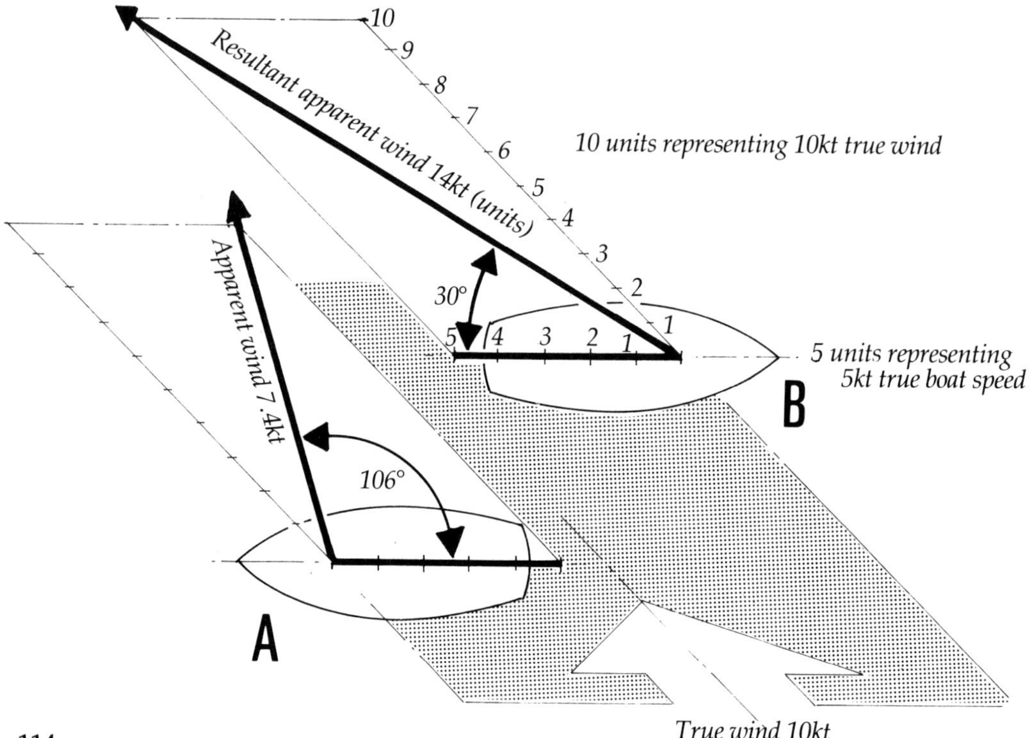

Resultant apparent wind 14kt (units)

10 units representing 10kt true wind

Apparent wind 7·4kt

30°

106°

5 units representing 5kt true boat speed

B

A

True wind 10kt

You can calculate the apparent wind effect by drawing the parallelogram of forces to scale. The length of the resultant line indicates the strength of the apparent wind; the angle, its direction.

In this example both boats are travelling at 5 kt with a 10-kt wind at 45° to their course. Boat A is broad reaching and feels an apparent wind of 7.4 kt. Boat B is close hauled and feels an apparent wind of 14 kt. The wind feels stronger to this boat, which may have to reduce sail to cope with the increase.

Bad sail setting

1. Baggy luff, headsail not hauled tight.

2. Mainsail not hoisted enough, leach badly stretched and disfigured.

3. Mainsail luff not tightened.

4. Peak of gaff rig sail too high.

5. Sheeting in headsail too hard on a reach causes luff of mainsail to flap.

6. Headsail sheet position too far forward, foot excessively curved.

115

OPPOSITE: Beating to windward.

I don't, of course, mean the word literally, but there often seems to be some uncontrollable urge among less experienced sailors to flatten in the sheets too hard and point up a bit too close to the wind. It may look as though the yacht is doing well so far as pointing up towards the wind is concerned, but in fact she is always losing speed and making unnecessary leeway.

If there is one secret about sailing close-hauled, it is to keep the boat moving at all costs. To do this the sails must be allowed to take up their proper designed curve, and this means that there must be flexibility in their sheeting. By all means, sheet them in hard when sailing on a wind, but not so hard that they are flattened right in. And they themselves will tell you when you are steering too close to the wind by lifting their luffs. As soon as you see them doing this, bring the tiller a touch up to windward to ease the boat away from the wind. The luff to watch is the luff of the jib; if the sails are properly sheeted to the wind, this will be the first one to lift.

There is something else that should be observed when setting and sheeting a sail and that is the strength of the wind at the time. The harder it blows, the flatter the sails should be set when sailing on the wind; but in light weather there is no profit in setting the mainsail up with much tension on luff and foot, and neither mainsail nor jib should be sheeted in so hard as to flatten the sail. With the main all you need is enough tension on the luff to give a slight crease all the way from peak to tack before the sail fills. If in a light wind the crease is still there the luff is too taut. Similarly, the foot should be drawn out just to the point where there is the smallest crease along it which disappears as soon as the sail is full. The sails will of course have been cut so as to establish their basic fullness or otherwise, but the amount of flow can be modified by luff and foot tension. The rule is that in light airs you can use the full flow of the sail to advantage but in stronger winds tension can be used to reduce the fullness. What you are doing with these adjustments is to change the shape of the sail from a low-speed aerofoil which will give the best lift in light winds to a high-speed aerofoil better suited to winds of greater velocity.

The time comes, after a little practice, when it is no longer necessary to watch the luff of the foresail to make sure that you are not pinching the boat. The feel of the tiller and of the wind on the side of your head will tell you when you are sailing with the sails full and as close to the wind as the yacht will go. You don't get this feeling so strongly when the wind is very light or fluky. When it is like this you will need to use your eyes as well as the feel of the tiller to make sure that you are getting the best out of your boat. One important point to remember is that for any yacht to sail at her best when on the wind, the luffs of the headsails must be set up taut. To get this, it is necessary to make sure that the backstay is doing its job properly. If it is badly set up, the mast will bend fractionally forward, and this means that the luffs of the sails will be slack by that amount. At the same time make sure the topping lift is slack. A mainsail which is obstructed cannot produce its full power.

Looking at the diagram of true and apparent wind opposite, it is obvious that the stronger the true wind, the broader the angle of the apparent wind to your course. So, when the wind is coming in stronger puffs, you can afford to eat up a bit to windward by luffing the puffs, as with the apparent wind at a broader angle, you can obviously sail a little closer. But the opposite is equally true. As a puff eases you will need to bear away a little to keep the sails full since, of course, the apparent wind is now making a smaller angle to your course. This little bit of knowledge is summed up in the jingle:

> In a puff, spring a luff,
> In a lull, keep her full.

The whole point of sailing a yacht close-hauled is to reach a point up to windward, either because that is the direction you want to go, or because you need to weather some particular mark, perhaps a rock or a shoal. If that particular point happens to be fairly broad on the bow you may be able to get there on one tack, although even if you can point to windward of your mark, you don't necessarily make it on one tack because every yacht makes a certain amount of leeway when sailing close-hauled. This is caused by that component of the wind which is acting at right angles to the fore-and-aft line, though its full effect is considerably modified by the yacht's keel which resists the sideways pressure of the wind on sails, hull and rigging. Leeway varies according to the design of the yacht, her draught, her freeboard, her speed

Luffing up to windward during a puff

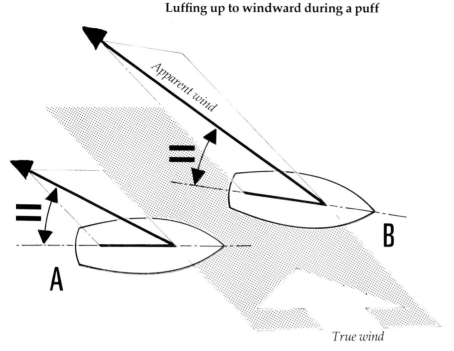

Apparent wind

True wind

Diagram of the parallelogram of forces showing why a boat can luff up to windward during a puff. Boat A is sailing as close to the wind as it can – that is, with the smallest possible angle between the apparent wind and its course. Boat B has been hit by a puff which has temporarily doubled the wind speed, only marginally increasing the boat's speed, but widening the angle between the apparent wind speed and its course. Here boat B has reduced this angle to the same as boat A's, the increase in apparent wind speed allowing it to point further up into the wind.

through the water, the strength of the wind, and the state of the sea. Obviously, a deep-draught yacht with a moderate freeboard will make less leeway than a shallow-draught yacht with a high freeboard. Less obviously, a yacht with a clean bottom makes less than one with a foul bottom – her speed through the water is greater – and yachts make more leeway in strong winds and heavy seas than in moderate winds and calm seas. Most leeway is made when sailing close-hauled, and it decreases steadily as the wind is brought aft until, when running directly before the wind, there is of course none at all.

In fairly normal conditions in an average cruising yacht, you would expect to make about 5° of leeway, which is the angle between the course you are steering and the course made good over the ground. That would be a minimum (other local conditions at the time could well increase this by a degree or two) and it needs to be taken into consideration whenever you are working up to windward.

Going about (tacking)

If you can't make the point you had intended, or lay the course you want to sail, on one tack, then you must beat up to windward first on one tack and then on the other. Changing a yacht's course through the wind from one tack to the other is a simple enough

process. There are really very few points to watch out for, the main one being a tendency on the part of many sailors to sheet the headsails across too soon. When this is done, they become backed to the wind and can cause a yacht to falter and fail to complete the manoeuvre. If your boat is a bit sluggish in the water it often pays to sail her a bit full before you put the helm down in order to get a bit of extra way on the boat. You need to keep your foresails drawing so as to use their power as long as possible, so don't let fly the foresheet too quickly. Be ready to sheet it in just after you cross the wind, and just before the sail fills on the new tack. If you leave it later than that you may have a job hardening it in if there is any real weight in the wind.

Finally, don't use too much helm as you go about. Ease the helm down a little as you start to tack to keep her sailing, and wait until the sails begin to shake before gradually increasing the rudder angle.

The reason for this is that every yacht will fore-reach a little as she comes up into the wind, and you want to use this to advantage when you sail her across the wind. If you use too much helm the rudder will act as a brake and you will lose this fore-reaching quality, often called 'carry'. At its greatest angle the rudder should not be over more than about 30°–35° to the fore-and-aft line.

OPPOSITE: On the starboard tack.

1

2

3

4

Going about (tacking)

Step 1: Boat on port tack prepares to go about. Helmsman warns crew to stand by sheets.

Step 2: The helmsman gives a warning shout and pushes the helm down to leeward to bring the boat's head into the wind. The crew lets go the jib sheet.

Step 3: Providing the boat is travelling at a good speed and the order and helm movement are smartly executed, the boat should remain no more than a matter of seconds with her head into the wind ('in stays').

Here the mainsail is already filling on the opposite tack. In light winds or heavy seas it sometimes pays to hold onto the jib sheet until after the boat's head has passed through the wind. This will help the boat to swing.

Step 4: The boat now pays off on the opposite tack, the helm is brought back to its usual position and the jib sheet pulled in and made fast.

There are sometimes occasions when your boat will need a bit more help to get her across the wind. If she has a long straight keel she may have lost most of her way as she comes up head to wind. You can then help the bows across by backing the headsail to the wind, which will help to blow the bows down towards the new tack. And if you are tacking in a rough sea and the boat pitches into a wave so that her forward movement is stopped, reverse the helm. Once she stops she begins to make sternway, and if you keep the original helm on she will merely sail off on the original tack, since the effect of the rudder when moving astern is the opposite to that when moving ahead.

Having made your tack, the next problem is how far to sail on that course before tacking again. Some of this decision will depend on the direction and strength of the tidal stream.

If you don't have this knowledge in your head, a glance at a tidal atlas will give it to you. Obviously you want to make the most use you can of the tide, and if you can use it to push you along to windward, then you adjust your tacks accordingly.

However, if the direction or strength of the tide is not going to make any appreciable difference, there are good and not so good ways of tacking to reach your objective. If, for example, it lies directly to windward of you, you could reach it with one long leg on one tack and an equally long leg on the other. This is not a good way, as you sail a longer distance and you risk a change in the wind heading you and leaving you badly placed. The better way is to make short tacks that get ever shorter as you approach your objective. If you reckon that your yacht will sail close-hauled at four points off the wind, and allow

Tacking procedures

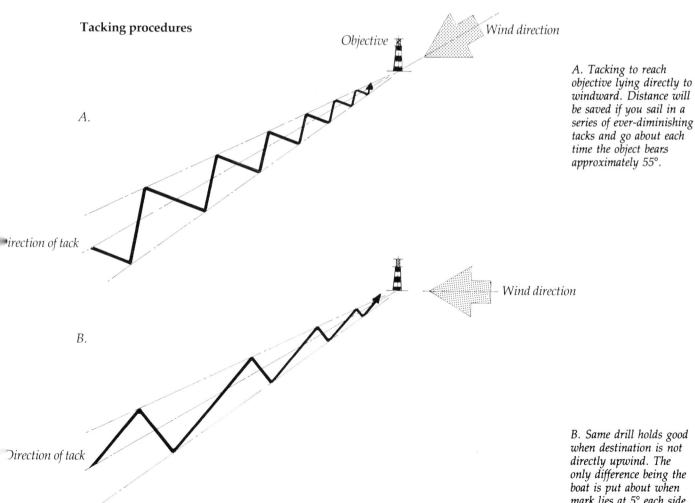

A. Tacking to reach objective lying directly to windward. Distance will be saved if you sail in a series of ever-diminishing tacks and go about each time the object bears approximately 55°.

B. Same drill holds good when destination is not directly upwind. The only difference being the boat is put about when mark lies at 5° each side of rhumb line.

OPPOSITE: Running with the wind astern and the sails 'goose-winged', that is, sheeted on opposite sides.

about 5° for leeway, you will be sailing at an angle of 50° to the course to be made good. Sail your first tack until your objective bears a bit more than that on the bow – about 55° would be fine – and then go about and continue on the opposite tack until you have the same bearing (55°) on the bow. Keep repeating this process until you reach your objective. By the time it gets there your yacht will have sailed an appreciably shorter distance than if you had made two long legs, and any change in the wind will have had the minimal effect. If you think of it as a long, narrow triangle with your windward mark at the apex and the two sides drawn at 5° either side of the course to be made good, all you have to do is to tack whenever you reach one of the sides of the triangle, keeping the yacht always within it.

The other tacking problem is when your objective is not directly to windward of you. Here the same final method holds good, but choose your first tack to take you down to leeward of the point you want to reach and not up to windward of it. Then, when it bears about 55° on the bow, go about until you reach the same bearing on the other bow. And so on. Obviously, in a case like this, the legs will not be of equal length; you will sail one longer leg and one shorter one, but you will get there just as quickly. The same reasons hold good – you sail a shorter distance and changes in the wind have much less effect on the final outcome.

Of course, if you are one of those clever seamen who can foretell changes in wind strength or direction (it is not always all that difficult) you need to modify these methods to take advantage of your knowledge. You may also see an area of calmer water which it would pay you to reach. A good seaman is never hidebound in following general theories of this nature; if he can see an advantage in taking another course, he should always seize it thankfully.

Finally, when sailing close-hauled (and indeed when reaching), try to trim your yacht so that she carries a little weather helm. This is an inbuilt safety measure, for if she is caught in a sudden squall she will automatically luff up towards the wind. Besides, a touch of weather helm gives you that lively feeling through the tiller which you need to cultivate in order to tell you that your yacht is going her best. You can induce weather helm by reducing headsail area, raking the

mast further aft or moving interior weights forward. It is more common, however, for boats to suffer an excess of weather helm and this has to be reduced by the reversal of these suggestions, and in extreme cases with a headsail set on a short bowsprit.

You won't get that feel of the helm if your yacht is so balanced that she carries no helm at all. But avoid lee helm like the plague; it is always dangerous. If you meet that same sudden squall with your yacht carrying lee helm, she will bear away from the wind and may even become unmanageable.

Reaching

Having done our close-hauled sailing, let us bear away a bit until the yacht is reaching. This is her fastest point of sailing and also the easiest for the helmsman; so easy in fact that it is known as sailing on a soldier's wind, which I'm sure is a grave libel on the many soldiers I have known who have been bitten by the sailing bug. All you have to worry about when reaching is the correct trim of the sails and steering the course you want to sail, whether by eye in relation to some mark, or by compass. With the wind just free a yacht is on a close reach; with it abeam she is on a broad reach.

To get the best trim of the sails for reaching, ease the sheets gently until the luffs of the sails begin to lift. Then harden in a fraction, and they will be set exactly right to get the best out of the yacht. The fault one can most often see when a yacht is reaching is the sheets hardened in too much. This provides an enjoyable angle of heel and much swishing of the water when the wind is fresh, and makes you think you are going great guns. In fact you're not; all you are doing is decreasing the speed and increasing the leeway.

Running

If reaching is comparatively easy for the helmsman, many people might think that running with the wind abaft the beam is even easier. If the wind is coming from the quarter there certainly is no difficulty; it is exactly the same as sailing on a very broad reach, and all that is necessary is to ease the sheets to keep the sails full. But if the wind is coming from dead astern, or very nearly dead astern, steering a yacht is a very different kettle of fish. What happens in this case is that the mainsail, eased as far forward as it will go to

present its maximum area to the wind, blankets the foresails so that they flap idly and can do no work. So you have an unbalanced rig with all the effective sail on one side of the yacht. This unbalanced sail plan will inevitably tend to keep pushing the yacht's bows round into the wind. If you don't want to set a spinnaker and the wind is steady and coming from well aft you can boom out the foresail to windward – this is known as running goose-winged or wing and wing. It works reasonably well but if the wind is fickle or blowing in puffs the sail needs a great deal of attention to keep it drawing. If you have a spinnaker and decide to set it, you can get a much better balance of the sails, but we shall deal with spinnakers on page 130.

Meanwhile let us go back to this tendency in a yacht running with the wind astern to keep trying to come up into the wind. After a little experience you will find that you can frequently anticipate the moment when she wants to do so and be able to correct it by using the helm. Often the yacht will give a sort of surge forward, and very soon after this, up she will try to come into the wind. It is when you feel the surge that you want to apply a little helm to hold her off the wind and to straighten her up.

Another thing you will find when sailing with a following wind is a great tendency for the yacht to roll, particularly if the wind is a bit fresh. Why yachts should do so I do not know, and there is very little that a helmsman can do about it. The worst thing is to try to keep her head permanently dead on her course as this will only accentuate the roll. If you allow her to wander a little either side of your course you may be able to check this tendency a little and keep her on a slightly more even keel.

Your next small problem when running on a long leg is one of chafe. If you have eased right away in an attempt to get the mainsail as square as possible to the wind, it will rub against the after lee shroud, and if the yacht is rolling, as she almost certainly will be, this will make the chafing worse. You can help a little by holding the boom down with a kicking strap, but the best answer, particularly if your cruising is extended, is to sacrifice a little of this sail angle and sheet the mainsail as far forward as it will go without coming up against the shrouds (see chapter four).

Gybing

And now to the last problem, which is running by the lee. The wind rarely blows from one direction without altering at all, and you may find that a small shift in direction brings the wind from dead astern to a little on the lee quarter. If the yacht is rolling as she runs, the apparent wind (which is the one we are concerned with) can vary quite considerably, and the movement of the boom and mainsail during the rolls accentuates this and can easily bring the wind onto the forward side of the sail and involve you in an involuntary gybe. If you let the boom swing right across, this is known as gybing all standing or, as a sailing friend of mine always calls it, an imperial gybe, which sounds pretty majestic and does, in an odd way, describe the awesomeness of a really heavy gybe. If there is any real weight in the wind it can also be

Goose-winged with genoa 'boomed-out'. A pole prevents the sail collapsing.

1

2

3

4

Controlled gybe

Step 1: Boat has the wind on the starboard quarter sailing on broad reach.

Step 2: Move helm to bring stern directly into the wind . . . at same time haul mainsheet tight and keep it under control.

Step 3: Boat's stern passed through the wind.

Step 4: Quickly release mainsheet.

Step 5: With wind now on port quarter, reset sail for broad reach.

Setting the spinnaker on a run

Step 1: Spinnaker set ready for hoisting. It will run up with a halyard, controlled on its leeward side by a sheet, and on its windward side by a similar sheet which is rove through the end of the pole and acts as an after-guy. The pole is also controlled by a topping lift and a fore-guy which also serves as a downhaul. The inboard end of the pole is clipped to the mast and can sometimes be adjusted here for height.

dangerous. It may sweep an unwary member of the crew overboard, strain the rigging and damage the boom as it brings up hard on the weather shrouds.

The immediate, automatic and unthinking reaction, if you do see the boom begin to swing, should be to put the tiller hard down to leeward in order to bring the bows up towards the wind. If this is too late to stop the gybe, it may be enough to break its full

force. But the better and much more seaman-like thing to do is not to run by the lee. As soon as you feel the wind crossing the stern, it is easy to bring the mainsail over on the other tack in a controlled gybe without any of the fearsomeness of the imperial variety. Start by luffing a little to bring the wind fine on the quarter and haul in on the mainsheet until the boom is nearly amidships. Then bring your helm up until the wind crosses

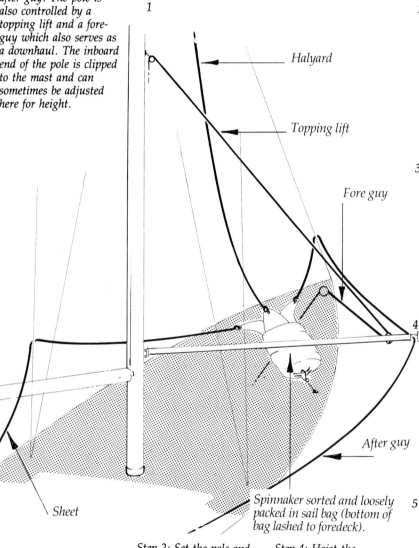

1

Halyard

Topping lift

Fore guy

After guy

Sheet

Spinnaker sorted and loosely packed in sail bag (bottom of bag lashed to foredeck).

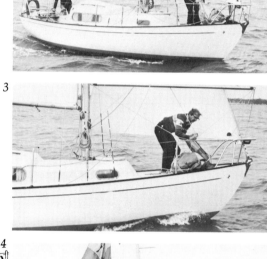

2

3

4

5

Step 2: Set the pole and reeve the windward sheet (or after-guy) of the spinnaker through its outer end.

Step 3: Hank on the spinnaker halyard as the final preparation.

Step 4: Hoist the spinnaker on the halyard, while the helmsman or crew tend the sheets.

Step 5: The spinnaker is now set and beginning to draw.

Gybing the spinnaker

Step 1: Gybing the spinnaker involves bringing the pole across and setting it on what was formerly the leeward side. The operation entails letting go the spinnaker sheet from the end of the pole, swinging the pole out to the other side and reeving the former leeward sheet. Most spinnaker poles are double-ended, which considerably simplifies the operation.

Step 2: Boat on a dead run with spinnaker pole on windward (starboard) side.

Step 3: Snap hook lanyard on the spinnaker pole to release the windward sheet.

Step 4: Swing pole across to leeward side.

Step 5: Snap hook on pole opens to connect leeward spinnaker sheet.

Step 6: With pole secure, gybe boat around. It is sometimes helpful to gybe the mainsail prior to the spinnaker as this will blanket the latter and take some of the weight out of it.

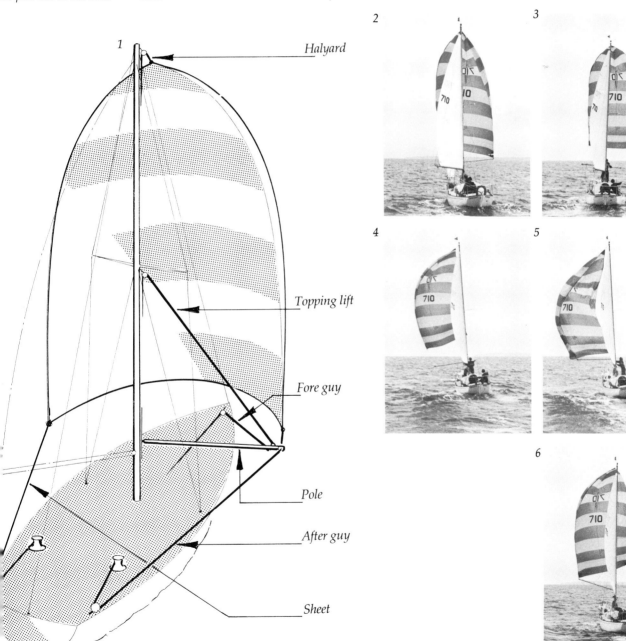

1   Halyard

Topping lift

Fore guy

Pole

After guy

Sheet

2

3

4

5

6

If you have a longish sail ahead with the wind abaft the beam you will do much better if you set a spinnaker.

the stern and the boom swings over. As it does so, pay out the main sheet smartly. This needs to be done quickly, otherwise the tendency will be for the yacht to luff right up; they always do after a gybe if there is any delay in letting the mainsail and boom swing right forward.

Sailing with a spinnaker

If you have a longish sail ahead of you with the wind abaft the beam, you will do much better if you set a spinnaker. It will balance the mainsail, make the steering much easier, and will also give you an extra turn of speed.

The most common type of spinnaker is the parachute, which is an isosceles triangle, cut with a huge belly. The names given to its parts are the same as for any other triangular sail. It is controlled by its three corners, as although you use a boom or pole, the spinnaker is attached to it only at its tack.

Parachute spinnakers are set high (the helmsman would be unable to see where he was going otherwise) and with an immense belly; they must therefore be set completely outside the forward rigging. With their great belly they need only a short boom, and because luff and leech are the same length and the whole sail is set outside the rigging, it is an easy matter to bring it from one gybe onto the other without lowering and rehoisting it, simply by making what was the tack on one gybe into the clew on the other. All that is necessary is to change over the short boom so that it bears out the new tack on the other side of the mast. The previous fore-guy becomes the new sheet, and the old sheet the new fore-guy.

If yours is one of the small cruisers, your spinnaker boom will be stowed on deck when not in use and will have a topping lift and fore-guy but no outhaul. The after-guy runs through the outboard end of the boom which will usually be fitted with a parrot beak to allow the rope to run but not jump out of

the end of the boom.

To set the spinnaker you should first bend the sheet onto the clew, the halyard onto the head and the after-guy directly onto the tack after it has been led through the outboard end of the boom. Make sure that everything is set outside the other rigging and will not foul it. The spinnaker boom is raised into position by the topping lift with the fore-guy already attached to the boom. You then hoist the sail, and trim it with the after-guy to get the sail filled and drawing. The fore-guy will be trimmed to stop the boom from lifting and will need to be adjusted with the after-guy.

As a general rule applying to parachute spinnakers, the heel of the pole should be at a height that makes it nearly horizontal when the sail is drawing. To achieve this the gooseneck should be in a slide. Any divergence should be upward at the outboard end, that is, slightly cocked up, rather than drooping. The foot of the sail should be kept parallel to the water.

When you want to hand or douse the sail, you must first spill the wind from it. This is done by easing the boom right forward. Remove the after-guy and lower the sail handsomely, gathering it in as it comes down. As with hoisting it, this is best done in the lee of the mainsail.

Nevertheless, when you have the wind behind you and your thoughts turn towards a spinnaker to help the boat along, never forget that these are light-weather sails, and as such are normally cut from lightweight nylon where the extra strength of that material is no bar to its use for this particular sail. In strong winds, if used for any length of time, it is frequently pulled out of shape and can get baggy along the luff and the leech. This does not mean that use of the spinnaker is restricted to winds of up to force 2 on the Beaufort scale, but it does mean that you may run into trouble if you use a spinnaker for long periods in strong winds.

Handing the spinnaker (opposite)

Step 1: Rehoist the jib.

Step 2: Ease windward sheet or after-guy and allow the pole to swing forward so that the spinnaker clew can be reached from the foredeck.

Step 3: Release snap shackle securing the sheet to the windward spinnaker clew, allowing the spinnaker to fly out to leeward. The helmsman or crew should meanwhile begin to pull on the leeward sheet.

Steps 4 and 5: The foredeck man should now begin to lower away the spinnaker halyard while the helmsman or crew quickly pull the sail down under the main boom and into the cockpit.

2

4

Handing a torn spinnaker.

Running aground

Having taken the boat out from her anchorage and sailed her close-hauled on a reach, and running with the wind abaft the beam, it is time to take her back and anchor her, or pick up her mooring. We are doing this, perhaps a bit pleased with ourselves after a good day's sailing, when, with all her sails set and the wind still blowing, the yacht stops moving. And what was that slight grating noise under her keel? We have run her onto a sandbank, or a mudbank, or just plain ashore. We have 'put her on the putty' as the accepted phraseology goes.

Really, there is very little excuse for putting a yacht on the putty. You should know the waters in which you are sailing, having previously studied the chart if it is the first time you are visiting them. You should be able to recognize the fairway buoys and any local marks, usually canes or withies, which are used to mark the unbuoyed channels. The local *Sailing Directions* almost always has this information. You should know the times of high and low water, as from these you can quickly estimate the height of the tide at any moment, using the rough and ready twelfths rule. The twelfths rule is a rough attempt to mathematize the unsteady rise and fall of the tide. It divides the six hour range of the tide (which is got by subtracting the low water from the nearest high water) into factors of twelve, and says that the tide rises (or falls) $1/12$ in the first hour, $2/12$ in the second hour and so on. It is usually set out like this:

Interval	Rise or fall
1st hour	$1/12$
2nd hour	$2/12$
3rd hour	$3/12$
4th hour	$3/12$
5th hour	$2/12$
6th hour	$1/12$

OPPOSITE: An alternative to the spinnaker is the 'blooper' or cruising chute, which is a very lightweight sail – somewhere between a spinnaker and a very baggy genoa. Since it requires no guy ropes, poles and so on, it is extremely popular for cruisers.

OPPOSITE: Down she comes. The big spinnaker is lowered and hauled over the deck.

Nevertheless, yachts do run aground, most frequently through trying to take a short cut, and so it is useful to know what to do to get them back into deep water again.

You always know where the deep water is because you have just come from it. You know the direction of the wind because you have just been sailing with it, and you ought to know the state of the tide and whether it is ebbing or flowing. If you are sailing one of the more old-fashioned type of boat with a long, straight keel when you go aground, you will have to come off in the same direction as you went aground. If you try to get the bows round to sail her off, all you will do is to pile up a bank of mud or sand or shingle, or whatever the bottom is, against the side of her forefoot. If you have the more modern design of cut-away forefoot and deep keel aft, you may be able to get her bows round and sail her off into deeper water. There are three golden rules to remember when you run aground:

Grounding on a lee shore demands quick and positive action.

1. If you run aground and do nothing with the sails, leaving them trimmed as they were, all that they can do will be to try to drive you yet harder ashore. So un-less you are actually in stays, that is, head to wind, at the moment of ground-ing, start by letting fly the sails.

2. If possible, make the sails do most of the hard work. If you are sailing a yacht with a cut-away forefoot, a backed headsail will help considerably to get the bows round towards deeper water. If it isn't quite enough, help it in its work by bearing away with a spare spar – a spinnaker boom, for example, if it is stowed on deck. Get as wide a purchase as you can with the end of the spar or the offending piece of ground and then lean back on the spar, facing the direction you want the bows to swing, pull-ing and not pushing.

3. Never allow yourself to get flustered. If you run aground with a falling tide, you have got very little time indeed to get her off and sailing again. If your actions are precise and quick you may just do it. If you panic and spend too long trying to decide what to do, you will almost certainly have to wait until the next flood tide rises high enough to lift her off.

On a rising tide

If you run aground on a rising tide you have little cause for concern. Unless you know you can sail off (for example by swinging the bows round with a backed headsail) lower the sails and lay out the kedge anchor in deeper water on the weather bow. There is no point in straining away on the kedge warp; in a few minutes the tide will lift her and you can haul her out to the kedge without any risk of subsequent backache.

In a river or estuary

If you are sailing in a river or estuary and you go aground on a river bank or the low ground stretching out from a sea wall, I trust it will be on the weather side of the river. It is an elementary rule of seamanship that when approaching a lee shore you should allow yourself an extra margin of room in case the wind shifts and heads you, and you should therefore be absolutely certain not to go close enough in to hit the bottom. There is rarely very much sympathy for anyone who runs his yacht aground; there is none whatsoever for one who does so on a lee shore.

On a falling tide

If you go ashore on a falling tide, you may be lucky and get off the mud before your yacht is sewed (in other words before the tide has dropped enough to make it impossible). This will almost certainly mean that you have reacted fast enough to get the wind acting on the sails to blow the boat's bows round and sail her off. If not, and if you have to lay out a kedge to haul her off, you are very unlikely to succeed and all that is left is to wait patiently for the next tide to lift her.

If you are in this situation the one important thing to do is to make sure that as the tide leaves the yacht she lists towards the bank on which she has run aground and not towards the deep water. If your yacht has a deep keel and relatively narrow beam, she will probably lie right over on her side as the tide ebbs, and if she is allowed to list the wrong way it is possible that the next tidal rise may not lift her far enough before it reaches the cockpit coaming and floods her. The best way of making sure she lists the right way is to stow the mainsail along the boom and swing it out towards the high ground, or to rouse out the anchor cable and lay it out along that side of the deck. If this

does not do the trick, then somehow you must get an anchor out abeam on the safe side, bend a halyard to the anchor, and haul the yacht over.

At high water

I think that many sailing people will reckon that this is enough; that as the next tide lifts her they will be ready to sail her off. I would myself at this stage take the additional precaution of laying out a kedge into the deeper water, securing the warp to the weather bow. A lot of people forget that what looks easy in daylight may not be quite so simple in the dark, and that with successive high waters a little over twelve hours apart, your yacht may

OPPOSITE: Gybing the spinnaker.

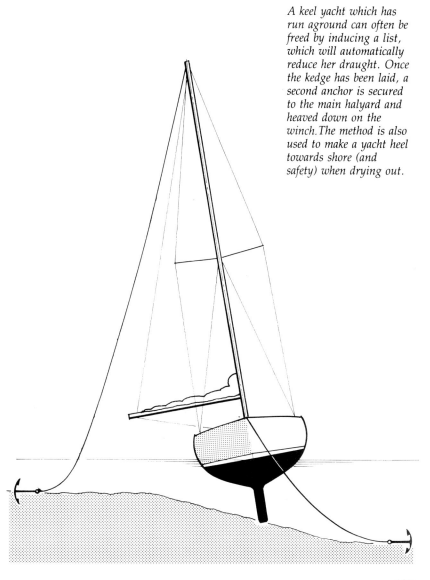

A keel yacht which has run aground can often be freed by inducing a list, which will automatically reduce her draught. Once the kedge has been laid, a second anchor is secured to the main halyard and heaved down on the winch. The method is also used to make a yacht heel towards shore (and safety) when drying out.

be lifting off during the night. I can remember, many years ago, going aground at about half ebb as we were returning after a day's sailing. All the right things were done and we settled down to wait the six hours or so for the tide to return. It was an opportunity to do a little serious cooking after a long day's sailing. We had an excellent hot meal, and then lay talking in the cabin while waiting for the new flood to do its work. The conversation dwindled, the tide rose, lifted the yacht gently, and imperceptibly deposited her higher up the bank, leaving her there at the top of high water. If we had had a kedge out, at least we would have been no worse off than we were before, even if we *had* slept through it all.

This business of going aground at the top of high water can be serious, for if the tides are taking off, the succeeding high water won't reach high enough to lift you. So, particularly in the period between springs and neaps, be doubly aware of the danger of taking risks as the flood approaches its full, or your yacht may be sitting on its sandbank or patch of mud for several days instead of for a single tide. From the top of springs to the next top of springs is fourteen and a half days, and that is a lot of sailing days to miss due to one incautious move. So always keep this danger period in mind when you are out sailing and give yourself an extra margin of safety. This is not the best time to try to take a short cut or to attempt to gain a little extra distance on a leg as you beat in to your anchorage.

Dried out and facing the correct way. If boat had taken the ground on her other bilge then the incoming sea could have flooded her cockpit.

Picking up a mooring

So we have done our day's sailing, run aground in our hurry to get back before the bar closes, got off again, and now really are approaching our anchorage. This time we will be picking up a mooring rather than letting go an anchor, since it is the more difficult of the two. Incidentally, both these operations come under the heading of 'bringing up'.

Unless you are coming in at slack water, which for our purposes may be said to lie between half an hour either side of the time of high or low water, it is essential to come up to the mooring buoy head to tide. Having had a day handling the boat on all points of sailing, you should by now have a pretty reasonable idea of how she reacts to the wind, how much she forereaches or 'carries' as you bring her head to wind, how swiftly or sluggishly she answers her helm, and how much leeway she makes when close-hauled and reaching. You should know fairly accurately the strength and direction of the tide from the time of day, according to how long an interval has passed since the last high or low water. You know the wind force and direction because you can feel it on your face. In fact, you have got the essential knowledge to enable you to pick up your mooring buoy under sail alone.

There are still one or two more things to do before sailing in and picking it up. Look at neighbouring yachts on their moorings and note the direction they are lying in relation to the tide and the wind. Your yacht will be lying in the same direction when she has her mooring chain on board. If, when lying in that direction, the wind is forward of the beam, you can keep your sails set until you have picked up the mooring; if the wind is abaft the beam, you can't, and they must be handed before you reach the mooring buoy. Lastly, unless you have got plenty of room for manoeuvring, have an anchor ready for letting go in case the proximity of other yachts makes it impossible to turn away and make a second run. It is far better to anchor than to charge down on, or even drift towards, an adjacent yacht and perhaps cause damage to both. No one will blame you if you have to let go your anchor; they are far more likely to commend you for having taken so seamanlike a precaution. If you have had to anchor, don't start thinking of weighing it

and getting under way for a second attempt; take a line in the dinghy over to your mooring, secure it to the ring of the buoy or to the mooring warp just beneath it, then weigh the anchor and haul yourself up to the mooring.

However, you must now make the attempt to get the buoy on board. You know that if the tide is running, you must arrive at the buoy head to tide; if it is slack water, head to wind.

You know too, because it is obvious, that you need to reach the buoy with all, or nearly all, way off the yacht.

At slack water

The easiest time to pick up a mooring is of course at slack water, when all you have to think about is the wind. So steer to arrive at a position to leeward of the buoy at the distance you estimate the yacht will forereach when brought up into the wind. When you get there, luff up into the wind, let the sails shake, and if your judgement has been correct, the buoy will arrive under your bow, with very little way left on the boat, ready to be brought aboard. If you have misjudged your forereach and you still have a good deal of way on when you reach the buoy, resist any temptation to pick it up and secure the warp; you will be in all sorts of troubles if you do, with your yacht sailing round the mooring and being brought up in all directions. Leave it, bear away, and come back for a second attempt.

Against the tide

If the tide is running and you are beating up against it, exactly the same procedure will take you to your mooring buoy, though because of the strength of the tide holding you back, you will need to be a bit nearer to the mooring before you luff up into the wind. If you are running up to the mooring against the tide, you will need to hand the mainsail before you come up to the buoy. So bring her head to wind a little way to windward of the buoy and lower the mainsail. Then bear away and run back over the tide with the headsails only. When you think you have enough way on the boat to reach the mooring buoy without the headsails, lower them and bring the buoy inboard. If the tide is running so strongly that you are only creeping along, keep the headsails set until you have picked the buoy up. It won't do any harm to have a little way on the boat when you reach the

1

2

4

5

Picking up a mooring buoy (downwind)

Step 1: Approach buoy downwind.

Step 2: Sail past.

Step 3: Start to round up into the wind.

Step 4: Do a controlled gybe.

Step 5: Sail upwind towards buoy.

Step 6: Secure line onto buoy.

Step 7: Let sheet fly.

Step 8: Lower sail.

7

buoy; in fact it will help you as it gives you a bit of a start in hauling the warp in against the tide.

With the tide
So far you have reached your mooring with the tide running against you; now you must think of how to do it when the tide is fair and running with you. You have to reach the buoy head to tide, so it is necessary to sail past your mooring and come back to it. If you are beating, sail past the buoy, come up to the wind and lower the mainsail, then bear away and run down to the buoy under your headsails. If you are running, continue a little way past the buoy, round up into the wind, choose the tack which will take you to leeward of the buoy, and forereach up to it.

These are the sensible and straightforward ways, but with experience you can try a shorter method when you are running up with the tide under you. Steer the yacht to leeward of the mooring buoy, and as the buoy comes abeam, begin to luff up to bring her right round head to wind. Your object here is to bring the yacht round in a semi-circle so that the buoy is brought under her bow as she comes head to wind (good judgement of distance) and so that the yacht has just about lost all way through the water when she reaches the buoy (good judgement of speed). You may be able to exercise some control of the speed by trimming the mainsail, hardening in the sheet if you are losing a bit too much, easing it away if you are going too fast.

Wind at right angles to tide
When the wind is blowing at right angles to the tide, you have the choice of sailing to windward of the buoy and running in under headsails or sailing to leeward of it and forereaching. If you choose the latter method, don't think that all is over as soon as you have the mooring buoy safely on board. Get the sails off her as quickly as you can, otherwise she is likely to take charge and you'll have a hard job of it getting the sails down without tearing them on some projection.

Picking up a mooring under sail is not merely for those who do not have an auxiliary motor in their yacht, it is also for those who enjoy the satisfaction of real achievement – and believe me, it is a very great satisfaction. But so immense in recent years has been the growth in the numbers of people who find their leisure and enjoyment in sailing that almost every yacht harbour or anchorage round the coasts is now densely crowded with yachts and picking up a mooring under sail can be a daunting prospect. With yachts moored all round you, there is no room for mistakes. So most yachtsmen, I suspect, are these days more concerned about avoiding the risks of collision than enjoying the satisfaction of well-achieved manoeuvres under sail and prefer the certainties of an auxiliary engine to the vagaries of the wind. If your chosen harbour is similarly crowded I would, though reluctantly, recommend motoring in on the engine.

Anchoring

Coming to an anchor is a much simpler operation, mainly because you need way on the yacht as you let go in order to lay the cable along the bottom and not drop it in a heap on top of the anchor. It doesn't matter if it is headway or sternway, but it is usual to lower the anchor with the boat moving slowly astern; let go the anchor onto the bottom, check the cable or rope, then when you feel the anchor bite, slack away the desired amount. If your anchor is of the fisherman type, check the cable running out as soon as the anchor reaches the bottom and then pay it out slowly as the yacht moves ahead or astern; if your anchor is a CQR or Mesh (Danforth), let it have a good deal of chain straightaway and then begin paying out in the normal fashion.

The main points you need to be sure about when you lie to an anchor are that there is sufficient depth of water at low tide for the yacht to lie comfortably, and that there is enough room for her to swing to her anchor. You will need to pay out a length of chain at the very least three times the depth of water at high tide, and this will give you an idea of the amount of room you will need to allow the yacht to swing without fouling any other anchored yacht or other obstruction. If, however, you use a nylon rope, then a 7:1 scope is usual and consequent with this increased amount so extra swinging space will be needed. If you are not sure of the nature of the bottom or suspect the presence of old mooring chains lying there, it is wise to buoy your anchor. As mentioned earlier, if you do decide to do this, stream the buoy and see

1

4

3

Anchoring

Step 1: Prepare anchor and cable for lowering, head into wind or tide and stop.

Step 2: Lower anchor to water's edge.

Step 3: Watch eddies around anchor for signs of boat making sternway, then lower anchor carefully onto the bottom.

Step 4: Veer little more cable until it 'grows' ahead to indicate anchor is holding.

Step 5: Let out intended run of cable. Secure and take anchor bearings.

that the buoy rope is running clear before you let the anchor go.

You may well find that in many of the anchorages you visit there will not be enough room for your yacht to swing to a single anchor. If so, I recommend you to put out a second anchor and middle the yacht between them so that she can swing only in her own length. This is also advisable in places where a strong tide runs, even if there is nothing close enough to restrict the yacht lying to a single anchor. The main point to remember when you are mooring with two anchors is that it is better to place the two anchors up and down stream rather than across the stream; this will give you a better safety margin if the weather deteriorates while you are lying there.

There are three ways of mooring a yacht. Let us take the easiest way first.

Laying out a kedge

Let go the bower anchor and lay the cable along the bottom, allowing the tide to do the work of dropping you down to the full scope of the cable, which is of course three times the depth at high water. Then, with a warp secured to the kedge, you take it out in the opposite direction in the dinghy as far as the warp will let you, and let it go.

But before going any further, let us have a quick look at the ways of doing this. First, the kedge. The seamanlike way is to secure it over the stern of the dinghy, clear for dropping with the warp bent onto the ring, and the anchor held in position with a short length of rope rove through the ring and secured inboard in a fashion that is easy to cast off. If, instead of securing it over the stern, you carry the anchor inside the dinghy you may find that you have got to stand up to lift it clear of the gunwales, which is not a good thing to do in a dinghy. Also, in the act of dropping it overboard, one of the flukes could catch in your clothing and provide you with an involuntary ducking, always a cause of great hilarity among onlookers.

Now for the warp. The best way of doing this is to bend one end onto the anchor and then coil it down in the dinghy so that the inboard end is at the top of the coil. Then take the inboard and secure it round the anchor bitts or some other convenient place forward in the yacht. Next, row the dinghy down in the opposite direction in which the bower anchor lies, paying out the warp as

3

Laying out a kedge anchor

Step 1: Secure kedge over the stern of the dinghy.

Step 2: Coil warp into dinghy.

Step 3: Allow warp to run out from dinghy.

Step 4: Row dinghy towards deep water or direction of expected weather.

Step 5: Lower anchor carefully – never throw!

you go. When all the warp has been paid out, cast off the lashing holding the anchor so that it drops to the bottom.

An alternative method is to take all the warp with you in the dinghy, let go the kedge when you reckon you are the correct distance away, and then pay out the warp as you row back to your yacht. To do this you will of course have had to coil the warp the other way so that the inboard end is at the bottom of the coil. Before you start the coil, take a turn with the inboard end round a thwart; I know of nothing more disconcerting than to see the inboard end running out over the dinghy's stern while you are still a little way short of your yacht. And any onlookers will split their sides when this happens. If you have misjudged the distance a little and the warp won't reach, there is no cause for despair. Get someone on board to veer a little of the bower anchor cable and let the yacht drift down to you. Haul the warp tight and bring it to the bower anchor cable, making sure that it is outside all the rigging. Next, secure it to the bower cable outside the cable fairlead with a rolling hitch, and finally veer the bower cable so that the hitch is well below the level of the yacht's keel. This is to make sure that as the yacht swings with the tide her keel will clear the two cables. If, after making the rolling hitch, you have enough of the warp left, bring the end inboard and secure it.

What you must never do when mooring is to lay out the kedge and bring the warp to the yacht's stern instead of her bows. The whole point of a moor is that the yacht may swing with the tide, even if in a very limited space. If you have one anchor holding her bows and another her stern, she will not be able to swing at all, for a yacht will not lie comfortably stern to tide. Moored like this she will sheer about and try to lie across the tide, putting so much strain on the kedge that it may begin to drag.

Running moors and dropping moors

The two other methods of mooring are known as a running moor and a dropping moor. They are not difficult provided that the wind is strong and steady enough to guarantee you enough way on the boat if you are mooring under sail. What you need to realize is that you will require twice the normal amount of cable, which is a minimum of six times the depth at high water, if you do a

running or dropping moor. If we take the running moor first, you approach the position in which you want the yacht to lie along the direction in which the tide flows, and when you are short of that position by the amount of scope of cable to which you want the yacht to lie, which is three times the depth at high water, you let go the bower anchor. Continue sailing (or motoring) along the same course, paying out the cable as you go, until you have got twice the required scope of cable laid out along the bottom; this is the six times the depth at high water mentioned above. Then take the sail off her or stop the engine, let go the kedge, and start heaving in on the bower cable while paying out the kedge warp at the same time. When the yacht is middled between the two anchors, secure the cables as before. No doubt the tide will help to drop you down to the midway position so that there is no need to exert undue effort at heaving in the bower cable.

A dropping moor is a running moor in reverse. The first anchor to be let go is uptide of your position, and as the tide drops you down from that anchor you pay out cable until a length equal to six times the depth at high water has been run out. Then the kedge is let go and the yacht middled by heaving in on the bower cable.

A final word about running and dropping moors. Always do them against the tide; you will have a very difficult job on your hands if you try to do them with the tide. It's not entirely impossible, but if there is no way of approaching your desired mooring position with the tide against you, use the dinghy and the first method described above. It will prove to be much less laborious and is just as efficient as either of the other two.

Mooring swivel

If you use a chain cable instead of a warp on your kedge, or have one of those super yachts with two bower anchors each on its own chain cable, don't attach one cable to the other by means of a rolling hitch when you middle between the anchors. If you are going to remain moored for only one night (two tides) bring in both cables through their own stemhead fairleads and accept the inevitable single twist you will get in the cables as your yacht swings round with the tide. You need to arrange the scope of one of your cables so that when the yacht is middled you have a joining shackle close inboard of the fairleads. Clearing the twist when you unmoor entails putting a stopper on that cable below the twist, breaking it at the joining shackle, clearing the twist by passing the end of the broken cable round the other, and connecting it up again with the joining shackle.

But if you are staying more than a night, which will mean more than one twist in the cables, it is much better to use a mooring swivel. This entails giving each anchor a scope that brings a joining shackle close to the stemhead. Each cable is then broken at the joining shackle, the end links of the outboard ends shackled to the lower links of the swivel, and the inboard end of one of them to the top link. With the swivel lowered clear of the keel, the yacht can then swing as often as she likes without putting a twist in the cables.

Backing up an anchor
There may be times, as you come into an anchorage, when a lowering sky, a falling barometer, a rising wind, or suspicions about the holding ground, may give you doubts about whether your anchor will be able to hold the ship if conditions turn really bad. You can often set these doubts at rest by backing up the bower anchor with the kedge. To do this, you secure the end of the kedge warp to the bower cable about 4 fathoms (7m) from the anchor, using a rolling hitch and then seizing back the end protruding from the hitch so that it cannot slip down the cable. Give the yacht all the scope you have on the bower anchor and lay out the kedge beyond and on the same line as the bower. Then dismiss your doubts in the assurance that, short of a hurricane, your yacht will not drag her anchor.

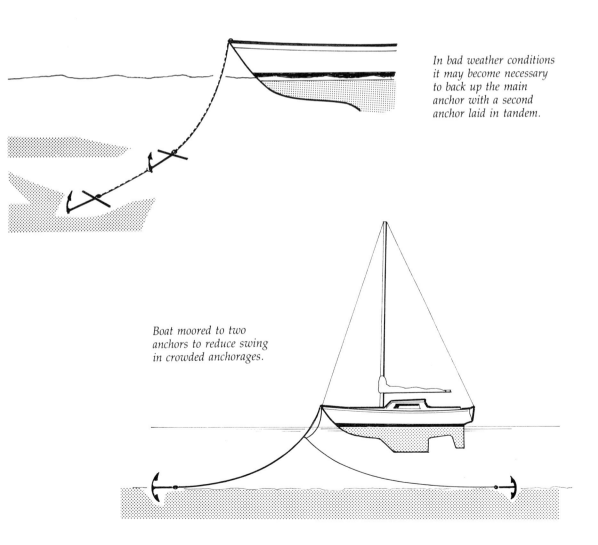

In bad weather conditions it may become necessary to back up the main anchor with a second anchor laid in tandem.

Boat moored to two anchors to reduce swing in crowded anchorages.

CHAPTER 9

Coping with wind and waves

As the weather gets bad, it is not really the wind that presents the greatest threat to a small vessel, but the waves. The huge waves of the great oceans, with crests up to half a mile (1km) apart, are majestic and awe-inspiring but present no real threat to a yacht. It is the steep, short seas that do the damage, or irregular seas caused by a wind shift – the new sea crossing the old one and causing occasional pyramid shapes which can fall down with great weight and little chance of forewarning. The worst seas come when the wind gets up against a strong current, as one finds, for instance, in the Alderney Race (8 knots at springs) in the English Channel, or in the Pentland Firth between Scotland and the Orkney Islands to the north.

Bad seas are also encountered when there is irregularity in the seabed over which the waves are passing. These can be found in various places around the globe, such as on the Continental shelf in the Bay of Biscay. Here the depth drops from 295ft to 19,700ft (90–6,000m) in the space of 20 miles (32 km). In strong easterly winds, fortunately rare, the waves here can take on a peculiar dipping formation, rather as if their troughs have become particularly deep. And it is this that can destroy. Similarly in the Agulhas Current, approaching Port Elizabeth from the Indian Ocean, there is a sudden drop in the seabed causing 'holes' in the surface of the sea into which liners have been known to pitch and not rise again.

The sight of a really big wave breaking is extremely frightening, and one imagines that it is in the welter of white water and the roaring that the great danger lies. It doesn't, of course. The greater danger is in the moment when the wave is still solid and rearing up preparatory to breaking. It is when a wave does that immediately astern of a small yacht

that things may get broken. A water-filled cockpit is not the end of all things provided that the volume of water is not too great and that the self-draining pipes are adequate. (They very seldom are, however. I think that, at the minimum, there should be two pipes of 2in (50mm) diameter, and you should never allow a strainer to be incorporated in a self-draining pipe.) The best cockpit drains I ever saw were of 3in (75mm) diameter, and one could see straight through them into the sea below. Also in the cockpit there should be no locker lids to fly off and form further weight-carrying water tanks. There should also be a means of pumping. If your yacht is built with a permanent bridge deck between cockpit and cabin, this is the occasion on which you will be truly thankful for it.

The reason for this emphasis on the cockpit is that, in almost all cruising yachts, the cockpit is in the stern. If your yacht is one of those built with the cockpit amidships, the danger is of course considerably less. With a normal cockpit in the stern, the weight of water held in it before it can drain away bears the stern down, and if the drains can't deal with it quickly enough, a succeeding wave may board the yacht in a big way and smash it up. It is only a yacht's ability to float up with her own buoyancy, and to keep on the surface of the heavy element in which she lives, that enables her to survive the blows aimed at her. Once she begins to lose her buoyancy her end is inevitable.

The worst waves of all are those that are actually breaking on a hostile shore, and once among them a yacht does not have much chance of survival and nor, indeed, has her crew. So let me repeat once again one of the golden heavy-weather rules. Once the weather has deteriorated it is extremely inadvisable to approach anywhere near the

4

8

Making a yacht watertight

When bad weather threatens, a small boat's best defence lies in her own inherent buoyancy. So at all costs this must be preserved and that means keeping the water out.

1. Ventilators should be taken off

2. . . . and fitted with blanks.

3. Skylights are vulnerable to leaks and damage . . .

4. and should be covered with canvas well secured.

5.. A chain opening this size could ship a gallon of water a minute!

6. A proper navel pipe with hinged cover is the best protection.

7. In emergencies stuff the hole with cotton waste.

8. More than one boat has been lost for failing to fit catches on the cockpit lockers.

9. Large wheelhouse doors like this are an invitation to disaster and the boat is suitable only for sheltered waters.

10. A canvas screen saves having to keep the washboards in place.

11. Large windows set in rubber grommet are also a threat to the boat's watertight integrity, there are many records of them having been pushed in.

shore if it can possibly be avoided, and the temptation to run for shelter must be resisted at all costs. Even if the shelter means the lee behind a headland, wave formations have a peculiar habit of passing right round a promontory and setting strongly into the bay beyond. What is more, a subsequent wind shift may turn what at first appeared on the chart to represent a sheltered anchorage into a trap of the most pernicious character and from which escape may be almost impossible.

GRP hulls of monocoque construction can sometimes survive a battering on rock or coral and live to sail again, but a better survivor is steel. Sadly enough, wooden yachts are the most easily sunk.

When the weather worsens

All this may sound formidable, but it must be remembered that the chance of a yacht on a normal long-distance cruise being caught in truly exceptional weather conditions – in the centre of a hurricane, for instance – is pretty remote, and there is really little to fear from the occasional gale at sea provided you have confidence in the stoutness of your yacht and her gear.

There is nothing like weathering a gale or two for gaining this confidence. But until you have dealt with it, the real question is what you can do about it in advance. And here is one golden rule that is well worth remembering. Don't go too fast. As soon as the wind gets strong, a small boat begins to go faster and faster. And before long it becomes increasingly difficult to steer, heels over further and further, and begins bucketing about in an unpredictable and dangerous manner. This is the exact moment when it is very easy to lose someone overboard. The skipper himself may be steering, and being in the cockpit will have something firm to hold on to. The rest of the crew, who have to get up on deck and start reducing sail, usually following shouted instructions, are the ones at greatest risk. This is the moment when you should reduce the speed of the yacht through the wind.

Let us now consider the main rules that should govern your actions at sea when the weather gets bad.

1. Have confidence in your yacht and in your ability to handle her, and realize that when the weather deteriorates, she is on her own and must find her own salvation before she and you can return to the harbour where you want to be.

2. Plan your voyages both in relation to the time of year and the availability of favourable winds.

3. Listen to the weather forecasts and, if for some reason you cannot receive them, watch your barometer carefully and try to anticipate any change in the weather which its movements may foretell. (See chapter thirteen.)

4. If the weather begins to deteriorate and you find your yacht becoming difficult to steer, reduce her speed by reducing her sail area. Also, if you have not already done so, put on lifejackets and safety harnesses.

5. If she is still difficult to steer under reduced sail, run her off the wind, but never far enough to risk gybing. If you are running before the wind, keep her on a straight course. Don't let her waver.

6. If the weather gets worse still, heave to or lie a-hull.

7. Resist all temptations to close the shore in search of shelter, particularly if the shelter lies to leeward. Never forget for a moment that you and your yacht are ten times safer at sea even in wild weather than you are battling off a lee shore.

8. Use a sea anchor if you are drifting dangerously to leeward when lying a-hull.

9. In a full storm with winds of force 10 or above, run before the wind under bare poles. And slow down by towing a warp or some other object if your yacht looks like hanging on the wave crests for longer than she should do.

10. If you are forced onto a lee shore, stay with your yacht until she actually begins to break up.

11. The most important rule of all. Keep thinking ahead and, as the weather

progressively deteriorates, know how to adapt to it and trust your own judgement as to when you do so.

Shortening sail

The way to reduce the yacht's speed is to take some of the sail off her, either by reefing or by the substitution of a smaller sail for a larger one. If, from a weather forecast over the radio or from your own reading of the weather signs, you expect the wind to strengthen into a really strong blow, shorten sail in plenty of time. It is far easier to roll down a reef or two and hoist a smaller jib or staysail when the wind is working up to its full strength than when it has reached it. And what you do then depends to some extent

on where you are. The one thing to avoid is to try to run for shelter unless it is close at hand. It is always a temptation, when the sea is rising and the barometer is falling, to look for some harbour or anchorage where you can escape from the pounding to come. If there is one to windward of you then, if you feel you must, you can go ahead and try to get there, but I would still recommend staying out at sea as the better bet. If the harbour or anchorage lies to leeward, resist the temptation with all your might, even if you know the harbour and its entrance well. This is particularly important if you look likely to get there when the tide is ebbing. To seek shelter to leeward is *always* a risky business, and doubly so with a tide running out of a har-

A spray hood can protect the crew from the elements and if this means preserving their efficiency and strength then it is obviously an important item.

bour entrance. It is always far better to face it out at sea.

When the wind begins to blow and you shorten sail, your main consideration must be that the vessel should remain balanced after the reduction. It is no good, say, reducing to just a small jib if you are trying to go to windward, because most yachts will carry too much lee helm under a foresail alone to make headway with any sort of efficiency. Better to have a smaller jib and a close-reefed main, or even trysail. Not that, in these days of terylene and dacron, I think it is really a necessity to carry a trysail unless your mainsail cannot be reefed down enough to cope with a strong wind. Still, if you have one, you might as well use it in a gale, even though you will need to be very careful when setting it. Naturally it involves lowering the mainsail and securing it to the boom, transferring the main halyard, and rigging the sheet, all on a violently tossing deck in sheets of spray.

Turning away from the wind
If you have unlimited sea room, the best thing is to turn away from the wind sufficiently to reduce the noise, spray and motion but of course not far enough to be anywhere near the risk of a gybe. One of the worst things, I always think, about a storm at sea in a yacht is the noise that the wind makes in the rigging, a perpetual roar varied with an occasional high-pitched scream when the squalls strike. Although you and your crew, after the first three or four hours, will be getting tired of the general tumult caused by a combination of violent motion, the shudder of the yacht when a big sea hits her, the continual sheets of spray driving across the deck, and the noise of the wave crests as they break alongside, it is the unceasing roar of the wind that really takes it out of you. So turning away from the wind is by far the kindest thing you can do for your crew, and indeed for yourself and the boat.

The moment at which you decide that enough is enough and the time has come to turn away from the wind is not difficult to determine. You will know by instinct when an increase in wind strength has become strong enough to endanger the ship and her gear, and that is the moment for decisive action. I can remember one occasion myself when there was no question that unless we should run off at once without a moment's delay, the mast would go. It is not often that you will encounter a wind of this strength, but when you do, trust your own instinctive feeling of the right moment to reduce the strain on boat and crew. In this sort of weather, no one will think you a coward for not carrying on a futile battle against the elements.

Running before the wind
If, instead of trying to go to windward, you are running before the wind, keep as much sail as you can forward, even to the extent of setting a small spinnaker if you find the steering becoming progressively more difficult. In a two-masted vessel, it is best to lower the mizzen entirely and rely only on the forward sails.

Running before a favourable gale is in many ways the epitome of exciting sailing. When sailing there is nothing quite as thrilling as when a yacht lifts to the advancing wave, seems to hold steady on its crest for a few moments as she rushes forward with the wave in a smother of white foam, and then slides down into the trough while another wave comes up from astern to repeat the process. It is a magnificent sensation and you feel that you can continue like this for as long as the gale lasts.

But watch it. If the wind continues to freshen and the waves to grow bigger, you may unwittingly be approaching a condition of great danger. The signs are generally that the yacht is going really fast, stays longer than usual on each wave crest, and has a tendency, as the wave crest at last passes, to try to round up to the sea. What is happening is that the yacht's stern, on or near the crest, is being pushed forward by the motion of the wave while her bow, buried in the trough between waves, is held back because the water between the waves moves in the opposite direction to the waves themselves. These are the conditions that can cause a yacht to broach, when she lies broadside to the seas, or pitchpole as she slides down the face of the wave. This is a moment of real danger, for if a wave takes her sideways her own speed may be enough to roll her over. Once upside down, the mast may be wrenched out of her by the force of the righting movement, and even in GRP yachts it has been known for the coachroof to be smashed.

So you must do one of two things. You

Preparing for a blow

Preparing for strong winds may mean more than just reefing, it can mean lowering sails altogether. These pictures show some of the options.

1. Mainsail deeply reefed with storm jib to replace the headsail.

2. Ketch making good speed under headsail and mizzen alone.

3. Yawl under reefed main.

4. Boat running before the wind with reefed mainsail and twin headsails.

5. In a strong following wind it can help to carry extra sail forward.

157

OPPOSITE: Boat hove to on starboard tack. Note headsail is sheeted to windward, mainsheet is eased, and tiller is being held down to leeward. Heaving to on starboard tack gives the boat automatic right of way.

must either increase the yacht's speed relative to that of the waves, perhaps by setting a small spinnaker as mentioned above, or you must slow her down by taking some of the sail off her. The purpose of both remedies is to give the rudder a better grip of the water so that she will steer easily. And if you think that there is more wind to come, it is not difficult to decide which alternative to take.

When a yacht is running in bad weather, both Slocum and Moitessier – and you can hardly ask for better authorities – consider that the safest course is about 45° from the general line of the waves. Whether this is so or not depends to some extent on the underwater conformation of the yacht, and some yachts run more easily than others. What I think is more important is that the yacht's course should be straight and controlled, and that she should be travelling at a manageable pace for steering.

Heaving to

If you do not have enough sea room, perhaps because of shoal water or proximity to a shipping lane, then the best thing is to heave to, possibly by going about without tending the foresail sheets. The effect of this is to reduce your speed through the water to nearly nil by having the mainsail driving against the foresail. If you ease the main sheet a little you can then lash the helm down to leeward and your yacht will sail herself, with the mainsail trying to drive her up into the wind and the backed foresail trying to keep her away from it. The angle of heel will probably increase but the rolling should stop, and your yacht will ride easily over the oncoming seas. But it is important to make sure that the sails and helm are trimmed in such a way that the boat never comes up into the wind enough to make the sails flog. Even the most modern sail materials cannot stand much of that, and

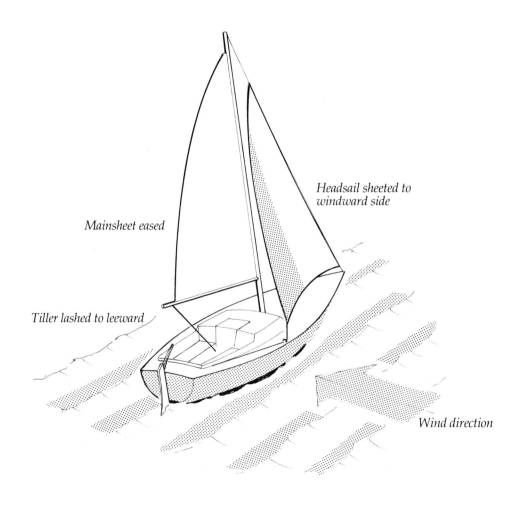

Mainsheet eased

Headsail sheeted to windward side

Tiller lashed to leeward

Wind direction

Hove to. By sheeting the headsail to windward and easing the mainsail the drive in each sail counteracts the other and the boat is made to stop. It is necessary to keep the helm lashed to leeward to maintain this equilibrium.

if you allow it to happen you will end up with sails torn and frayed to bits. Having hove to, and as soon as the uproar dies down, you can gather your wits and decide what to do next and how to do it.

Lying a-hull

If the gale continues to increase in strength, blowing, say, at force 8 or force 9, you may find it necessary to lie a-hull, that is with all the sail off her, leaving the wind to act on masts and rigging only. Here again you need the helm lashed down, so that the wind will blow from the beam or a bit abaft of it. You will naturally make a lot of leeway, but this causes a smoother patch of water to windward, something like an oil slick without the oil, and the crests of the advancing waves are reduced when they meet the slick. A yacht lying a-hull is apt to roll considerably, but the pressure of the wind on masts and rigging will probably prevent the roll to windward, so that it very rarely passes the vertical and is all to leeward.

Running under bare poles

If the gale is determined to develop into a storm, which is force 10 or above, I am sure that the safest thing to do is to run before the wind under bare poles. But to do this successfully you need to have a reliable and expert man on the helm, for it is absolutely essential that the yacht is kept exactly stern on to each advancing sea, since even a small deviation can lead to a risk of broaching. A good grip of the rudder on the water is essential, and so you must not only watch your steering very carefully but also your speed through the water, for if the water in which the rudder is immersed is travelling at the same speed, or near it, as the yacht herself, there will be no grip at all and any small aberration in the waves will knock her off course and you won't be able to get her back.

Slowing down with no sails

If the force 10 wind persists, you will almost certainly find it necessary to reduce speed even more. Once again when you find the yacht hanging on the crest for long periods and being very difficult to steer, that is the moment when you *must* slow her down, and since she has no sail at all on her, you must find some other way of doing so. Chapter three mentioned the value of carrying a length of coir rope, also known as grass rope,

on board, and this is an occasion when it comes into its own. You need to use all its length, secured at each end on either counter so that it forms a bight as it is towed, and this makes a fairly effective brake to slow you down. Nylon or terylene (dacron) rope is too smooth for this purpose and is not nearly so good. Perhaps the ideal thing is to tow a large wickerwork basket – but how many yachts would ever have such a thing handy at the crucial moment? Failing a basket, an old sail, towed at the end of a rope, would serve much the same purpose, though it would not do the sail any good. I have often wondered why no one, so far as I know, has tried towing the anchor on a length of chain cable, and I think this would be effective. But of course you would have to take some precautions to protect the taffrail where the cable rides over it, and also make provision in advance for eventually retrieving the anchor. With the weight involved, the difficulties might be considerable.

Lying to sea anchor

Next, one comes to the business of lying to a sea anchor. This has become a matter of considerable debate, and although I don't like a sea anchor, there are times when I would certainly use one.

But first of all, let us clear up the confusion over something that many people call a sea anchor – a sort of tapered canvas bag held open at the large end by a metal hoop. This is in fact a drogue, towed astern to slow a yacht down, and is not, and never was, a sea anchor. It is very little use as such unless it is really big, and it is not nearly as effective a brake on speed as a grass rope towed in a bight, as mentioned above.

The best sea anchor is something sizeable which you make yourself from stuff carried on board; wooden gratings, an old sail, cushions, anything else you have that floats, firmly secured together at the end of your thickest warp, to which the yacht will lie head or stern to the sea. I see no point in stowing on board something specifically called a sea anchor, which must be pretty large to be effective and which you will very rarely need, when you can very quickly put together something that will be equally effective from gear you already have in the yacht.

Some yacht skippers say that you should lie bows-on to a sea anchor, others that you should lie stern-on. The bows-on enthusiasts

say that a yacht lies easier with her bows pointed towards the advancing seas, which I think must be true; those who prefer to lie stern-on to the sea say that to do so creates less strain on the rudder (because the yacht will be making headway, not sternway) and that if you lie bows-on, the yacht will tend to turn away from the wind. This may equally be true. If your yacht has a canoe stern, then I imagine that it would pay to lie stern-on to the seas because it is kinder to the rudder, but with any other design of stern you will have sheets of water flooding into the cockpit and down the companionway unless you can make the doors really watertight.

The main use of a sea anchor is to check excessive leeway when you are lying a-hull in a storm. If you have plenty of sea room to leeward, I see little point in bothering to put out a sea anchor, for you will come to no harm provided the conditions do not worsen.

And if they do, then you stop trying to lie a-hull and run before the storm under bare poles. The one situation in which the use of a sea anchor is essential is when you have some danger to leeward of you, such as a tidal race, shoal water or land, making it necessary to slow down your rate of drift to leeward. If this is the case you *must* use one. And if you use one, then it is only sensible to include an oil bag. This is a canvas bag fitted with cotton waste soaked in vegetable oil – although any oil can be used – which seeps out and spreads itself over the sea surface. This has the effect of calming the waves to windward of the yacht.

Foundering

It is probably true to say that the best chance of survival for the crew is to stay with the yacht until she is actually sinking beneath the surface. As a classic example of this, there is

Unless sinking, it is better to stay with a foundering yacht. A life was lost and this boat severely damaged when the crew attempted to abandon her and transfer to a freighter. In spite of the damage, the boat remained afloat for days and finally had to be sunk as a hazard to navigation.

The ultimate disaster. An inflatable dinghy will give the crew a better chance of survival.

the haunting memory of the one crew member of the South Goodwin Light Vessel who remained incarcerated in the forecastle when she dragged her anchors and rolled over on her side on the sands with the waves breaking right over her. He could still breathe in there and was sheltered from the wind. The remainder of the lightship's crew were never seen again, but after three nights this man was rescued. And there is the equally true story of a merchant vessel drifting off Cape Finisterre in a storm with her engine broken down. The captain and six of the crew took to the lifeboat and perished in the waves; two crew members remained on board and, three days later, they and the ship were saved. Several similar stories could be told of some of the yachts in the disastrous 1979 Fastnet race. A liferaft can begin to look attractive when a yacht is being smashed by waves but until she is on the point of foundering, she is still the safer option.

If a yacht is being broken up on a lee shore in bad weather, the crew will almost certainly have a better chance of survival if they can keep with an inflatable rather than with a solid dinghy. An air dinghy will stay afloat for a long time even after being punctured, which is always a possibility on rocks. You can increase the chance of survival by making everyone secure himself to the dinghy by a line, because when exhausted it is only too easy to lose your grip of the dinghy and be swept away from it in the waves. It goes without saying that by this stage of an emergency everyone on board should be wearing an inflatable lifejacket, which will increase their individual chances of getting safely ashore. Another consideration is temperature, and the last thing anyone ought to do if preparing to be immersed in the sea is to follow convention and remove clothing before taking the plunge. Even shoes should be retained; they may save your life if you are obliged to clamber up rocks.

Mid-sea collision and lifting off
One of the worst dangers to a yacht in bad weather is that of being run down by a big ship. A yacht becomes progressively more difficult to handle as the weather gets worse, and she also becomes increasingly difficult

for the large vessel to sight, either by eye or with the ship's radar since the yacht becomes hidden in the ground clutter caused by echoes from the surrounding waves. In bad weather, a yacht's best hope of recognition by radar is to have aloft at a height above sea level of more than 12–13ft (4m) a large undistorted radar reflector on a firm mounting with one of the hollows pointing straight upwards. This is in the 'rain-collecting' position where maximum reflectivity is achieved. The modern types enclosed in a plastic capsule are the most practical.

It is sometimes tempting in bad weather to imagine that help might arrive in the form of a large ship that could come alongside and take you off. The seeds of disaster lie in this pattern. It is extremely difficult to manoeuvre even quite small vessels with any degree of accuracy in bad weather. There are only two possibilities for the rescuing vessel; either to lie across the wind and hope that the yacht will be able to take advantage of the lee thus formed or else to try to go alongside the yacht on her lee side. In the first instance the larger hull will be sweeping sideways over the surface of the sea towards the yacht, and the water on the lee side, though admittedly relatively smooth, will suck the yacht, or anyone who falls into the water, right up to the big ship's side and smash the yacht or drown the man. In the second, the yacht will be rolling to such a degree in the rough water that the mast at least will roll against the bigger ship's side, be snapped off and fall, endangering everyone in the process. In either event, anyone who tries to mount a boarding ladder up a ship's side will risk being crushed between the small vessel and the large one as the smaller rises and falls in the waves relative to the larger one.

Becalmed!

We have looked at the problems of heavy weather and at the measures we can take to deal with them. Very light weather, too, presents problems to exercise us, though they are neither so hazardous nor so pressing. One of them is water. If you have been plagued by bad luck with the winds – for example, when making a transatlantic crossing in the low latitudes – the fresh-water supply can become a cause of anxiety and it is advisable to be extremely cautious about its use

for anything other than drinking, and to limit even that. Salt, of course, will make you thirsty, but at the same time you should not cut down on it too much in order to eke out your fresh water; lack of salt in the tropics quickly results in skin conditions such as boils, prickly heat, and so on.

The lightness of modern metal spars is a great saving on gear in calms. In the Mediterranean, in particular, one frequently finds choppy sea conditions left by a dying wind, and there is nothing, I think, more agonizing to the spirit than a really, big, heavy, old-fashioned wooden boom crashing about from side to side, fit to pull the blocks out of the deck. In such conditions, night or day, it is essential to get preventers on the spar and bowse it down until it is safely captured, and this holds good also for the lightweight metal boom. Continual jerking is bad for terylene or dacron, not so much for the cloths themselves as for the thread where it passes through the seams, and it is here that the sails are most likely to fail.

The yachtsman's worst enemy in calms is chafe on gear, and even the most modern rig can suffer from it if the skipper neglects to be observant. I once lost a nearly new terylene genoa sheet through chafe. During the course of a single night it became almost severed at about the mid-points – which goes to show how quickly continual rubbing can eat through even the strongest materials. Good design and good materials are a great help, and you can protect them from the rigging in various ways (described in chapter four) where they fall short. If a sheet or halyard is subject to chafe at one particular point, you can as a temporary measure slip a piece of slit plastic piping over it.

Prolonged periods becalmed, especially in hot weather, are ideal conditions for the growth of weed on the bottom, and it is tempting to go over the side and try to scrub it off. In most places this is an excessively stupid thing to do, however still the air. Maybe it sounds melodramatic, but I have always been somewhat apprehensive of being taken by a shark since a man swimming next to me in Australian waters once lost his foot to one. But I expect this fear is uncalled for unless the swimmer, for one reason or another, is bleeding. That really is fatal, for by some miracle of Nature sharks are able to sense blood in the sea from a great distance. They can swim extremely fast, too.

Fog

I suppose that winds and waves and calms are sent to try us, or allow us to exercise any particular skills we may have, but one of the greatest curses for the seaman is fog, and fog with wind and waves at the same time is probably the worst of the lot. Fog is no more than a form of cloud at sea level, caused when air which has acquired humidity by passing over the sea meets a cold patch so that the humidity begins to precipitate, turning into tiny suspended droplets of moisture. Some parts of the world are more subject to fog than others, and one of the more notorious is the Grand Banks of Newfoundland where water-charged air may move up from the warm Gulf Stream to the ice-cold current descending from Greenland and the Davis Strait. Another is the western coast of Europe, which is swept by prevailing southwest winds that have gathered their cargo of water on their journey across the Atlantic and are cooled down on reaching the winter continent.

If caught in fog, your best aid is an echo sounder (depth sounder see page 202) or a leadline, and usually a great deal can be deduced from changes in depth as you move across the sea-bed. The worst anxiety is about other shipping, and if you are near a shipping lane when fog comes down, it is advisable to hoist your radar reflector and clear the lane as soon as you can. It is true that a big ship's radar should be able to spot a small vessel at sea, but then again it may not, as even radar is to some extent impaired by humidity. And even a radar set is no good when nobody is watching it. Next, bring your position up to date, entering on your chart time, course and speed upon hitting the fog, and updating this every fifteen minutes.

It is particularly unfortunate if you have to run your auxiliary engine in fog, because your next best aid, after the echo sounder, is your hearing, and the sound of your own engine will drown out everything else. It is wise to stop your engine every so often, to listen to outside sounds for a minute or so. Admittedly, there are few more terrifying sounds at sea than the steadily increasing beat of a big ship's propellers as she approaches in the murk, but it is better to know that she is there and to steer away from the sound as best you can than to be unaware of her proximity and take no action.

Sound waves can be bent in fog and may seem to come from a direction other than the true one, but a little detective work on what you can hear often helps to give a guide to your position. Light vessels hoot, some buoys ring bells, whistle, or make other noises, and with the aid of a chart or a nautical almanac you should be able to identify them. Sometimes you may be lucky in other ways – I remember being anchored in the English Channel once, and out of the clammy silence we suddenly heard the strains of a brass band playing 'Anchors Aweigh'. 'Ah, the Royal Marine Barracks at Deal', we guessed. And when half an hour later the sun came and ate up the fog, we saw that we were right.

Thunderstorms

One further weather condition not yet mentioned is an electrical storm or thunderstorm. And to these should probably be added a waterspout. Such conditions characteristically prevail towards the end of, and at the breaking up of, a prolonged period of high pressure. The land and the air have become dry because of the heat from the sun and the clear skies during the early part of the 'high'. Above the land where it is hot, columns of air begin ascending with great power and sometimes to enormous heights. Cumulus clouds form, often extremely beautiful to the eye. And eventually beneath their darkening bases the wind tears in to replace the rising air and you are faced with line squalls. The onset of these squalls can be sudden and vicious, and you may be faced with the necessity of taking in all sail to avoid losing it. It is in these conditions, due to the previous dryness and the build-up of electric charge, that you may get electrical phenomena such as sheet lightning, flashes of forked lightning, or St Elmo's fire. You would think that a yacht with its metal mast, the highest point for miles around, would be a natural target for lightning. Unfortunately, little is known about the reason why lightning takes the course it does. Suffice it to say that though yacht radios have been burned out by lightning and other parts of yachts shattered round a localized area, the number of vessels lost at sea due to lightning is minimal. Thunder storms and electrical storms are probably a good deal less dangerous than their appearance suggests.

Salvage

Let me now move on to the aftermath of bad weather. Your yacht may have been damaged and someone may come along and offer you a tow to safety. If the offer is from another yacht you can generally accept without further ado, for most yachtsmen help one another without thought of salvage or monetary reward. But if it is a commercial ship make certain, before you accept any assistance, that you know exactly what is involved. There is a big difference between a towage charge, which is a fixed sum agreed in advance between the two parties, and salvage, which is based on the value of the vessel brought in to safety. So if you are in trouble, arrange for a tow to a mutually agreed place and fix in advance the amount to be paid.

If you cannot get such an agreement, do at least observe the following rules. Pass your own hawser to the vessel which will be towing you; never accept his. Do not allow any member of the rescuer's crew on board your yacht unless, of course, you are too short-handed through injuries to manage on your own. Always steer your own yacht while being towed and retain your command over her at all times. And make sure that you give the orders throughout the whole operation. Provided you do all this, any subsequent claim for salvage is very unlikely to stick.

Should you put to sea when the weather looks rather frightening? And having got there, should you put back for shore before the weather gets worse? These are questions that a skipper is continually forced to decide, often when he is being hag-ridden by an irresponsible crew, or driven on by friends who are stuck somewhere waiting for things to get better, or even prompted by the thought of the cost of failing to get back to his home port or of his deadline for getting back to work. There is no definite answer, of course, except to say that it is better to put a reef in before departure, and then shake it out, rather than the other way round; that things outside are seldom as bad as they look from the shore; and that a well-designed and well-found vessel can survive most things at sea provided she has sea room and is not driven into shallow water.

You would think that with such a catalogue of disastrous conditions to be faced no one would ever risk going to sea for the misery of it all. And yet, what can better the days when everything goes just right? When the sunshine melts away the fog, when the expected gale never develops, when the possibly foul wind turns out to be capable of being used to best advantage, when the unexpected speed of a passage enables you to catch and use a favourable tide, and finally when a strange landfall turns out to be recognizable and the navigator has the joy of entering a new harbour faultlessly to the astonishment of his admiring crew? Those are the moments that make all the trials and tribulations of other days supremely worth while.

British lifeboat crews do not usually claim salvage, although they are entitled to.

CHAPTER 10

Safety at sea

The first thing you need to know about safety is what equipment you should have aboard. I have summarized here the recommendations of the British Department of Trade and Industry, and think that this list (intended to cover sea-going craft of 18–45ft or 5.5–13.7m loa) should be regarded as the basic minimum on a cruiser. In the USA new federal regulations are coming out on safety equipment and you should keep up to date on them by checking with your local Coast Guard. In Australia minimum safety requirements for sea-going craft are set by a separate marine board authority in each state. In New Zealand they are laid down nationally by the New Zealand Ports Authority.

Safety equipment

1. One safety harness and one lifejacket or 'wearable personal flotation device' (both of an approved safety standard) for each person on board.

2. Equipment for rescuing a man overboard:
   ● At least two lifebuoys (PFD Type IV in the USA), one of which should be within reach of the helmsman. If you intend sailing at night it should be fitted with a self-igniting light.
   ● A buoyant line 100ft (30m) long with a minimum breaking strain of 250lb (115kg) placed within easy reach of the helmsman.

3. One liferaft or dinghy (either rigid, inflatable or collapsible), made to DTI or equivalent specification, carried on deck and provided with permanent buoyancy, with oars and rowlocks adequately stored. In the case of an inflatable dinghy with two compartments, one compartment should

be kept fully inflated. (For vessels that operate only in the summer months and never go more than 3 miles (5km) from the shore the requirement for additional flotation is reduced to one 30in (0.8m) lifebuoy or equivalent for every two people on board.)

4. General equipment:
   ● Two anchors, each with a warp or chain of appropriate length. (Where warp is used at least 3 fathoms (5.5.m) of chain should be inserted between the anchor and the warp.)
   ● Bilge pump
   ● Compass and spare
   ● Charts covering every area you intend to visit
   ● Six distress flares, two of which should be of the rocket/parachute type
   ● Two ropes of adequate length
   ● First-aid box, including anti-seasickness pills
   ● Radio receiver
   ● Water-resistant torch
   ● Radar reflector, as large as can be conveniently carried and preferably mounted at least 10ft (3m) above sea level
   ● Life-line
   ● Engine tool kit

The boat's name and number, or sail number, should be exhibited prominently in letters or figures at least 9in (0.2m) high. In the USA the Federal Boat Safety Act requires all motor-driven boats to register and to display their registration number on the bows.

5. Fire-fighting equipment:
   a) For craft over 30ft (9m) in length and smaller boats which are fitted with powerful engines and carry quantities

More and more boats are now equipped with dan buoys usually attached to the lifebuoy and used to mark the position of a man in the water. The thin mast carries a flag and self-igniting light.

of fuel: two fire extinguishers each of not less than 3lb (1.4kg) capacity dry powder, or equivalent, and one or more of 5lb (2.3kg) capacity dry powder or equivalent. In this type of craft a fixed installation may be necessary.

b) For craft up to 30ft (9m) in length equipped with cooking facilities and engines: two fire extinguishers, each of not less than 3lb (1.4kg) capacity dry powder or equivalent.

c) For craft up to 30ft (9m) in length equipped with cooking facilities only, or with engine only: one fire extinguisher of not less than 3lb (1.4kg) capacity dry powder or equivalent.

In the USA all fire extinguishers used on board should bear a label to say that they have been approved as 'marine type' by the Coast Guard, and any boat with an inboard engine must have adequate back flame control for each carburettor.

Note: Carbon dioxide or foam extinguishers of equal extinguishing capacity are acceptable alternatives to dry-powder appliances. BCF or BTM types may be carried, but make sure everyone on board knows of the danger of using them in confined spaces.

All the craft mentioned above should carry two buckets with lanyards and a bag of sand.

I suppose that the most frequent cause of loss of life in cruising yachts is when people fall overboard and fail to get picked up. It is by no means always in heavy weather that the disaster of falling overboard occurs; in fact heavy weather usually makes people more conscious of the dangers and therefore less likely to take a risk when working on deck. It is, I am sure, much more often in moderate weather, when you are not so acutely on your guard, that a careless step or a sudden and unexpected lurch of the yacht can send you into the drink. The proper procedures for picking up under sail a man who has fallen overboard follow a little later in this chapter, but it is worth having a look at what can be done on board to make it easier to recover the man and more difficult for him to fall overboard in the first place before we get on to the more dramatic scenes of rescue at sea.

Lifebuoys

An overriding essential is the lifebuoy, and it should be permanently stowed somewhere within quick and easy reach of the helmsman. There is always a convenient place in the neighbourhood of the cockpit in most cruising yachts – perhaps on top of the sliding hatch, if one is fitted, or on the coachroof, but better still, if the boat has a stern pulpit, stowed vertically in a holder attached to the pulpit rail. If it is stowed flat it will have to be prevented from sliding about by suitable chocks but should never be lashed down. If you have a man overboard the few seconds spent in unlashing a lifebuoy may spell the difference between life and death.

It is extraordinary how difficult it is to locate a lifebuoy in the sea, even in daylight and in quite a moderate chop. So it should be painted in a bright colour in sharp contrast to the sea. Bright orange is the most visible and is the recommended colour. If you sail at night, the lifebuoys should be fitted with a self-igniting light. Most modern lifebuoys are U-shaped; they support a body in the sea just as efficiently as the traditional circular

shape and are easier for anyone in the water to slip into. The usual filling is cellular plastic in a PVC cover, but cork in a canvas cover will give a man in the water plenty of support to keep his head above the seas.

In addition to lifebuoys I would suggest that the cruising yachtsman might consider providing kapok-filled cushions for the cockpit seats. These are made with rope binding to provide handholds, and since you will probably want cockpit cushions anyway it is not a bad idea to have ones which can also serve a second purpose in an emergency.

Lifejackets

Every yacht should carry on board one lifejacket to DTI or BSI (British Standards Institution) approval for every member of the crew. It is important to recognize the difference between these and personal buoyancy aids (PBAs). The latter can be in the form of a blouse, bib or vest and are either inflatable or have built-in buoyancy. They will keep you warm as well as providing buoyancy for some hours. They are more comfortable to wear than the standard lifejacket, but unlike the lifejacket, they are not approved for prolonged immersion. In Britain the Ship and Boat Builders' National Federation now requires that approved PBAs be marked: THIS

The U-shaped lifebuoy is easier for a man to climb into and is more easily stowed aboard.

OPPOSITE: In a small cruiser with a family crew, foredeck work calls for the utmost vigilance and care. This man is sensibly sitting down to it.

Children should wear lifejackets at all times when outside the cabin and cockpit.

IS A PERSONAL BUOYANCY AID – NOT A LIFE-JACKET. The Standards Association of Australia has a similar requirement.

Guardrails

Every seagoing yacht today has a pulpit in the bows to provide safety and support when working forward and most also have a pulpit at the stern. The pulpit, I suggest, should set the height at which guardrails are fitted round the deck. Most seamen are sensible enough to realize that a low guardrail is more of a danger than a safety measure, yet one does occasionally see some deep-sea yachts with an adequate pulpit combined with a guardrail of only half its height – just perfect for tripping someone up on deck and depositing him overboard. Most pulpits rise above deck level to a height of about 2 to 2½ft (60–76cm) and this is the right height for the guardrail if it is to serve any useful purpose. And it should have its stanchions very firmly secured on deck, by through-bolting if possible. A man thrown against a guardrail in a rough sea exerts a considerable lateral pressure on the stanchions, and it is imperative that they are anchored firmly enough to the deck to withstand these pressures.

A guardrail of this height will of course exact some penalties, particularly in the matter of the main sheet which may chafe on the

Netting is useful, especially with small children; it also prevents handed sails from falling over the side.

Guardrails and stanchions should be solid and secure to withstand all expected weights.

173

wire rail. But this has to be accepted in the interests of crew safety, which is the paramount consideration in any yacht on an extended cruise. Sometimes you see guardrails abreast the cockpit which have been lowered to about half their proper height in order to provide a clear run for the main sheet, but this is a risk which ought not to be taken in a cruising yacht. It is a simple matter to use plastic tubing to encase the wire of the guardrail between stanchions in the line of the main sheet, and this will minimize the chafe.

Tow ropes

It is a good plan if you are alone in the cockpit either by day or night with everyone else below decks, to take a turn round your waist with a rope and secure the end inboard. Sometimes, particularly on a hot day with little wind, you may well want to sit up on deck and perhaps steer with a foot on the tiller in order to get a breath of air round your body. It is possible in these circumstances, particularly when running before a fitful breeze, for you to get knocked overboard by the boom during an involuntary gybe and for no one to be any the wiser. Similarly, if you are sailing single-handed, don't take a swim even on a windless day without a rope round your middle with the other end secured inboard. A tiny breeze getting up is enough to start a yacht sailing and it is by no means unknown for an owner enjoying a cooling dip alongside to see his yacht sail away and leave him. If you are an exceptionally good swimmer and don't fancy such an elementary precaution, at least veer a rope over the stern with a lifebuoy at the end before you dive in. And also have steps or a rope ladder over the side before you start, for it is extraordinarily difficult to get back on board up the side of a yacht without some sort of help. Again, all this is very elementary, but accidents and misjudgements do sometimes happen, and it is so very little trouble to make sure of being on the safe side.

Lifelines and safety harnesses

If, instead of a hot, still day that tempts you into a dip overboard to cool off, you are sailing in really rough weather that calls for a good deal of work on deck, you should have lifelines rigged up on deck and should wear a safety harness. A lifeline is no more than a length of wire or rope rigged tautly along

the deck from the cockpit to the forestay. Make sure everyone working on deck also wears a harness with a rope that he can snap on to the lifeline. This not only means that each man is attached to the boat but has the additional merit that if he should fall overboard it will hold him upright in the water.

OPPOSITE: Lifeharness worn with hook ready to snap on should wearer need to leave the cockpit.

'Man-a-board' lifeline system presents no hindrance and keeps crew attached to the boat at all times.

The Latchway device negotiates lifeline fixing clips on lifeline without detaching itself.

Liferafts
In an emergency the item of safety equipment most likely to prolong your chances of survival is the gas-inflated liferaft. When properly packed a four-man liferaft does not take up a great deal of room – it is roughly the same dimensions as a normal sized kitbag – and it weighs less than a hundredweight (50kg). It inflates automatically when it is thrown overboard as the line attached to it operates the gas cylinder. It is fitted with a canopy which is automatically erected when the liferaft inflates and all the necessary gear, such as baler, paddles, flares, a repair kit, and sometimes food and water, are included in it. The liferaft is attached to the boat with a line of a specially calculated breaking strain so that it will not float away before the crew have been able to climb into it but it will not be dragged down if the yacht sinks.

No skill is required to inflate it but, since the only time you will use it yourself will be

1. *Valise*

2. *Liferaft*

when it is really needed, it is a good idea to send it back to the manufacturers from time to time to be serviced and checked to ensure that it is in working order and that none of the parts have perished.

Do not think that if you carry a dinghy aboard this means that you would not do well also to have a liferaft. Certainly a rigid dinghy is useless for lifesaving unless your yacht sinks in a calm sea within rowing distance of the shore or of another yacht. However, a normal inflatable dinghy which has automatic inflation and is equipped with a handpump, canopy and oars should be serviceable in an emergency if you have a good reason for not wanting to invest in both a dinghy and a liferaft.

Man overboard!

If, in spite of the guardrail, a man has gone overboard it is then up to you to pick him up. He will depend for his survival on your judgement, skill, and speed of reaction in handling the yacht, and so you should know the proper procedures without having to think what to do or to look it up in a book.

The first and immediate thing you must do is to throw him the lifebuoy. Try to make sure it lands in the water close beside him; but not so close that you risk hitting him with it. And at the same time yell for all hands on deck, making sure to get a note of urgency into your yell so that everyone below decks knows that it is an emergency. An ordinary cry of 'All hands on deck' can often result in some precious seconds being lost.

Tell someone already up on deck (or else the first one who appears from below) to keep his eyes on the man in the water – preferably also pointing at him with his arm – and never let him stray from sight no matter what is happening on board. Make sure that he can see the man before you turn your attention to anything else, and impress on him that his information will be vital when you bring the yacht round, for you yourself will inevitably lose sight of him in the process of trying to bring the yacht alongside the man in the water, head to wind, and with all way stopped, in the shortest possible time. Tell the next one up from below to clear away and man the boathook, and the next to prepare a heaving line in case you don't get the yacht within boathook range. But don't just go sailing on while you are organizing the watcher, the boathook and the heaving line; the yacht must already be making her turn as you do all these.

I imagine that everyone who sails any sort of boat has had it impressed on him or her that when you have a man overboard you gybe round and never turn to windward. This is fairly obvious, I am sure, because it will save a lot of time – if you turn to windward, you will be to windward of the man you want to reach and it will therefore take that much longer to get to him because you will have to gybe in any case at the other end of the turn. This is an emergency when every second counts – the longer it takes to reach him, the greater the chance of losing sight of him in the water. Unless there is a reasonably calm sea, it is always much more difficult than you think to spot a lifebuoy in the water, and the longer you take to reach him, the greater distance away he will be and the more difficult it will be to keep in sight of him.

So always gybe round. The only case where it is not necessary to gybe is if a man falls overboard when the yacht is running directly before the wind. What you do then is bring the yacht up to the wind, judge when

Man overboard!

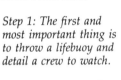

Step 1: The first and most important thing is to throw a lifebuoy and detail a crew to watch.

Step 2: Manoeuvre boat downwind, throw buoyant heaving line.

Step 3. Heave man alongside.

Step 4. Secure him to boat. (Continue opposite)

A. When a man falls in, immediately throw him a lifebuoy, post a lookout and gybe the boat around.
B. Complete gybe and proceed downwind while crew prepares for recovery.
C. Turn into the wind and bring boat to a stop to effect the rescue.

BELOW RIGHT: If after sailing downwind you cannot see the casualty, instigate a search by sailing the boat on a series of broad reaches to and fro within the downwind arc (or downstream arc) of the man's last-known position. It may be necessary to time the boat on each leg.

Man overboard drill

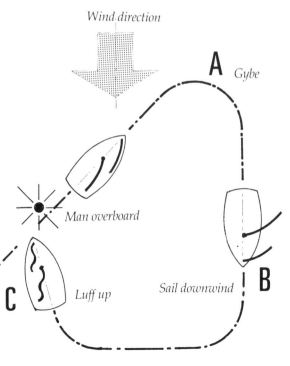

Wind direction

A *Gybe*

Man overboard

Luff up C

Sail downwind B

Wind direction

Man overboard

Search pattern of broad reaches

Step 5. Provide ladder or large bight of rope.

Step 6. If unable to heave himself aboard . . .

Step 7. get him to lie flat and with two ropes . . .

Step 8. 'parbuckle' him aboard.

Step 9. It may help forcibly to heel the boat.

you need to tack to bring the yacht close to leeward of the man in the water and then turn the boat, head to wind to bring the man alongside. You need to think of how far the yacht will forereach as you bring her head to wind so that she has lost her way when you get the man alongside, and at the same time remember that a yacht loses her way when she forereaches much more quickly in a rough sea than in a smooth one.

If you try to visualize this business of getting your yacht as quickly as you can alongside the man in the water, think of turning a full circle away from the wind, which is gybing, and ending up head to wind at about the point where you started your turn. Except when on a dead run, this will be the appropriate pattern of your movements to achieve the desired result. Immediately you have thrown the lifebuoy, you must, if possible, gybe all standing, as there will be no time to ease the severity of the boom's swing as it comes over. Obviously, if the wind is so strong that you are going to risk losing your mast in a gybe, you must then take the only alternative of turning to windward and gybing at the other end of your turn, by when there will be someone to ease the boom over with the sheet. But whichever way you decide, don't hesitate, and do it at once. A man's life is hanging on your decision, and if you take your time in deciding which way to turn, you risk losing him altogether.

Having made the turn and brought the boat up head to wind within boathook range of the man overboard, the next obvious move is to get him out of the water. First, bring him close alongside with the boathook and immediately pass the bight of a rope over his head and under his shoulders, and bring him to the place where the yacht's freeboard is least.

Then secure both ends of the bight firmly, either to a handy cleat or to the base of the stanchions. This will hold him well above water while you work out the next step. If the person who has gone overboard is fairly far gone and too exhausted to help himself, it is always a difficult job to lift him up. The actual weight of the man himself will be increased by the weight of his waterlogged clothing, which is considerable. The best way is to lift him in a parbuckle. To do this you make the end of a rope fast to the rail, pass it over his body, down round it, and bring

An exhausted man can be got aboard in the belly of a sail if crew heave on halyard.

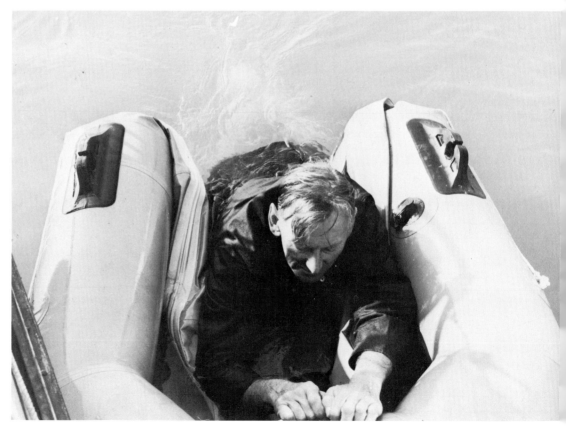

Or it may be possible to float him into the rubber dinghy which is usually ready on deck in half-inflated condition.

Fire

the end back on board. It is easier with two parbuckles, one round his chest and the other round his thighs. If you then haul in on the ends his body will be lifted up to deck level. If he is not too exhausted to need a parbuckle and can help himself, tie a bowline in the end of a rope and lower it overboard to form a step into which he can get a foot. And then, if necessary, a second bowline, not lowered so far, into which he can get his other foot and take a step upwards.

If he has swallowed a lot of water while he has been in the sea, he will need emptying out. The correct procedure for this, and for resuscitation if necessary, is included later in this chapter.

While still on the subject of man overboard, I feel that there is a danger in wearing seaboots while you are sailing, even the short ankle-length ones. I know that these are popular wear nowadays, but if you go overboard with seaboots on your feet, they will fill with water and drag you down. And they are almost impossible to kick off when you are in the water and using your arms to help you keep afloat until you can reach a lifebuoy.

I suppose that one of the most desperate things that can happen on board a yacht, or in any ship for that matter, is fire. I don't mean by that the occasional flare-up from a pressure-cooker or lamp but the real thing caused by a leakage of petrol used for the auxiliary engine or of heavy gas used for the cooking stove. Both these are explosive when they mix with air, and a fire started by an explosion is usually away to a very good start indeed.

So, first of all, minimize this risk by making certain that all the pipe joints for the engine and the stove are tight and leakproof. This is a small chore which needs doing regularly, not just at the start of a long passage in the belief that if they are tight at the start then they will remain tight until you come to an anchor again. So far as the auxiliary engine is concerned, try to ensure that if there are occasional drips of fuel or oil they are unable to drain away into the bilge. A good drip tray will ensure this but it ought to be cleaned regularly with cotton waste in order to remove any fuel or oil that may have collected

If all else fails tow the exhausted man into shallow water.

there. As advised earlier, your fuel tank filler pipe should be on deck. Always use a big, deep-sided funnel when filling it so that any splashes – and you can't avoid splashing a bit when filling – are caught on the sides of the funnel. If you have a diesel engine you have somewhat less cause to worry because the fuel will not vaporize readily like petrol, but it is still an inflammable liquid so you should wipe up any spillage.

These sorts of precautions will greatly minimize the risk of fire, but you still need to carry fire extinguishers, making sure that they are kept reasonably close to the main danger points (the auxiliary engine and the galley) and are instantly accessible – but not so close that they may be engulfed in the fire.

All extinguishers, whether liquid- or powder-filled, act on the principle of smothering the source of the fire so that oxygen, without which nothing will burn, is excluded. Extinguishers have various types of chemical fillings and all are reasonably efficient when properly used, but some are toxic and you need to know which kind of filling you have. Most fires start below deck, and often in a confined space, so you need to exercise caution if you are using a toxic mixture. A small fire blanket is a worthwhile addition for dealing with galley fires.

Bigger boats may have an automatic extinguisher or warning system installed in the engine compartment. The latter may be actuated by either heat or smoke to give an

audible warning.

If you should have a fire on board, you will need to act quickly to prevent it spreading. It is not much use seizing the nearest extinguisher and spraying generally in the direction of the flames; you need to find the source of the fire and cut it off. So get as close as you can and spray as low as you can, for the source of the fire will be at the bottom of the blaze.

Illness and accident

From time to time when you are at sea for long periods someone may fall sick or fall over and break a bone, or just suffer from seasickness. So there should be someone on hand with some knowledge of first aid. Preferably this will be you yourself, for if you have this knowledge it won't be necessary to look for someone who has it when making up a crew for cruising. In general, I think that the rudiments of first aid are largely common sense, which most sailors seem to have in generous measure, but there are a few pitfalls so that a book on first aid is a useful addition to your yacht's library. Here are one or two of the pitfalls which a little extra first-aid knowledge may help you to avoid.

Kiss of life

First, everyone on board should be familiar with giving what is known as the kiss of life or mouth to mouth resuscitation. The rudiments of this are to make sure that there is a clear passage for air to reach the patient's lungs by seeing that his tongue is lying flat and not blocking his airpipe and that his neck is properly extended. Having verified these, close his nose with your fingers, support his chin, fill your lungs with air, and breathe out mouth to mouth so that your air goes into his lungs. Go on repeating this, but not too

It is important to carry a fire extinguisher in the engine compartment or nearby.

The kiss of life

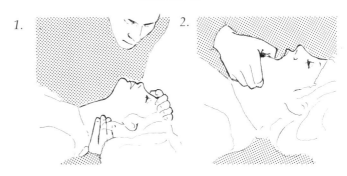

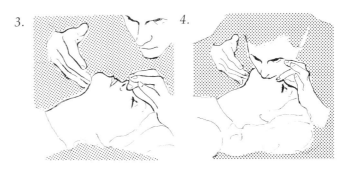

The kiss of life

1. Lay casualty on his or her back, pull head as far back as possible.

2. Clear any obstruction from mouth, make sure tongue is forward.

3. Pinch nose to close it, take normal breath.

4. With lips around casualty's open mouth exhale forcibly to inflate chest. Allow chest to deflate then continue.

fast: about ten to twelve breaths per minute is the breathing rate for an adult; twice this for a child. If the patient shows no signs of breathing under his own steam, do not give up hope too soon; there are cases of the kiss of life being successful after as long as an hour of trying. But if the patient does start breathing on his own, roll him over quickly. He will almost certainly vomit, and if he is lying on his back when he does so he will choke, and all your efforts to restore life may have been in vain. This rolling over is the most important moment of resuscitation, an action which must not be forgotten. Once you have got him breathing normally, get him into a warm bunk, get him to drink some warm tea or coffee, and keep him there for at least twenty-four hours. And keep more than an occasional eye on him, for the danger of collapse hasn't passed just because he is breathing again.

Broken bones
If you have to deal with a broken bone, don't try to set it. This is something much better done later with the help of an X-ray photograph. If it is a simple fracture of a limb, straighten it out as well as you can and get splints onto it, making sure that the splints are well padded on the inside. (Inflatable, clear splints are also now available.) Don't try to move the victim until the splints are in place and firmly bandaged. If it is a compound fracture, which means that the bone has broken the skin and is protruding through it, cut away the clothing and clean the wound with disinfectant before applying splints. Don't try to bandage broken ribs; you may well do more harm than good if you do. In all cases of broken bones, abandon your cruising plans and make for the nearest doctor.

Cuts and wounds
If you have to deal with cuts or other wounds, first establish whether the bleeding is venous or arterial. In the first the blood is dark red and oozes out of the wound; in the second it is bright red and comes out in spurts. Treat a venous wound by cleaning it with an antiseptic solution and using a pad and bandage, or a plaster if it is small, while it is still bleeding. An arterial wound is treated by stopping the flow of blood before it is dressed.

The quickest method to stop bleeding is strong, direct pressure on the wound itself. Grab the wound and squeeze, and keep on squeezing for as long as fifteen minutes. Send someone else for a compress or do without it for a time. Do not release pressure frequently to see if the blood flow is easing up.

As soon as possible, and without releasing direct pressure, get a compress bandage and place it under your hand. This will absorb some of the blood and aid in clotting. Try to raise the bleeding portion of the body so that it is higher than the heart, which lets gravity help stop the flow.

If direct pressure doesn't appear to be working, try to find the artery feeding the wound and apply pressure there, too. However, do not stop direct wound pressure.

About tourniquets: they work and they are dangerous. According to the American Red Cross, '. . . the decision to apply a tourniquet is in reality a decision to risk sacrifice of a limb in order to save a life.' If you must use a tourniquet, make sure it is at least 2in (5cm) wide. Place it just above the wound and tighten down using a stick as a lever. Note the time you applied the tourniquet by either writing it directly on the patient's skin or clothing or attaching a note that will travel with him. *Do not* loosen the tourniquet once it is applied.

Another good technique to halt or slow bleeding is to use an air splint. These clear, plastic envelopes can be blown up around a wounded area and can exert considerable overall pressure to control bleeding.

Shock
One of the things that many first-aiders often fail to realize is the incidence and effect of shock following an accident. A great many people seem to think that once you have sorted an accident out and dressed the wounds, the worst is over and a stiff tot for the patient is the order of the day. Some sort of shock follows every accident, and if it is intense, some patients can die of it. Quite a few people display no symptoms of shock after an accident even though they will inevitably be suffering from it to some degree. You can diagnose shock from such symptoms as pale lips, grey face, a cold sweat, a weak or unnaturally fast pulse, or a tendency to vomit. So, after any accident and the relevant immediate treatment, deal with any shock by lying the victim down flat on a bunk without

a pillow or cushion under his head, keep him warm with a blanket, and give him hot tea or coffee to drink. And don't give him that stiff tot until you are sure that the shock has worn off.

Stomach pains
Unless you happen to be a doctor and know about diagnosis and treatment you may occasionally come across some diseases on board which you can't recognize and so can't treat. But there are some where your guess can at least be informed.

Any pain in the stomach or lower intestinal area should receive your full attention. *Do not* pass it off as indigestion. Do not give pain-killers to your patient – they can only mask the problem. Do not give enemas to relieve pain.

Diarrhoea
Stop all food intake for at least six hours and begin large amounts of isotonic-type fluids (Coca Cola, weak tea). Avoid dehydration. Pepto Bismol can help as it contains compounds that decrease fluid output.

Vomiting
Stop all food intake for at least four hours. Then start taking isotonic fluids or a mild sugar solution in small frequent amounts.

Seasickness
There is, so far as I know, no known cure for seasickness though there are various proprietary medicines which are advertised as specific. Fatigue, diet, fear, time at sea, roll, pitch, yaw, surge, or any combination of all these can produce seasickness. What is actually happening is called neural overloading: fluid in the semicircular canals in your ears reacts to change in balance and orientation. When you are on board a boat, sometimes too many contradictory signals reach this internal stabilizing machine and it begins to shut down. In time the system will sort itself out and you get your sea-legs.

It is excellent therapy to do something that involves concentration or a view of the horizon. Steering is good medicine.

The only other advice about seasickness I can give is that since it is always less uncomfortable to be sick on a full stomach than an empty one, try to encourage the sufferer to get something down inside him even if it is going to come up again shortly afterwards.

Frequent small nibbles of bread or biscuits, barley sugar, sips of hot tea or soup, are better than trying to stuff him with a slap-up meal.

Fortunately most people who know themselves to be prone to seasickness don't often offer themselves as crew members in cruising yachts, but in some cases the joys of sailing soon outweigh the painfulness of seasickness, particularly as the sea can't be rough for ever. I suppose such sufferers deserve the sympathies of the luckier ones with strong stomachs, but seasickness is not a pretty sight, and the removal of one member of a working crew in conditions when usually all are needed is hardly likely to endear him to his companions. But be patient with him, and when the sea goes down no doubt he will dig in as efficiently as the remainder if he hasn't been discouraged by your scowls during his period of incapacity. If he is up on deck and needs to vomit, slap a safety harness on him or get a line round him and secure it inboard. It is very dangerous to let him be sick over the side unsecured.

First-aid kit
Of course every yacht should carry a comprehensive first-aid kit, well stocked with bandages and dressings and the simpler universal drugs for making up such things as eye lotions, treatment for burns, calamine lotion for sunburn, kaolin, aspirin, mild painkillers such as codeine, and so on. It is better to be overstocked than understocked, but stick to the simpler drugs whose action you understand. Illness at sea is no time to start experimenting with exotica in the drugs world.

Many years ago I crewed in a Fastnet race with a tearaway skipper who believed in getting the last inch out of his yacht and his crew. He had an idea that ocean racing was a relatively sedentary occupation and likely to lead to constipation. Naturally, a constipated crew could not give of its best, so every morning there was a compulsory issue of something resembling a small nuclear bomb, known in those days as a 'number nine'. Maybe his boat was the overall winner of the race because of them, but it was a drastic affair. However, despite this experience, I would suggest you keep some sort of laxative in your first-aid kit – albeit something a bit more gentle and civilized than a 'number nine'. Constipation is no fun on a long cruise.

CHAPTER 11

Laying up and fitting out

I suppose that the natural sequence of these two annual practices would be fitting out a yacht at the start of the sailing season and laying her up for the winter at the end of it. But I am going to take them in the reverse order because so much of the work of fitting out in the spring will depend on how much has been done to the yacht when laying her up at the end of the season.

Even boat owners who sail in waters where winters are mild enough to allow sailing all the year round need to take time out between seasons to carry out maintenance and repairs. Many people in Australia and New Zealand, for example, choose the cooler weather of early winter or spring to do this work, although they usually keep their boats in commission through the winter.

Where to lay up

The first decision to be made is where you propose to lay your yacht up and the second is how much of the work involved you feel you want to do yourself and how much you will leave to experts. This, I think, must depend to a certain extent on what you have experienced during the season, particularly whether any radical weaknesses, which will involve structural renewal, have revealed themselves. I am sure that these are best done in the boatyard where all the proper facilities exist, but if you have nothing that is structurally wrong, there is no laying up or fitting out work that you cannot do yourself if you feel so inclined. And of course if you can do it all under your own steam, it will certainly save you a lot of money, for no good boatyard these days is cheap.

There are several possible places in which to lay up your yacht: under cover, supported by legs on a hard, in a mud berth, on her own moorings, or in a marina.

Under cover

If you lay up under cover it will almost certainly be in a boatyard (for which there will obviously be a charge), and if you intend to work on your yacht yourself during the winter and early spring, you will also need to get the agreement of the yard to do so. (You will need to get similar agreement in a marina.) One advantage of having the yacht hauled up under cover is that the whole hull is exposed so that work on any part of it can easily be undertaken. But the only time full hull exposure is really needed, unless other repairs are required, comes when you are fitting out in the spring and need to apply anti-fouling paint. If your boat is wooden-hulled and you lay her up under cover you may find some of the seams opening up as she dries out, but they will take up again when she goes back into the water after fitting out.

On a trailer

In these days of large boat trailers, it is possible that you can lay your yacht up under cover in your own home. If it is your intention to trail your keel yacht home, you will need the services of a boatyard with a slip to haul the yacht onto her trailer out of the water, but that should be all the outside assistance you will need.

The new breed of trailable yacht – or trailer-sailer – really comes into its own for laying up as it can be kept at home and worked on during the week. However, even trailer yachts need special attention if they are to be laid up through the winter or for any lengthy period. First make sure the boat is being properly supported on the trailer and

Trailer-sailers save money by taking boats home.

BELOW RIGHT: A home-made cradle can be useful when storing a boat ashore.

Properly made covers are essential in colder climates where snow can fill a boat through the smallest cracks.

the interior is properly ventilated. Ideally the boat will be covered and set up so that any water that collects in the bilge will drain away or be removed regularly.

On a hard
Your next two choices – supported by legs on a hard or in a mud berth – are really alternatives that depend on the nature of your local coastline. (Neither system is much used in North America.) I would find it difficult to believe that if a mud berth were available, anyone would want to lay his yacht up on a hard, supported by legs. But if there is no mud, it is not difficult to lay up on a hard beach.

You need four stout spars, long enough to reach from ground level to well above deck level of the yacht, and they need to be planted firmly and also held steady by guys so that they cannot move. They also need to be positioned so that the forward pair is abreast the foremast and the after pair abreast the cockpit, and each should have a tackle fitted on the top. Bring your yacht up between the two pairs at the top of high water springs, hook the lower blocks of the tackles to the chainplates or other convenient places, and then set up the tackles so that the yacht is held upright. Some older yachts are in fact fitted to take legs with holes bored through the topsides (plugged when not in use). The legs are bolted on through these holes, and being held rigidly in place by the bolts, provide all the support required to hold the hull upright.

In a mud berth
A mud berth, found mainly (if you are lucky) among the mass of small creeks along any low-lying shore, at one time cost you nothing, but nowadays you will probably be paying rent if someone owns the foreshore. Here again, you bring the boat up at the top of high water springs and settle her down as high up as she will go in the mud. Unless it is very hard mud, which appears to be a contradiction in terms, she will soon dig herself a hole shaped to her hull where she will lie happily upright throughout the winter. But you must moor her up with chains or wires secured to posts driven into the ground (or you could use anchors in place of these), one on each bow and one on each quarter, making four in all. This is to guard against a freak high water, which occasionally occurs

when a strong onshore gale holds up the outgoing tide so that the following flood tide is swollen by the water that failed to get away. If you are lucky with your mud berth, you may find the adjacent saltings firm enough to support a gangplank so that you can get on board dry-shod throughout the winter.

On your own moorings
If you lay up on your moorings, the only precaution you need to take is against floating ice. It will only damage a wooden hull, and if you have one of these the best protection is a couple of stout planks screwed to one another to form a V shape and secured at the bow just above and below the waterline. It is surprising how much damage to wooden planking even a thin film of ice can do when carried along by the tide, particularly when it lasts for a week or so.

In a marina
If you moor in a marina, the boat will very likely remain in her own berth during the winter, to be lifted out only for attention to her bottom.

Provided the winter temperatures are not too severe, you can prevent ice from forming by hooking up a bubbler system that will agitate the water around the boat's hull. There are two basic types of bubbler systems available – the agitator type and the compressor type. The agitator type consists of a sealed submersible electric motor, propellor, power cord, and mounting pipe. The motor is filled and sealed with a special dielectric oil and no further lubrication is required. The motor is mounted on the pipe and then lowered into the water to the proper depth. The power cord is waterproof and is attached to the pipe with waterproof electrical tape.

The compressor system usually consists of an electric compressor, temperature sensor and control, leader hose, bubbler hose, safety valve, purge valve and other necessary fittings. The compressor unit pumps air to perforated hoses creating the necessary circulation with air bubbles rising from the hose to the surface.

Masts
Wherever you lay your boat up, if you have a wooden mast you will need to lift it out

A boom tent helps keep essential parts dry when laying up afloat.

with a pair of sheerlegs rigged on deck, or by a boatyard crane if it is too long and heavy to be lifted with sheerlegs. A metal mast can be left stepped in position (unless of course you are laying up under cover) and it will come to no harm provided the mast rigging is stainless-steel wire. But I would prefer to lift the mast no matter whether it is wood or metal, or the rigging stainless or galvanized, as the winter is the time to examine all the rigging, standing as well as running, and you won't be able to do this thoroughly if you keep your mast stepped.

Hull covering

There is one other thing you must do when you lay your boat up in the open, and that is to rig a ridge pole along the whole length of the boat, about 3–4 ft (1–1.2m) above deck level for choice, and rig a waterproof tarpaulin or awning to cover the hull. This covering should reach down well below the topsides and be held in place with synthetic rope passed completely under the hull. You can work these down even when lying in a mud berth without any great difficulty. And make

sure that when you rig the covering you leave an opening both forward and aft so that the air can circulate and ventilate the yacht.

This is most important, as without ventilation you can easily get dry rot in a wooden hull or rust in a steel one.

Moveable gear

The next step in laying up is to remove all gear from the yacht which might be affected by damp and take it home, or to local storage if you have no suitable shed or garage.

Label all the bits of rigging you take home so that no confusion can arise later. The electric battery needs to go ashore as it will require an occasional charge during the winter, and if you have any electronic equipment that operates on dry cells the batteries should be removed (put in new ones when you fit out in the spring). Your sails will go home with all the other gear, but if they are very dirty and you are unable to cope with them at home, you will find that many sailmakers have laundry facilities.

Engine

Attention to the auxiliary engine is important to prevent deterioration during the winter months. If you think it needs a mechanical overhaul, it will of course have to be lifted out, but apart from that you can do all the normal maintenance work with it still on board. If you have a petrol engine, run it for a few minutes and squirt some oil into the air intake just before you stop it, then remove the spark plugs and pour a little oil into each cylinder; turn the engine over by hand for a few revolutions and then replace the plugs.

In the case of a diesel engine you can also leave a little lubricant in the cylinders but you should not inject any into the engine before you stop it. According to the number of hours the engine has run during the season you might wish to drain the oil in the sump and gearbox. If you do it is advisable to fix a notice on it saying NO OIL so that you are reminded before you start the engine again.

If the engine is sea-water cooled you should ensure that the whole unit is drained from the lowest point in the system, and if you have access to flush it with fresh water so much the better. An engine with indirect cooling will probably have anti-freeze in the fresh-water system, but if not it must be completely drained.

With a petrol engine it is best to drain the fuel system completely, including the tank, to avoid accumulation of water through condensation and you can clean the filters at the same time. In the case of a diesel engine, unless you believe that the fuel system needs a complete clean out, it is best not to interfere with it since it will not take in water through evaporation and condensation as will a petrol engine. The diesel is however extremely sensitive to foreign matter and entrained air in its fuel system, so it is best simply to fill the tank right up, add the appropriate amount of diesel fuel stabilizer and leave the system intact. If you have had a falling-off in performance or a smoky exhaust, the injector or injectors can be removed for recalibration, as can the fuel pump, but this is specialized work requiring proper equipment and clinical precaution against the ingress of any foreign matter. You are strongly advised to get the assistance of the appropriate service agent who will be equipped to give proper attention to these components and reinstal them.

Stepping the mast with a crane.

A wipe over with an oily rag and some grease on any linkages will complete the protective treatment for the engine but other maintenance jobs recommended by the maker's instruction manual, such as renewing the filter elements, should be carried out when you are fitting out.

Tanks, heads and bilges

Next, empty the fresh-water tank and drain the pipes and the heads. This is necessary in case there is a freeze-up during the winter which could result in burst pipes or even a burst tank if it is left full of water. You will not in any case wish to leave water to stagnate in the system. Pump out the bilge and get it as dry as possible before you start to scrub down as much of the inside of the hull as you can reach, not forgetting the bilges themselves, the insides of the lockers, and every other corner you can get at. You will need to give the bilge another pump out after this, then mop up any remaining water lying around with a sponge. Most important, fix all doors, including locker doors and lids, in the open position, and if possible lift up part of the cabin sole. This will ensure that everywhere is ventilated and will remain dry during the winter months.

Metal parts and timbers

Door hinges, winches and any other metal parts that move should be oiled, and if you have any brasswork on or below deck give it a coating of petroleum jelly.

You may save yourself much work later if you attend to any parts that need revarnishing. Any varnish that has been scratched or damaged during the sailing season is an open door for moisture and any subsequent frost will extend the damage considerably, necessitating a lot more scraping and rubbing down in the spring. It is wise to attend to these areas promptly by rubbing down and giving a first coat of varnish before the frost can make an entry. The top coat can then be put on with little preparation when fitting out.

GRP hull

If you have a GRP boat there is another job which is better done when the vessel is lifted out. Wash the hull thoroughly and apply gel coat or polyurethane to any deep scratches or abrasions after cleaning the affected area with dry rubbing-down paper. If dirt, oil stains and so on are difficult to remove they can be shifted with a mild rubbing-down compound, but don't rub down the gel coat except where you are touching-up damage. If you carry on from this immediately and wax polish the whole of the hull and any other external GRP areas you will have done

most of the work required on the outside of the hull before the boat goes back into the water and also given it protection during the winter. I always feel that as a general rule it is advisable to do as much as you can before the onset of winter weather – neglect at this stage can cause more damage than you get during the actual sailing season.

With all this done, you can say that your boat is well and safely laid up for the winter. Virtually all the moveable gear is out of her and she is an empty hull with only her fixtures left inside. All the rest – sails, running rigging, cushions, sleeping bags, cooking utensils, and everything else down to the boathook – is ashore, preferably at home where it will be easier for you to do all the winter work that will be needed.

Sails, rigging and spars

I have always found it best to try to pace myself over the winter work. The sailing season generally ends in the autumn and starts again in the early spring, leaving around five months in which to fit in the work needing to be done. At the top of my list I enter the things that are beyond my capacity and need to be sent away. Among these are any sails for repair or alteration requiring the skill of a sailmaker and any wire rigging that needs replacement – this should only be necessary very occasionally if the rigging has been properly looked after.

First, then, look through your sails and put aside those for major repair and any that need renewal. Get them to your sailmaker as soon as you can to avoid disappointment, for the usual rush of orders in the spring may overwhelm him. If you have taken out your mast and the standing rigging – and this is not always necessary, it depends upon how recent and how thorough the last overhaul was – go through the wire rigging, looking especially for rust and broken strands if it is galvanized; bend it backwards and forwards if you see any sign of rust and if a wire snaps mark the whole length for renewal. There won't be any rust if it is stainless steel rigging but if you find a broken wire you will need to replace the whole length. Look carefully at the spliced ends whether tucked or Talurit (Nicopress) and particularly where the wire runs into the splice.

1. *After several seasons'*
use a fibreglass hull may
become dull and scuffed.
2. Spray painting
restores the shine.

RIGHT AND FAR RIGHT: It is sometimes necessary to go aloft to inspect the rigging, and this is the correct way to do it. The man in the bosun's chair helps to lift himself by the rigging; this is also an insurance in case the chair should slip. One man turns the winch and keeps his eye on the man in the chair, while the third man 'tails' the winch and watches that the turns are properly made.

Look through all your running rigging – warps, hawsers, and odd lengths of rope. Be ruthless and condemn any rope that is getting frayed or long-jawed, (rope in which the twist has been pulled out through continual use and has not resumed its normal tightness of lay). Don't keep any such rope; either cut it up into lengths for making baggywrinkle or ditch it completely. One of the worst faults of many yachtsmen, I have found, is to keep lengths of suspect rope in the belief that it may come in useful some day. If you do this, you can be sure that it will let you down one day and, in the malign nature of things, will choose to do so at the very moment you need its strength most. Make a note of all you have condemned and put in a replacement order with your yacht chandler.

Another home job is to strip down all blocks with metal sheaves and grease the pins, though there is no need to touch any blocks with Tufnol sheaves as these require no maintenance. Clean down all rigging screws and apply a little grease thinly to their threads. If you have any wooden spars at home, strip off the varnish, rub them down with sandpaper and revarnish.

General repairs

The next step I would take is to look in my diary and put aside four or five weekends to spend working down at the boat. If you have any small repair work, do this first. If you want to strip down the heads, a pump or part of the engine, or overhaul the cooking stove, do this next. Also take a look at your anchor chain, clean it and wipe it over with an oily rag. If you notice a worn link in the cable or suspect a weak one take out that length of chain between the joining shackles. You might be able to get a blacksmith to re-place the worn link, but if you do, it won't be galvanized, so if you have a galvanized chain it is probably best to cut out the link yourself and replace it with a galvanized join-ing shackle, remembering that the bow should face forward.

Preparing for painting

If you have a wooden boat you now start on the paint, burning off if necessary but other-wise rubbing down, stopping and under-coating. If you are down to the wood, don't do any more at a time than you can undercoat immediately – the outside air is not kind to exposed wood. And as you go clean up any mess you make before you leave the boat. There will also be the dinghy to repair, re-paint or revarnish.

These occasional visits down to the boat will not only ease the labour of final painting and varnishing in the spring, when you will have a mass of such work, but also reassure you that your yacht remains dry and properly ventilated throughout the months of being laid up.

Painting

By the time all this has been completed the old year should have turned and the new one will be under way. Now is the time to pray for a few days of still, settled weather for the last and longest of the fitting out jobs still to be done. It can't be done in rain, and wind is almost sure to spoil it – so make your prayers good and strong.

*Because of its poisonous
properties, old anti-
fouling should always be
removed with plenty of
water.*

I am assuming that every yachtsman who does his own laying up and fitting out knows how to wield a paint brush and is knowledgeable about the intricacies of laying on, laying off, and striking off, which I believe is the jargon with which professional painters describe what I call slapping on a coat of paint. All I can usefully say about painting and varnishing yachts internally and externally is that it will pay you handsomely to use the paint enamels and varnishes of one of the firms that specialize in the manufacture of marine paints. The paints are a good deal more expensive than household paints but they will more than repay their extra cost with their lower water permeability and greater hardness and durability. And if you are not an expert in their application, you will probably find that the manufacturing firm will be only too pleased to send you a manual explaining the correct method of applying them.

But there are one or two points about painting generally that are perhaps worth making. It does not help if you have to keep breaking off the actual painting job to look for a piece of sandpaper to rub down an uneven spot or a rag with which to wipe up any drips. See that they are all there before you start. And never try to burn paint off a steel hull, if you do you may blister the inside paint as thin steel is a formidable conductor of heat. The safest method for a steel boat is to use a chemical paint stripper that can be neutralized with water. And finally, have a different paintbrush for every colour; it is a waste of time having to clean a brush in turpentine whenever you make a change of colour.

The most difficult part of painting a yacht is painting in the boot-top line. Nothing shows a yacht off better than a neat line that has a certain amount of sheer, though not as much as the deck line. If you are satisfied with the one you already have, all you need to take care of is that you don't lose it in the initial rubbing down or burning off and painting. Scribe it in a bit deeper if there is any risk of this. If you are not happy with the one you have, try some variations with a long, thin and flexible batten which you can secure to the sides with tacks. Always stand well away from the hull when you look at this new line, and when you are happy with it, scribe it in. Get the topside enamel on first, painting an inch or so beneath the line, and then cut the line in with the bottom undercoat and anti-fouling paint. If your hand is not very steady, use a strip of masking tape to protect the enamel above the line while you apply the bottom paint. It is important, just for the good looks of a yacht, that this line is sharp and not smudged or wavy.

It is here that you may come up against a small snag. Most yachts have their boot-top line a few inches above the actual waterline so that their topsides do not pick up the dirt that so often floats on the surface in harbour. You cannot use anti-fouling paint right up to the boot-top line if this is above the waterline as this type of paint is liable to flake when exposed to the air. You will need a special boot-top paint which you apply in a band extending from the boot-top line to a few inches below the waterline. It means cutting in two lines parallel to each other, and the paint will not be anti-fouling, but it sets very hard and will stand hard scrubbing to keep it clean and free of weed.

Naturally, when you are painting the bottom and topsides, you will have to bring your yacht up from her mud berth or moorings, if that is where she has been laid up, and get her up on a hard for the painting. And this is also the time to step her mast if you took it out when laying up.

You have now reached the final stage of fitting out. With the mast in her you can set up all the standing rigging and reeve the running rigging. Where you can, turn your ropes and wires end for end so that the wear is spread equally. You are ready then to bring down all the rest of her gear which you have overhauled during the winter or kept dry in store. When this is done, or perhaps when the mast is stepped, she will need to come alongside to fill up with fresh water. When she is afloat, you should carry out the normal trials and tests to make sure that everything is working, such as the auxiliary engine, the heads, and everything else that moves. If all is well, she is ready for the new season.

CHAPTER 12

Navigation equipment

This book is not intended in any way to be a manual of navigation; there are surely enough of those already in existence to teach a would-be navigator how to take bearings and sights, how to work them out and how to apply the results to a chart to give a position. All I shall discuss in this chapter will be the varieties of charts available to a navigator and the sorts of instruments he will need to get him where he wants to go.

The task of a navigator is to get his vessel safely and economically (that is, by the best available route) from the place of departure to the place of intended arrival. In the case of a sailing vessel this does not necessarily mean by the shortest route geographically, for the sailing man needs to consider prevailing winds and currents when he is planning a voyage. So if you are intending to go foreign in your cruising yacht, you need to do a bit of preliminary investigation before you weigh anchor and plunge off into the blue. Look for the areas of prevailing winds and see whether they can help you on your way and which ones will hold you back.

Charts and publications
Old pilot charts of the oceans, if you can get hold of a set, will give you the answers; if you can't find a set, the *British Admiralty Pilots* and *Sailing Directions*, published by the Hydrographic Department, will have much of this sort of information. Similar publications are produced by many other national authorities. *Ocean Passages of the World*, which you can get from most chart agents, is another publication that will be helpful with detailed information about weather and ocean currents.

As far as charts are concerned, my own preference is for British Admiralty charts, of which the main selling agent is J. D. Potter Ltd, 145 Minories, London EC3. They keep a stock of every Admiralty chart for every part of the world, and they have sub-agents who stock these charts in every major port. They also keep a stock of the *Admiralty Pilots*, mentioned above, and all other hydrographic publications. I have found these Admiralty charts give more information than any others, are extremely well engraved and printed, and that the paper used is tough enough to withstand a great deal of wear. They have, perhaps, two drawbacks for the yachtsman: they are not cheap and they are large, measuring up to 52 × 28in (132 × 71cm) overall for the largest, the chart area being 48 × 25in (122 × 63cm). But when folded in two, they can be stowed in a reasonably small space (charts should always be stowed flat, never rolled).

For Admiralty charts, local coastal charts and *Ocean Passages of the World*, sailors in Australia and New Zealand should contact their local Hydrographic Office or A Class Chart agent. The address of the Australian Hydrographic Office, which publishes the AUS series of charts, is 161 Walker Street, North Sydney, NSW 2060; that of the Hydrographic Office of the Royal New Zealand Navy (NZ Series), Burns Avenue, Takapuna, Auckland.

In the USA, harbour, coastal and ocean passage charts, available at numerous marine supply stores, are published by the National Oceanographic and Atmospheric Administration (NOAA), 6010 Executive Boulevard, Rockville, Maryland 20852.

There are smaller charts specially produced for yachtsmen, of which perhaps the most widely known in Britain are the Y series of charts, produced by Norie & Wilson of Glasgow. Similar spiral-bound series, produced in the USA by the Better Boating Association, are called Chart Kits. These measure 22 ×

15in (55 × 42cm) and are printed to be readable under a red night-light. They do not cover ocean passages, but are standard equipment aboard US yachts and with commercial fishermen. Another Norie & Wilson series, backed with blue paper and somewhat obviously known as the Blueback series, does cover most of the world though on a smaller scale than the Admiralty charts for Europe or the NOAA charts for North America, and in less detail.

I have often been asked what a yachtsman should do about the *Notices to Mariners*, which contain regular periodic corrections to charts caused by such things as temporary work in harbours and ports, the withdrawal of navigational buoys and lightvessels, alterations of the seabed, new wrecks which form a danger to navigation, and so on. The great majority of these notices really apply only to big ships, and a yacht that may draw only about 6 or 7ft (1.8–2m) is more often than not unaffected by them. When you plan a voyage, it is probably enough to read through the *Notices to Mariners* that have been issued since you last consulted them and make a list of those that might affect the charts you will have to be using. You should then be able to tell from the list which of them are likely to

be important to you and your yacht for the voyage you have planned and which are not, and if one or two do look important, get out the chart and put the correction on it. I have never found it necessary to do more than that; to enter up every correction on all your charts is a long and tedious labour unlikely to pay you any real and permanent dividends. It is largely a matter of degree; what is vital chart information for a super-tanker may not always be so vital for a small yacht.

Charting tools

Next come the navigational instruments you will need, first for the actual chart work and then for the art of navigation itself. All you need basically for chart work are a pair of dividers, a parallel ruler, a pencil and a soft eraser. The dividers you should get are the type you can use with one hand, bowed at the top so that you can open them by pressing the sides of the bow. As for rulers, I prefer a heavy brass or gunmetal parallel ruler with rollers, but the sliding perspex kind is equally efficient if you hold it on the chart with enough pressure so that it cannot slip. And unless you want continually to be bending down to pick up your pencil when it rolls off the chart table, get three-sided ones, either B or 2B so that they don't leave thin indentations on the chart when you rub out the pencil marks. These are minimum requirements, but it will make chart work easier if you add a course-setting protractor and a station pointer, both very useful for coastal passage-making.

Compass

Unless you already have one, I would suggest that you get a magnetic compass with the card marked in degrees rather than in points and quarter-points as it is easier to apply the variation and deviation corrections, which are always quoted in degrees. There are some sailing people who prefer a compass with a prism to magnify the lubber's line, particularly in yachts with wheel steering when the helmsman is directly abaft the compass; there are others who prefer a compass with a perspex dome which also magnifies the card; and yet others who swear by the grid type of steering compass. I have

Prime instruments for chartwork: dividers, protractor and chart.

found that the grid type is the easiest to steer by (particularly with tiller steering where you have the compass to one side and below you), even though it does mean altering the ring for every change of course, but this compass must be positioned so that you look down on it, otherwise it is difficult to read accurately.

But more important than the type of compass you prefer is where you place it in your yacht. It must, of course, be in a position where the helmsman can see it easily. If you can combine this with a position where you can get a good all-round view from it, so much the better as this will be ideal for taking bearings. You can often manage to find such a position in a large yacht but very rarely in a small one. So, if you can't mount your compass where you get an all-round view, you will have to take your bearings with a pelorus or a separate hand-held compass. It is a simple matter to make a pelorus from the compass rose cut from an old chart, mounting it on a wooden base, and fitting a brass strip with turned-up ends, each bored with a small hole, as your sights. If you set the card to the compass course being steered, you can read off the bearing as soon as you have aligned your sights on the object of which you want the bearing. But unless you are only an occasional sailor, it is far better to invest in a hand-held compass. You don't have to worry then if the yacht strays a little from her compass course while you are taking the bearing, which you would do if using a pelorus. The only precaution to take when using a hand-held compass is to keep it as clear as you can of all metal objects, including all wire rigging. Any metal in the vicinity produces deviation, and as you will never know how much it has produced, you will not be able to trust the accuracy of any bearings taken with it.

Deviation

Many yachtsmen, I fancy, do not worry about deviation in their compasses. It rarely runs to more than two or three degrees either side of the reading, and according to them, not many helmsmen can steer a course in a sailing vessel within that margin of error. But deviation does make a difference in coastal navigation when you are continually fixing your position by compass bearings, and as it is not difficult to work it out, I think it is always worth doing. The easiest way for a yachtsman is to borrow a corrected compass and mount it temporarily where no metal can influence it, perhaps on a wooden stool on deck, and line it up exactly with the yacht's fore-and-aft line. Then turn the yacht's head to each ten degrees all the way round the compass – you can get someone in a dinghy to tow the stern round if you are lying at anchor – and at each ten degrees read off both compasses. The differences will be the deviation of your own compass, and you can tabulate them on a card. If you find that your deviation exceeds about five degrees on any heading, it will pay you to call in a professional compass adjuster to alter the position of the corrector magnets in your binnacle. One small point to remember when applying deviation to a compass bearing: always use the deviation for the point of the compass on which the ship's head is lying and never for the compass bearing itself.

Variation

There is no difficulty in finding the variation; the compass rose on your chart is always slewed round to the variation in force when the chart was printed, and within the rose is printed the amount of variation, the date of printing, and the annual rate of increase or decrease in the variation. All you have to do is to multiply this rate by the number of years since the chart was printed and apply the results to the variation quoted on the chart.

When using a hand-held compass keep well clear of metal objects to avoid deviation.

A modern echo sounder fitted with depth alarm which gives audible warning of shallows. The depth alarm is a standby system, so only minimal current is used.

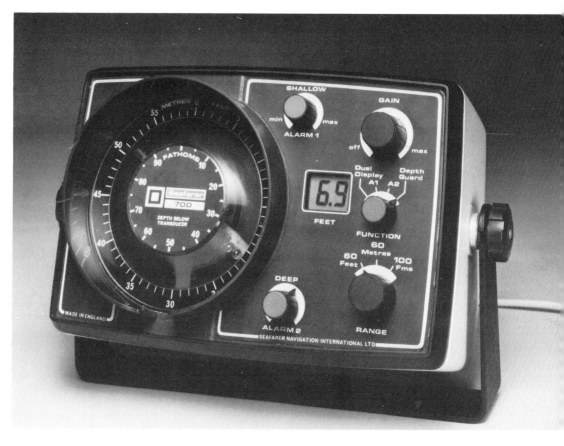

Sextant

You should have a sextant, for although many coastal passages may be made without one, it is not only useful for observation of sun, moon or stars if you are navigating deep sea but also for horizontal and vertical angles when navigating in coastal waters. Choose a robust one without too many additional frills, and although it is not quite so easy to read, I prefer a vernier to a micrometer for the minutes and seconds of arc; not that you will be navigating to seconds of arc in a sailing yacht. The only error you have to consider in a sextant is its index error, and you can easily find this by selecting some distant object on the horizon and bringing the direct and reflected image together. Your sextant should then give a reading of 0°, and if it does not, then the difference shown on the scale is the index error, either plus or minus according to which side of 0° your reading lies.

It is not easy to take an altitude of a celestial body with a sextant when there is any motion on a yacht, and it is only in a flat calm that you can count on having no motion at all.

Some people recommend using a bubble sextant which is supposed to give you a steady horizon and so make it easier to take a sight on a tossing deck, but I would much sooner persevere with an ordinary sextant whatever the difficulties, and am sure that in the end you will be able to get an accurate altitude.

The sextant used to be an expensive instrument; well made and in brass, it still is. However, dependable models are now available made in plastic and these are quite suitable for the coastal cruiser although the deep-sea sailor may prefer something more robust.

One essential when using a sextant is to know the exact time. Radio time-checks are helpful for synchronizing ordinary watches, or you can use a quartz watch – these are so accurate there is no need for radio time checks.

Log

Two other pieces of information you need for accurate navigation are the speed of the yacht and the distance run. There are several sorts of gear available for recording speed and distance. Most are electronic, but my own taste is for the sort of patent log you tow astern at the end of a plaited line. Very little can go wrong with it: it is accurate provided the rotator is kept deep enough in the water (you can make sure of this by giving it plenty of towing line), and of course it does not require any electricity to make it work. I have heard of the rotator attracting large fish such as sharks, who may consider it a tasty morsel much as a mackerel does a spinner, but I am confident that this is a rare occurrence. However, although I can vouch for the reliability of the patent log I nonetheless acknowledge that electronic logs are increasingly accurate and for many yachtsmen the best alternative.

Echo sounder (depth finder)

Another piece of essential information when navigating is the depth of water. Charts have soundings marked on them showing you the available depth at mean low water springs. Below the title of the chart it will be stated whether this is given in feet or fathoms: large-scale charts often give soundings in feet and small-scale charts covering larger areas in fathoms, but the more recent publications will have the soundings marked in metres and this will become universal for all Admiralty charts.

But if you are entering a harbour or navigating in shoal waters you can't know immediately what depth of water you have beneath your keel because it would require reference to both the chart and the tide table. So another essential piece of equipment to give you prompt information is the electronic echo sounder or depth finder. It is available with different displays – neon, meter or digital – so choose whichever you find easiest to read. It is more accurate than the lead line in inexperienced hands and has the advantages of speed and a much greater range; also, the read-out is continuous. After the compass and a good pair of binoculars (choose 7 × 50s – anything more powerful will prove impractical at sea), many yachtsmen would say that the depth finder is the most useful instrument aboard. It can be a very valuable aid to navigation in thick weather on coastal passages.

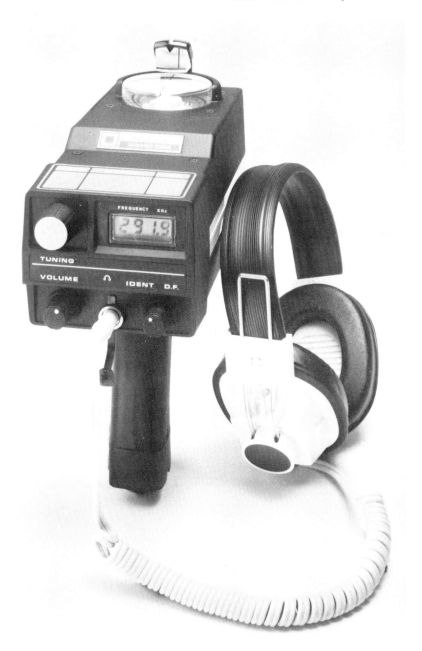

Radio direction finder (RDF)

The majority of cruising yachts today have a radio direction finder (RDF) for receiving bearings from radio beacons, some of these being of the compact, hand-held type. Most of the table-mounted models now have a built-in directional aerial instead of an outside loop and some have a sensor to eliminate

Hand-held radio direction finder with own prismatic compass. It is claimed to be accurate within 2°. Instrument has a digital readout, and the user can write group bearings on the casing of the instrument.

OPPOSITE: Spot-on navigation! Large genoas can make things difficult, but the man lying down on the bow is taking no chances.

Radar is becoming increasingly popular, although the small cruiser can have difficulty accommodating an aerial weighing up to 151lb (213kg).

the possibility of 180° error. They are becoming increasingly compact and efficient in their design but I would never try to navigate a yacht solely by fixes obtained from radio beacons. Although they can be most useful as a periodic check on more conventional means of navigation, and are certainly a real help in fog, they are liable to distortion at or around sunrise and sunset, often by several degrees, and are also unreliable when they cross land or cross the coast at a narrow angle. Still, if you choose beacons that avoid crossing land, particularly if the ground is high, you should be able to get a reasonably accurate fix if the angle of cut is fairly wide.

Hyperbolic aids
Radio position-finding systems such as Loran, Consol and Decca can be used by yachts, but require either special receivers or overprinted charts, or both. This limits their popularity. Also, few give universal coverage. More suitable, although expensive, is Omega, which can be picked up world wide. For the coastal yachtsman the most recent and useful innovation in this field is the Radio Lighthouse from which very accurate positions can be received using an ordinary transistor radio!

Radar

Radar is becoming increasingly popular. An enclosed scanner unit or radome with a low current consumption is suitable for sailing yachts (particularly two-masted craft where the scanner can be mounted on the fore side of the mizzen at spreader height). Short-range accuracy is the most desirable feature in a small yacht where the horizon may be only a few miles away – radar cannot 'see' further than that. Since radar operates just as well at night or in thick weather it is a most valuable aid in crowded waters, and its ability to give bearing and distance of vessels in the vicinity can often give the skipper welcome reassurance. The rigging requirements in small sailing cruisers obviously make it difficult to accommodate a radome and so for the time being only larger yachts can enjoy the facility.

VHF radio telephone

Another electronic facility now much in use is the small multi-channel VHF radio telephone transmitter and receiver which can be used ship-to-ship or ship-to-shore. Clearly this is a means of communication rather than navigation but it is valuable for a variety of purposes, not least emergency calls where plain language as distinct from a signal can give information as well as an alert.

Log book

Some yacht skippers go to sea with a proper log book, in which they regularly enter up information on navigation, pilotage, sea

state, weather, rig, boat behaviour and everything else! Such meticulous navigators deserve high commendation as their logs give them a permanent record of every voyage they make.I have known people at the other extreme who jot down the information on scraps of paper, transfer it straight onto the chart, and then destroy the evidence. No doubt this method works, but such navigators cannot conduct any post-mortems if things go wrong and they don't find themselves at the end of the day where they think they ought to be..

I must confess to a mild dislike of the formal log book with its large number of columns to be filled in, even though I recognize the wisdom and correctness of such a navigational record. I prefer a navigator's notebook which fits into a pocket and in which you can enter times, bearings, alterations of course, distances run, and all the other items of information needed to plot positions on a chart. It is a semi-permanent record which can later be summarized in the official log book. By this, I do not mean in any way that a log book is unnecessary. It is essential to keep one on board if you are cruising, as it is in effect the yacht's passport when you are going foreign. It is, I am sure, enough to write it up daily from a notebook without filling in all the multiplicity of columns watch by watch.

Leeward drift and currents

Finally, two small points to be kept firmly in mind when navigating a boat under sail. Don't forget that there is always a certain amount of drift to leeward when you are sailing and that you must allow for this when you lay off a course to steer. I have seen some yacht navigators carefully making the proper allowance for the tidal stream, applying variation and deviation correctly, and then wondering why they don't end up where this course says they ought to. An average allowance for leeward drift is about 5° in normal sailing weather, rather more when the wind is strong. If you forget to allow for it you will be miles out in your dead reckoning at the end of the day. The other point is that although you must work out the tidal streams and allow for them in coastal passages, they will cancel themselves out when crossing seas and oceans, so you can forget them until you are nearing the other side. But currents don't cancel themselves out. So try to work out your currents and apply them when ocean sailing in the same way as you would with tidal streams in coastal sailing. Both these small points are obvious enough when you think of them, but they are sometimes forgotten.

OPPOSITE: Red sky at night. Sky colourations are not the most reliable predictions but this orange setting sun, reflected through a dust-laden atmosphere, is a sign of good weather. (See next chapter.)

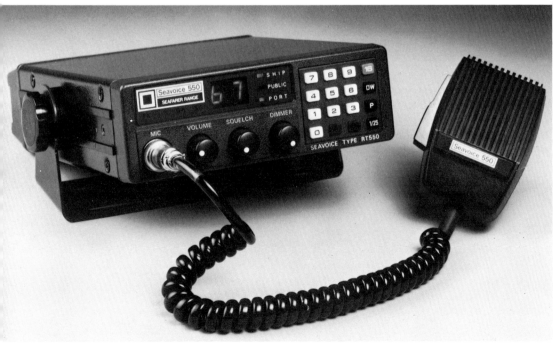

VHF radios are becoming smaller, cheaper and ubiquitous. This model has fifty-five international channels.

CHAPTER 13

Weather patterns and prediction

Meteorology, the study of weather patterns with the object of predicting changes, is something in which every yachtsman takes a great interest, even if his interest amounts only to listening to the local weather forecast to discover how wrong it can be. It is a complex and still inexact science, but with the growing number of reports now flooding into the various meteorological offices around the world, particularly those received from satellites which monitor conditions in the upper atmosphere and provide a continuous picture of cloud formations over huge areas, it is a science that is becoming daily more reliable.

This vast network of observations does not, of course, come to the yachtsman out at sea in his relatively small craft, but if he has some understanding of how weather patterns are formed and their effect on the wind and weather, he should be able to predict with at least some degree of confidence the sort of weather he can expect to meet in the next day or two, provided that the local pattern has not become too complex for prediction. It will always be something of a hit and miss affair, but the simpler and more obvious weather patterns should allow you to make generally accurate forecasts provided that you have the basic understanding to read and interpret the signs.

Atmospheric pressure

The real cause of all weather change lies in the property of a gas to rise when it is heated. Air is of course a gas, and when it is heated by the sun or by an extensive hot area such as a desert, it rises, creating an area of low pressure as it goes up. Colder air from the surrounding area flows in to take its place, and this action causes variations in the atmospheric pressure at sea level. The most important guide that any navigator can have to the probable behaviour of the weather in the immediate future is the atmospheric pressure in the vicinity of his position at sea.

So your most important weather-prediction instrument on board is a barometer, which gives you a continuous read-out of the current pressure. In a yacht you are unlikely to be able to hang a mercury barometer, which is the most reliable indicator of atmospheric pressure, but an aneroid barometer or a barograph will both do the job accurately enough. Of the two, I much prefer a barograph as it provides a visible picture of the way the atmospheric pressure is rising and falling, and this is something you need to know in any forecasting of change. But it does entail remembering to change the chart on the revolving drum every week and to keep the small receptacle at the end of the arm filled with ink. You can get the same picture if you plot out a series of readings from an aneroid and join them up, but you need to take plenty of regular readings.

Atmospheric pressure is measured in inches of mercury or in millibars, 3.4 millibars being equal to $1/10$ in of mercury. The average pressure at sea level is 29.9in of mercury or 1,013 millibars in winter and 30in or 1,016 millibars in summer. Variations above or below these levels indicate areas of high pressure and low pressure, and on the principle that nature abhors a vacuum, air from a high pressure area will always tend to flow in to fill a low pressure area. But because the earth is spinning on its axis and at the same time hurtling through space at an immense rate, the movements of air from high to low pressure areas are twisted so that they tend to blow round the areas instead of directly into the middle of them.

Anticyclones and depressions

There are two main weather systems in the general weather patterns – anticyclones and depressions. In the northern hemisphere an anticyclone is a system of wind that blows spirally in a clockwise direction around an area of high pressure, sometimes covering an area of immense size. In the southern hemisphere the anticyclonic wind blows in an anticlockwise direction, though still around a high-pressure area. The stronger winds blow at the outer limits of the anticyclone, gradually reducing in strength until at the centre they are very light or even nonexistent. Anticyclones in both hemispheres are fair-weather systems, with the wind never much more than moderate and the sky reasonably clear of cloud. They are slow moving, sometimes stationary for days on end. You can usually tell when you are running into anticyclonic weather when you see the barometric readings rising steadily and the sky clearing of cloud.

In a depression the wind blows in an anticlockwise direction around an area of low pressure in the northern hemisphere and in a clockwise direction in the southern hemi-

sphere. The winds are high and sometimes violent, frequently accompanied by heavy rain, and are strongest near the centre of the low pressure area where the barometric gradient is steepest. Depressions usually move fast at an average rate of about 25mph (40kmph), and the general signs of an approaching depression are a falling barometer, a backing wind and the formation of high cirrus cloud in the sky, the well-known 'mare's tail' sky so distrusted by sailors. Further indications of an approaching depression are a white luminous halo around the sun or moon, and low heavy cloud breaking up.

Buys Ballot's law

Depressions are bad-weather systems, and because the strongest winds are in the centre of them, you will if you are wise try to avoid taking your yacht there. You can find out in which direction the centre lies by applying Buys Ballot's law, a rough and ready method set out by a Dutch meteorologist of this name 120 years ago. If you find yourself in the path of an approaching depression, face the direction of the true wind and the centre of low pressure will be between 8 and 12 points (90°–135°) on your right-hand side if you are in the northern hemisphere and in the same angle on your left-hand side in the southern hemisphere. Knowing roughly in which direction the centre bears, you should be able to get out of its path. Starboard tack in the north, port tack in the south, could be the yachtsman's watchword when he anticipates a depression.

Barometric rises and falls

It does not necessarily follow however that because there is a rise in barometric pressure above the average level you can predict an anticyclone or that a fall foretells a depression. Provided that you are not sailing in the tropics, a rise or fall of three or four millibars above or below the average (1,013 millibars in winter and 1,016 in summer) are fairly normal and do not necessarily indicate any change in the current weather pattern. But a rise or fall of five or more millibars should arouse your suspicions. If you have a barometric reading of five millibars below normal, and the barometer then holds steady or continues to fall, you have a definite indication of a period of unsettled weather ahead of you. Similarly, a rise of five millibars above normal, with a steady or still-rising bar-

Being able to read a synoptic or weather chart will help to understand why past, present and future weather trends occur. The chart shows isobars, which are lines drawn through places of equal pressure. Where the isobars are close together winds will be strong; conversely widely spaced isobars indicate light winds. This chart shows a typical low-pressure system in the North Atlantic. It will be moving eastwards at considerable speed of between 25 and 40kt. The movement of this air will also create a temperature difference which in turn causes the cold and warm fronts to occur.

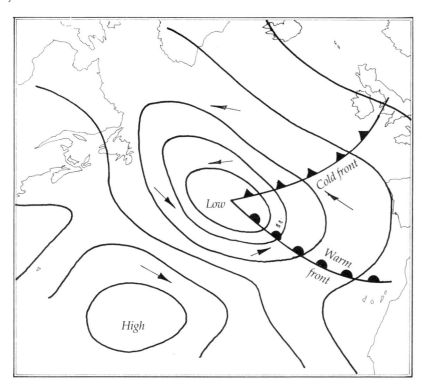

ometer, should make you believe that you are running into a period of fine weather with light or moderate winds.

If you are sailing in the tropics, a fall of three millibars is enough to cause you some concern, particularly if it persists for two or three days. When this happens you can be pretty sure that there is a tropical storm somewhere within a range of 250 miles (400km). The reason why a smaller fall in the tropics should make you suspect weather change is because variations of atmospheric pressure in those latitudes are generally limited to a small diurnal oscillation of no more than a millibar or two, so that a change of three millibars is quite a bit above the average.

Barometric readings can generally tell us some other things about the weather. If you have a reading of less than 1,000 millibars with the barometer falling rapidly at a rate of one or more millibars in an hour you can be certain that you will be meeting strong winds and rain; conversely, a rapidly rising barometer is a sure indication of fine weather for a day or two, which will be followed by a fall in pressure and unsettled weather. You can make other reasonably safe predictions from the behaviour of the barometer, which are best summed up in two simple rhymes every sailor should know and remember. The first is:

> Long foretold, long last,
> Short notice, soon past.

In other words, a steady fall in pressure over a long period will mean a long period of bad weather; a rapid fall indicates that though the weather will generally be severe, it will be over fairly soon. The second rhyme is:

> First rise after low
> Foretells a stronger blow.

This is a phenomenon common to all gales at sea, where the full force of the gale is felt after the centre of a depression has passed. The 'first rise' of the barometer mentioned in the rhyme indicates that the centre has passed and that the gale's full force is still to come. And gales with a rising barometer are invariably squally.

Even if we are aware of these general principles, most of us, I suspect, don't take the trouble to read the barometer frequently or accurately enough to work out what weather is in store for us. But it is possible to gener-

alize, and I don't think that you would go very far wrong if you associate high pressure with continuing good weather, low pressure with unstable and changing weather; a steady rise with good weather on the way, a steady fall with approaching bad weather; a rapid rise with an indication that the better weather will not last, and a rapid fall with a probability that stormy weather will be with you very soon.

Warm front

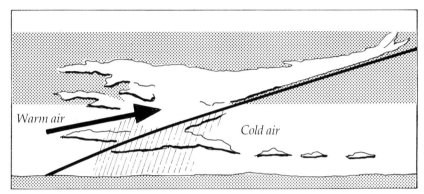

Warm front. A large wedge of advancing warm air overlays existing cold air. Usual signs: cumulus cloud scatters and dies to be replaced by thickening cloud and perhaps a fully overcast sky. Wind veers and increases, barometer falls steadily, strong possibility of rain.

Cold front

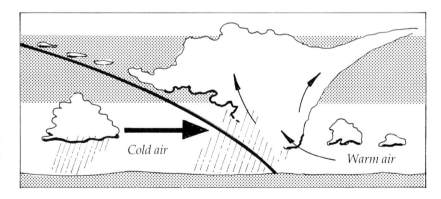

Cold front. Advancing cold air drives a wedge beneath existing warm air. Usual signs: barometer jumps; wind veers and increases with chance of gusts; heavy showers and line squalls.

Cloud formations

So much for what the barometer can tell us; now let us see whether we can try to predict anything from the shape and formation of clouds.

There are four main types of cloud formation – cirrus, cumulus, stratus and nimbus – and each of them may provide us with some information. There are in addition combinations of these four main formations which can also indicate the weather ahead. I don't think that cloud formations can give as positive an indication of weather change as can changes in barometric pressure, but this does not mean that you should totally disregard them.

Cirrus

The highest of the cloud formations is cirrus, which appears in the form of light wisps stretched across the sky. If there are only a few of them and they tend to disappear fairly quickly, it is probable that fine weather will continue. But if there are many and they appear to group themselves in long streaks radiating from a common centre, then the probability is that a depression accompanied by strong winds is approaching. If cirrus cloud takes the form of a thin film covering the sky which produces a halo round the moon at night, you can be pretty certain that violent weather is coming your way and you would be wise to prepare for it.

Cumulus

Cumulus cloud is the one that looks like masses of puffed-up cotton wool billowing upwards in the sky. Most people take it as a sign of fine and settled weather, and when it behaves itself, disappearing in the heat of the summer sun, it is just that. But if it appears to increase at the end of the day, it should be taken as an indication of a change in the weather; and if it builds itself up into large pyramids that look as though they are toppling over, you can confidently expect thunder.

Stratus

The lowest of the cloud formations is stratus, and in general it has little information for the seaman. It usually appears as a bank of low-lying shapeless cloud, forming mainly in the evening and dying away at dawn, and though sometimes it may look dark and

1

4

6

Cloud formations that can aid forecasting

1. Cirrus 'mares tails', ice crystal cloud. Should this cloud spread to become a continuous veil across the sky, perhaps producing a halo round sun or moon, it would indicate the approach of a warm front.

2. Altostratus, water drop cloud which therefore does not produce a halo round the sun – here almost obscured. Rain soon, particularly if sky in 1 has changed to this sky rapidly.

3. Stratocumulus beneath altostratus giving rain near a warm front.

4. Small cumulus with crisp tops developing during the day in thermals over the land. Characteristic of a warm sector in summer.

5. Small cumulus with blurred tops characteristic of subsiding air in high-pressure weather and shallow thermals. Clouds likely to disperse soon, leaving cloudless sunny day.

6. Large cumulus with billowing, crisp top and dense white colour indicating glaciation and imminent shower. Typical of unstable air.

7. Cumulonimbus at limit of convection, with top spreading out into characteristic anvil shape and bringing showers. Anvil cirrus of adjacent shower cloud visible in left of picture.

8. Sea fog, formed by condensation from air passing over a cold sea surface which has a temperature at, or below, the dewpoint of air.

213

threatening, it doesn't mean any harm. The only time it can tell us anything is if, as dusk is falling, its top edges look torn and twisted to windward and it meets cumulus cloud as it advances across the sky. The probability then is that a spell of bad weather is on its way.

Nimbus

The last of the main formations is nimbus – the rain cloud. It is the darkest in colour, sometimes even inky. If it has a hard lower edge which is broken with vortex-like wisps and is moving fast, it indicates a line squall coming with the cloud. If you see this approaching, don't hesitate; turn towards it to meet it bows on unless you have time to get the sails off the yacht before it reaches you.

There is still a bit more you can guess from clouds in connection with the weather, as much from their general nature as from their shape and actual form. When they look nice and soft and reasonably low you can expect fine weather with moderate breezes; when they have hard edges and look a bit oily, you can expect the wind to increase in force; when they are small and black, rain is certainly coming.

Fog

Sometimes you can foretell fog, which is in effect cloud that has formed at ground level. Cloud is formed when air is cooled below its saturation point, and this happens when warm, moist air is blown over a cold sea, which cools the lower layers of the air. So you can expect fogs at sea mainly in the spring and early summer when the sea is still cold and the adjacent land areas have been warmed by the sun. You can also expect to find fog in those areas where there are cold ocean currents. It is the temperature drop that causes fog to form, so that if you have a wind which has been warmed up by blowing over a warm area and then cooled by blowing over a cold area of sea, an area of fog should form. Mist, of course, is no more than thin fog – the difference between them is purely one of degree. Most people accept a visibility of about 1,000yd (915m) as the borderline between the two: above that visibility it is mist; below it is fog.

Weather lore

All the above are, possibly, the more scientific ways of trying to predict changes in the weather; there still remains what is generally known as weather lore, expressed in old beliefs and old wives' tales – or, for our purpose, old sailors' tales. Some of them work; some of them don't; but as they are usually expressed in jingles they are fun to contemplate and there may even be more than a grain of good sense in using them. Some of them repeat what we have already learned from looking at the clouds, such as:

> Mackerel sky and mares' tails
> Make tall ships carry short sails

This is the cirrus formation of long, radiating streaks of cloud, which as we have seen may indicate the approach of a depression with strong winds. Another of these well-known rhymes runs:

> When the wind shifts against the sun,
> Trust it not for back it will run.
> When the wind follows the sun,
> Fine weather will never be done.

These are the typical wind shifts associated with a depression (first two lines) and an anticyclone (last two lines) in the northern hemisphere (the other way round in the southern hemisphere).

A similar rhyme which more or less describes conditions in a depression runs:

> With the rain before the wind
> Stays and topsails you must mind,
> But with the wind before the rain
> Your topsails you may set again.

As you enter a depression you will often experience rain accompanying the warm front before the cold front catches it up, a phenomenon known as occlusion. This indicates that the strong winds of the depression are still to come.

If you have sailed into these winds without experiencing the rain of the warm front, occlusion has already taken place and the strong winds of the depression are passing and you are sailing into an area of steadier winds.

Some of these weather jingles seem to have little or no basis in normal weather prediction methods based on prevailing weather patterns. If you live in the northern hemisphere, you may have heard this one:

> If the wind is north-east three days without rain,
> Eight days will go by before south again.

Oddly enough you often get long periods of north-easterly weather in European waters when the wind refuses to budge; it is I believe something to do with the habit anticyclones have of remaining stationary, as opposed to depressions which always move along smartly. But I would doubt if you could accept this as an adequate forecast, or at least not a good enough one to bank on.

Two more charming little ones are:

> When the sea-hog jumps,
> Stand by at your pumps.

and

> Seagull, seagull, sit on the sand,
> It's never good weather when you're on the land.

The sea-hog is the old name for a porpoise, and it used to be believed among sailors that porpoises could foretell a coming storm and would jump out of the water for joy at the thought of all the extra fish that a storm would sweep in towards them. As for seagulls seen inland, people still believe that they fly inland to escape the discomfort of a storm at sea. I think it is more probable that they come inland (a) during the ploughing season because it's easier to pick up a worm than to dive down and catch a fish, (b) during the breeding season because they can't build their nests on the waves, and (c) because they've discovered an inland sheet of water where people throw them bread and other scraps. Seagulls never seem to me to be unduly worried by bad weather at sea.

Radio forecasts

Almost every yacht these days carries some form of wireless reception on board, and it stands to reason that official weather forecasts must be more accurate than your local ones based on barometric readings, cloud formations and jumping sea-hogs simply because they have much more detailed data to work on. So if they predict a gale while to you everything looks set fair, act on the assumption that they are more likely to be right than you are. But there may be occasions when you are sailing out of wireless range of official forecasts (in mid-Atlantic perhaps), and there will be an obvious bonus for you if you have enough of the rudiments of weather prediction at your fingertips to keep you out of the path of the fiercest storms. Don't forget Captain MacWhirr (mentioned in the Preface) and his horrid fate.

Not many yachtsmen try to take this business of weather forecasting too seriously, probably on the grounds that if the expert can get it wrong so often, what chance has an amateur of doing better? Besides, it is a distinct chore obtaining the information on which reasonable forecasts can be based, and whatever information you get will be infinitesimal in comparison with what comes into the national weather centres from weather ships, satellites, and a host of other sources.

Most nautical almanacs provide a list of stations all round the world which send out weather broadcasts, together with their frequencies and times of broadcasting. And for the long-distance voyager in all parts of the world it is well worth listening regularly to the stations that cover the area in which you are, or shortly will be, sailing. If you don't speak the home language of your chosen sailing area, it may not be much help to receive a broadcast in that tongue. I would suggest, however, that you do continue to listen to them regularly, for it is surprising how quickly you will begin to get the hang of a forecast in a foreign language. The meaning of words used most frequently for wind speeds, directions and sea states can be acquired with familiarity.

To avoid the feeling of despair you get if you only remember to listen to a weather broadcast just as it is finishing, it's a good idea to keep an alarm clock near the radio and set it for the next forecast. Or better still, you may have a radio that will automatically switch itself on with its own built-in clock, or even switch itself on and begin recording the forecast to play back later. This will enable you to take your own weather notes at leisure and not have to sit alongside the radio with pencil and pad and perhaps miss a vital figure because someone asks you a question at the crucial moment. North American sailors may happily avail themselves of two full-time VHF weather channels. If you have time, it is worth making your own weather map, from the notes you have taken, of the entire system covered in the broadcast. This will enable you to track existing lows, or areas of disturbed weather, and subsequently check their behaviour by keeping watch on your own barometer and on the wind direction and cloud patterns overhead.

World weather patterns

Generally speaking, the weather of the world is, so to speak, left behind by the earth as it spins. This means that weather is passing continually from west to east, and the prevailing wind is off the Atlantic Ocean in Europe; off the continental land mass in US waters, and in Australia off the Indian Ocean. Carrying this a bit further, the western coast of Europe therefore becomes a lee shore and the eastern seaboard of North America a weather shore. You can therefore generally reach up and down the eastern American shore as the prevailing wind blows across it. This is, in turn, doubtless the reason why the traditional American rig is the schooner, which is so admirable for reaching. In the same way in the southern hemisphere the unfriendly rocks of Western Australia are buffeted by westerlies (making it a lee shore). Beyond Australia the huge waves of the Great Southern Sea, the longest fetch in the world, build up under the prevailing westerlies towards the narrows of

Cape Horn, which is therefore so difficult to pass from east to west.

Imposed on this 'left behind' pattern on a global scale is the influence of the sun. Where the sun's rays are vertical, the earth gets hottest. This occurs in a belt round the earth: above the equator at the equinoxes of March and September, moving north to the Tropic of Cancer in June and south to the Tropic of Capricorn in December. Here the air is rising because of the heat, and drawing in supplies of cooler air beneath it as it rises. You might expect these supplies of cooler air to rush straight in towards the equator and, relative to outer space, they do so. But since a person on the earth's surface is himself hurtling through space from west to east with the spinning of the earth, the apparent wind that he feels is not straight towards the equator but coming in at an angle. In the case of the northern hemisphere the result is the North-East Trade Wind, so called because it hastened the sailing merchantmen with some degree of certainty across the Atlantic Ocean. In the southern hemisphere the result is the South-East Trade Wind, which brought the spice ships home from the East Indies across the Indian Ocean.

Air pressure over the cold North and South Poles tends to be high and, contrary to what one might expect, the air of the poles is often still and undisturbed for long periods, at least in summertime. And no doubt many Arctic and Antarctic explorers have been able to achieve their amazing journeys as a result of this fact. The late Major Tilman, one of the world's last explorers in the heroic sense, managed his many voyages because of this. And, of course, in calm weather you can be near ice without too much danger. In windy weather pack ice soon gets pushed away to a lee shore by the wind. Provided it is not also pushed down and trapped with the ice, a small boat can escape.

Between the high pressure of the polar regions and the low pressure of the equator (the region known as the doldrums) is an area of variable weather where cyclonic winds are frequent. Cyclonic, or circulating, winds are started by a wavy formation of the imaginary line that divides two weather systems. The wave becomes more pronounced, and as time goes by it 'breaks', much as a wave of water rears up as it approaches a shallow and then breaks or turns into a roller on the shore. Once the wind is actually re-

Pattern of prevailing winds throughout the world. Detailed wind maps are available and some knowledge of these expected winds is essential when planning an ocean voyage.

Prevailing winds

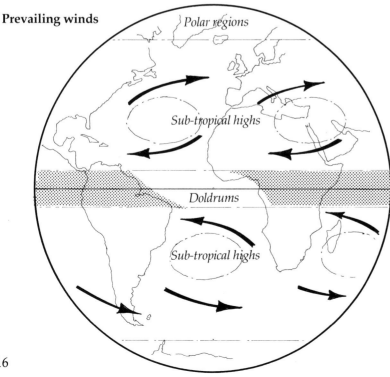

volving, centrifugal force tends to keep the area of low pressure in the centre. The winds are blowing towards the centre to try to fill it up, but as the earth revolves on its axis, the particles of air furthest from the equator receive less impulse from the movement of the earth than the particles nearest the equator. So, like a huge wheel with its lowest rim being shoved round by the moving equator, it begins to revolve, one way if it is in the northern hemisphere and the other way if it is in the southern.

Tropical revolving storms (hurricanes and typhoons)

This rather complicated analogy is included here because it applies not only to the usual 'lows' or cyclonic weather formations, but also to tropical revolving storms, which are, I suppose, the ultimate in what you can expect to have to face at sea in a small vessel. The reason why it is so important to remember which way the wind blows towards an area of low pressure is that if you do have the misfortune to find yourself at sea when a tropical revolving storm is approaching, you may be able to avoid the centre of the storm where the winds are highest by steering a course leading away from it as soon as the onset of the storm becomes apparent.

As I am sure everyone knows, the course taken by a hurricane (as this form of storm is known in the western Atlantic) or a typhoon (as it is known in the western Pacific) is completely unpredictable, and this is why they are so dangerous. It may veer east or west, double back on its tracks, or proceed as straight as a die for miles beyond its expected limits. Only one thing about it is certain, and that is that the winds in the vicinity of the eye of the storm are of unparalleled ferocity. Luckily, this form of disturbance seems to depend for its strength on the humidity of the revolving air, and once the humidity goes – for instance when it passes over dry land – the strength is usually dispelled. Hurricane and typhoon damage is worst on islands, which are engulfed in the pattern as it passes overhead, and on low-lying islands in particular, which are smothered by the waves beaten up by the violence of the wind. Never-

theless, regardless of these damage-prone islands, get out of the way of any such storm if you possibly can as they are no fun even in the open sea.

Taking into account the fact that the route of a tropical revolving storm is fairly unpredictable, you can, provided you have enough sea-room, apply Buys Ballot's law (this, as previously explained, states that in the northern hemisphere, if facing the true wind, the centre of the storm will lie on your starboard hand, and on your port in the southern hemisphere). You can therefore take it that if you are in the northern hemisphere and a tropical storm is approaching it is best to be on the starboard tack, and on the port tack if you are south of the equator.

Tropical revolving storms are confined to a predictable season and region. They occur in the western sections of the major oceans during the latter part of the summer: June, July and August in the northern hemisphere; December, January and February in the southern. So, if you are planning to cruise in these otherwise delectable waters, it would obviously be wise to work out your dates with the hurricane season in mind.

As an example of the kind of planning a seaman might make, let us take, say, a sailor from Britain wanting to enjoy the maximum cruising time in Caribbean waters. He might leave Britain in September, hoping to reach the Canary Islands in October. Or he might leave his departure until October, or even November, but he would then be asking for trouble in the Bay of Biscay, which is frequently encountering the onset of winter gales by that month. Leaving the Canaries in November, he would then sail south until he could pick up the North-East Trades, and they should carry him safely to the West Indies by January at the latest. So he would then get at least four months of good cruising before needing to think of finding a safe 'hurricane hole'.

Local winds

The world weather pattern is complicated on a local scale by the effects of land masses, their physical conformation and their temperature.

Land and sea breezes
The simplest illustration of this kind of modi-

fication to normal, expected weather is the common land and sea breeze – off the land at night, off the sea during the day. This is most likely in calm weather, particularly during a prolonged period of high pressure, because in such conditions the skies are usually clear and that means that during the day the sun will have the maximum effect in heating up the earth and that during the night there will be no cloud cover to cocoon the earth and retain its warmth. Since the earth warms and cools much faster than the sea, the air rises over the land as the morning sun gets hotter, and air from the sea is drawn in to replace it. At night, the reverse takes place. The earth cools quickly after sunset, while the sea retains its temperature, and air from the land is drawn out to replace the rising air over the sea. So you sail out of harbour against a breeze in the morning, and back to harbour against a breeze after dark. Or, if you are sailing along the coast, you may be on one tack during the main part of the day and on the other tack, still sailing in the same direction, by night. But there is never any venom in these breezes, and all that can happen is that you may be becalmed as these breezes replace each other. When sailing in the Adriatic, I have often found that you can almost set your watch by the regularity with which one breeze fades and the opposite breeze builds up. One other small point to notice about them is that they may often modify a prevailing wind.

Mistral

Land masses can have a constricting or expanding effect on wind movements, and the Mediterranean, especially in the western half, is peculiarly susceptible to these dangers. Conditions can change from a complete calm to a tearing wind in the space of a few moments, and all the while the sky remains a deceptive clear blue with no warning signs to help the hapless weather prophet.

One of these winds is known by the French as the Mistral, and it is a result of high pressure in the Atlantic coupled with low pressure in the central Mediterranean. The wet wind moves across central and northern Spain, funnelling between the central plateau and the high Pyrenees, then it spews out into the wide spaces of the Golfe de Lyons. Here it seems to acquire added beef as it blows across that particularly saline sea, producing short, dangerous seas almost to the coast of

Africa. These can be vicious waters in which to sail at times, because here you can sometimes get a breaking sea which is so much worse than breaking crests.

I learned an early and very valuable lesson in the Golfe de Lyons many years ago during a single-handed passage from Ajaccio to Toulon when, after a heavy buffeting, I began to have doubts whether the boat could stand the strain. My boat taught me that I need not have feared for her strength and ability to take punishment, and that if there were any weak link, it lay in me and not in her. I found, too, that if you have confidence in the robustness of your boat and its gear, it seems to transmit itself to your own handling of the boat so that you don't make the silly mistakes, or the wrong decisions, which can lead to deep trouble.

Katabatic squalls

Katabatic squalls are really blocks of cold air, if one can imagine such things, falling down off high ground. Barlovento (Portuguese), Tramontana (Italian), Meltemi (Greek), Bora (Yugoslavian), all these names would seem expressive enough to warn the voyager that the locals know the form and have found out how to live with it. These squalls are generally unpredictable and violent but do not normally last long. You can sometimes get a little warning of their imminence if you notice a sudden and unexplained drop in temperature.

Katabatic wind

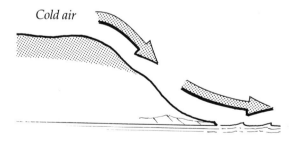

Cold air

Katabatic wind is a local wind often experienced along high coasts or in fiords where the air above is cooler and therefore heavier than air below, and so rushes across the sea speeded up by the force of gravity.

It would be wrong to think from all the above that cyclones, Mistrals in the Golfe de Lyons, mountainous seas off Cape Horn, and Boras and their ilk are normal conditions with which the cruising yachtsman has continually to contend. They are exceptions rather than rules; nevertheless they do happen at times and so it is wise at least to recognize their existence. It would be equally wrong to think that all rough weather must be one of these exceptions and that if they are not in the offing, all must be set fair. You should expect some bad weather in any long-distance cruise, and while with a little luck you can avoid a cyclone, you will be incredibly fortunate if you don't sometimes sail into bad patches of strong winds and big seas.

Bad weather always seems more frightening than it proves in the event. The seas may look particularly ferocious when you go doubtfully to the harbour entrance and stare gloomily at them from solid ground. Of course, if the morning's weather forecast has predicted a contrary gale, it would be stupid to ignore the warning, but it should always be remembered that our sailing forebears actually used to pray for a favourable gale. And to miss one might well prove to be a profligate waste of free motive power. So unless it is patently impossible, the best advice is to go out to sea and make the best of the weather.

This may sound pretty foolhardy advice, but you should take heart from all the thousands of small-yacht sailors, from Joshua Slocum in 1895 to the present day, who have proved that a small yacht of good design and sound construction is capable of surviving really ferocious gales. The basic structural design of a yacht is one of immense strength, and as long as she and her gear are sound she will not let you down when the going gets really bad. So when you feel you are up against it with an unrelenting gale, remove that doubt from your mind and concentrate entirely on your handling of your ship.

CHAPTER 14

Sailing regulations and etiquette

Rule of the Road

The authority for drawing up what we call the Rule of the Road is the International Committee for Safety of Life at Sea, and the official title of their rules is the International Regulations for Preventing Collisions at Sea. They are mandatory for every vessel that uses the sea, even if it is only under oars. You will find them set out in full in your nautical almanac, and there is no excuse for not knowing them. However, when yachts are racing they have additional racing rules laid down by the International Yacht Racing Union. When racing, yachts fly a square racing flag at the masthead to indicate that these additional rules apply, but the Rule of the Road overrides the racing rules in cases where a racing yacht may be approaching a sailing vessel that is not herself engaged in a race and is not flying a racing flag.

There are thirty-eight rules laid down by the International Convention, of which the last one lists some exemptions to the previous thirty-seven by allowing some vessels laid down before these rules came into force in 1972 a period of up to nine years to comply with the repositioning and visibility of some of the mandatory navigation lights carried at night. But there is nothing in these exemptions that need concern the skipper of a yacht. So let us have a look at those that apply to sailing vessels, but before we do so there is one important definition we need to recognize. If you are in a yacht and are using your auxiliary engine you are a vessel under power, even if your sails are still set. And as such, you must give way at sea to every vessel under sail only.

The rules that indicate which sailing vessel has the right of way when approaching another sailing vessel have been simplified in the 1972 regulations. Under the old rules you had to decide when a sailing vessel was running free, as one doing so had to give way to one that was close-hauled. This rule could cause confusion because it is sometimes difficult to decide the difference between, say, close-hauled and a close reach. All that is needed now is to know which tack you and the vessel you are approaching are on. All sailing vessels on the port tack – with the wind on the port side and the boom over to starboard – must keep out of the way of all sailing vessels on the starboard tack – with the wind on the starboard side and boom to port. It doesn't matter whether you are close-hauled, reaching, or running, or which point of sailing the other fellow is on; if you are on the port tack, it is your duty to give him the right of way and keep clear of him if he is on the starboard tack. If you are both on the same tack, the vessel to windward keeps clear of the vessel to leeward.

There is however one rule that overrides this, which is that an overtaking vessel must keep clear of the vessel being overtaken. It applies to *all* ships, and if you are under sail and coming up on an ocean liner, or anything else, you must keep clear of her, irrespective of which tack you are on. Overtaking itself is defined as approaching a vessel within the sector of two points abaft one beam and round her stern to two points abaft her other beam. So if you are not within this sector you are not an overtaking vessel, and the other rule applies.

A general rule is that a vessel under power gives way at sea to a vessel under sail provided that she is not using an auxiliary engine. But don't take this one too literally. When a vessel under sail is approaching or being approached by a large tanker or a container ship for instance, you don't argue as

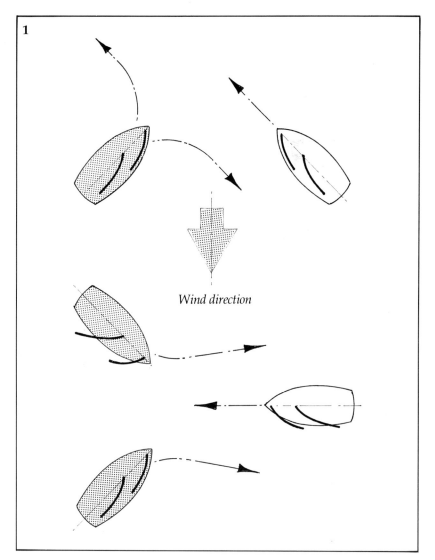

Wind direction

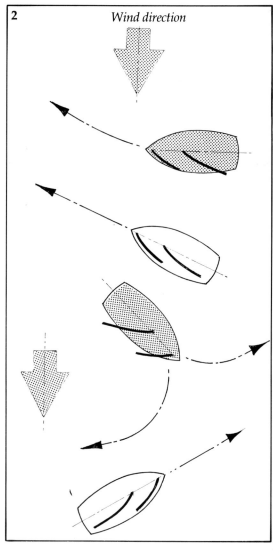

Wind direction

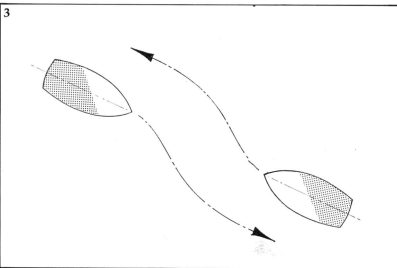

1. When two sailing boats meet on opposite tacks the boat on the starboard tack has right of way. The boat on the port tack (shaded) must get out of her way.

2. When vessels on the same tack meet and there is danger of a collision the boat which is to leeward has right of way. The windward boat (shaded) must take avoiding action.

3. When two power-driven vessels meet end on, or nearly end on so as to risk collision, each must alter course to starboard.

OPPOSITE: *In confined waters, the laws require small boats to keep clear of large vessels.*

to your right of way; you recognize that she is an unwieldy monster to manoeuvre and keep clear of her. In fact, in such a situation she is probably covered by the rules as 'a vessel restricted in her ability to manoeuvre', and if she is, it is your duty to keep clear of her. There are two other vessels of which you keep clear notwithstanding right of way – those not under command and those engaged in fishing. They can be recognized by the marks they hoist by day or the lights they carry at night.

The rules lay down another area in which the normal rights of way enjoyed by sailing vessels are modified. If you are sailing in a traffic lane of a recognized separation zone, you must not 'impede the safe passage of a power-driven vessel' if it is using the lane. This means that you must keep clear of her. I would doubt whether the skipper of any yacht would ever want to sail in a separation zone, except perhaps to cross it, as there is always plenty of depth of water inshore of the main traffic lanes for any yacht.

Navigation lights

At night, ships identify themselves by the lights they carry. The compulsory lights that a sailing vessel must exhibit are red and green sidelights and a white sternlight. The red (port) and green (starboard) lights are visible over an arc from dead ahead to two points abaft the beam; the sternlight is visible over the arc not covered by the sidelights, thus completing the full circle. You may, if you like, add to these compulsory lights two all-round lights at the masthead, red above green. It is wise to show these lights if you can; the other lights you are burning are all relatively low down close to the water (though it is wise to position them as high as you can), and the further away you can be seen by other vessels in your vicinity, the less chance there is of being run down by ships with drowsy lookouts. If your yacht is less than 34ft (12m) in overall length, she may carry a red and green combined lantern at the masthead in place of the sidelights, and if she is less than 23ft (7m) she may navigate at night without lights but with a strong torch or lantern which she must exhibit in sufficient time to prevent collision. Obviously, if you are between 39 and 23ft in length and are carrying a combined lantern at the masthead, you cannot at the same time carry the optional red and green all-round lights.

I cannot think that any yacht skipper in his

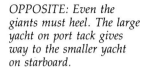

OPPOSITE: Even the giants must heel. The large yacht on port tack gives way to the smaller yacht on starboard.

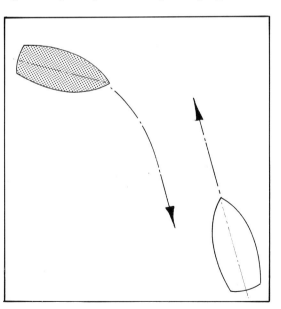

LEFT: When two power-driven vessels meet at an angle so as to risk collision the vessel which has the other on its own starboard side must keep out of the way, and must as far as possible avoid passing ahead, in other words the shaded boat alters to starboard.

RIGHT: An overtaking boat must give way to the boat it is overtaking. A vessel is considered to be overtaking when approaching from anything more than 22½° abaft the beam of the overtaken vessel.

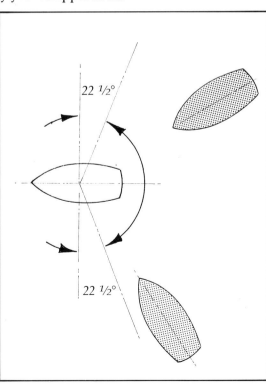

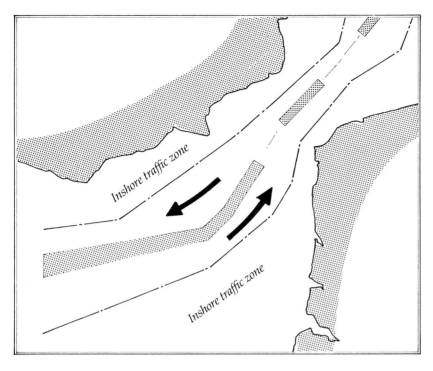

Traffic separation schemes have been introduced in busy shipping areas to regulate the flow of traffic. They are similar in principle to highways, with up and down lanes and a central reservation. This area must not be entered by any vessel other than those wishing to cross the zone, and this must be done at right angles. Except when crossing, small craft are required to keep out of the main traffic flow and to navigate within the inshore zones where no restrictions are imposed.

senses would rely on a torch or lantern at night unless it is impossible to burn the proper lights because of an electric breakdown or some similar reason. In the older days most yachts, I think, relied on oil-burning lamps for their navigation light, but thankfully those days are pretty well over and electric light has taken their place.

If you are having a combined red-and-green lantern at the masthead, insist on the bulb having a vertical filament as this is the only way that the cut-off point between red and green can effectively be differentiated.

You need to know not only the navigation lights that you have to carry under the rules, but also those that other ships must carry. The lights which they show at night are designed to enable you to judge the course the other ship is steering by means of the sectors through which they are visible. Obviously, if you can see a red light, a green light, with one or two white lights above them, they can only mean that a ship under power is steaming towards you; if all you can see is one white light, it must mean that a ship under power is going away from you. If you can see only one sidelight, red or green, and one or two masthead lights, it is not difficult to work out roughly which way the ship carrying them is steering. This is the kind of information you need to know when

navigating at night in company with other ships.

Don't forget that the lights you are carrying are there for other ships to see. They have a lower visibility distance than those of bigger ships, 1 mile (1.6km) for the sidelights and 2 miles (3.2km) for the sternlight. You are probably carrying them not much more than 6ft (1.8m) above sea level, unless in addition you are carrying the optional masthead lights. If you are sailing on a wind you may be heeling over, which will reduce the visibility of the lee sidelight still further, and at times you may even have a sail blanketing some of them, particularly if you have a spinnaker or a genoa set. So it is wise to make sure that the bulbs you use in your lights have a big enough wattage for their purpose and that the outer glass of all the lights is always kept clean and polished. The main purpose of all your navigation lights is to give other ships as much notice as possible of your presence, and they won't know you are there unless your navigation lights are bright enough for them to see.

Fog signals

If you are sailing in a fog and measure more than 34ft (12m) in overall length you must have a 'whistle' (a foghorn will do instead) and a bell on board, and sound the prescribed signal of one long blast of four to six seconds' duration and two short blasts of one second each every two minutes. If you are less than that overall length you need not make that signal but must make some sort of noise every two minutes. Every other ship in the vicinity is also making noises indicating the sort of vessel she is, and with luck you can pick up an approximation of her bearing from you from the direction from which the sound is coming. But don't rely entirely on the ability to do this, as apparent sound direction can be quite badly distorted in fog. Unless you are in a tearing hurry to get to your destination, it is far better, I always think, to make for shallow water where you can anchor until the fog lifts. As a vessel at anchor you have to ring a bell for five seconds every minute, but even this is better than risking your yacht in waters where there may be a fair amount of big-ship traffic which you can't see. And since all ships now carry radar, I get the impression that a lot of big-ship skippers, relying on this means of seeing in the dark to give them due warning of approaching danger, seem, in fog, to become afflicted by a form of 'motorway madness'. All ships should of course reduce speed in fog, but not all of them seem to obey this normal precaution.

Because these skippers rely on their radar to show them the position of adjacent vessels, it does not mean that you can rely on them as well. A yacht of comparatively small freeboard does not show up well on a radar screen and can very easily be confused with the wave returns, or clutter, which every radar operator expects to see on his screen. So if you must continue on your course in fog, hoist a radar reflector to the masthead. It will give other ships a more reasonable chance of recognizing what you are in time to avoid disaster.

Flags

International Code signals
As well as knowing the sectors and colours of navigation lights and the meanings of the various combinations, you should be prepared to recognize and read signals made in the International Code. Most nautical almanacs have a coloured representation of the flags and the meanings of single flag hoists; there are publications in all languages which give the full code meanings of two and three flag hoists. I am sure that every yacht engaged in long-distance cruising ought to carry a full set of International Code flags, which includes the numeral flags and substitutes, and of course a code book as well. But I often wonder quite how valuable these flags really are in a smallish yacht, as the individual flags themselves will probably be too small to be read at any distance, and the code is designed for distant signalling. There are forty flags and pendants in the International Code, and if they are to be large enough to be seen at a distance they will take up a fair amount of precious space on board. And, of course, you will also have on board three or four ensigns, particularly those of any foreign countries you may be visiting, and a few club burgees. But if you do carry a set of International Code flags on board, it is essential that each has its individual stowage in a lettered or numbered pocket or pigeonhole and that after use it is returned to its proper stow-

age. You can't really afford the time to sort through a heap of flags for the one you want each time you plan to make a signal.

Ensigns and burgees
Every British yacht must by law carry two flags on board – an ensign and a burgee – even if, because of her small size, she is not a registered yacht. The ensign (worn at sea) is the national flag of the yacht's nation, the burgee is the flag of her yacht club. In Britain all yachts of 15 tons Thames Measurement (TM) and over are required to wear their ensign on all proper occasions; yachts of less than 15 tons TM have the option of doing so or not, but must still carry an ensign on board at all times.

Normally, when a yacht is in commission, she wears her ensign while in harbour on a small staff at the stern between the hours of 8.0 am (25 March to 20 September) or 9.0 am (21 September to 24 March) and sunset. At sea, in a gaff-rigged boat, the ensign is worn at the peak of the gaff; in a bermudan-rigged ketch or yawl at the mizzen masthead; and in a single-masted bermudan-rigged boat about two-thirds of the way up the leech of the mainsail, using the nearest cringle to that position to hoist it to. This is the correct position, but a growing number of yachtsmen, holding that this position looks very like an

Every yacht should display its own national flag, either at the mizzen mast or the ensign staff, as here.

Flag stopping

Flags can be troublesome to send aloft, often wrapping themselves around shrouds and other rigging. One solution with most flags is to hoist them in a ball, although on a point of etiquette you are not supposed to hoist national flags and ensigns by this method.

1. Fold the flag in half, roll tightly then bind it several times with the underneath part of the halyard. Secure it by tucking the loop under the turns.

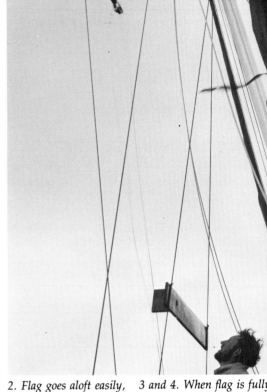

2. Flag goes aloft easily, avoiding snags.

3 and 4. When flag is fully hoisted, jerk the lazy part of the halyard to free the turns and the flag will break open.

Even the smallest vessel must hoist a courtesy ensign when she sails into a foreign port. This shows American Gerry Speiss after sailing his 10 ft (3 m) sloop across the Atlantic in 1979.

Squadron flag. The yacht ensign is flown at the stern staff when the boat is at anchor or underway under power. If the boat has an overhanging boom or some other reason why the staff cannot be on the centreline, the flag staff should be offset to starboard. Under sail, on a marconi-rigged boat, the ensign flies two-thirds up the length of the leech above the clew on the aftermost sail. On a gaff-rigged boat, it is displayed at the peak of the gaff on the aftermost sail. The ensign should not be flown from a stern staff when you are under sail. Only one other flag can be flown in place of the national ensign – the US Power Squadron ensign. It may be displayed only by members in good standing of that organization.

The yacht club burgee or private signal is flown at the truck of single masts and at the foremast truck of sailboats with more than one mast. It is displayed both when you are at anchor and underway. Only one burgee may be flown at a time.

Whenever a boat enters US waters from abroad, it must carry a yellow Q flag.

Dipping the ensign

There are certain customs at sea which ought to be observed by all yachtsmen. Unless in confined waters you should salute royal yachts (you can tell them because they fly a Royal Standard at the mainmasthead), all naval ships, and the flag officers of your own yacht club. And when you are at sea it is today a growing custom to salute any ship that is passing close to you, provided that she also is wearing an ensign. You salute in harbour by lowering the ensign down the staff until the lower edge is level with the rail, keeping it there until the ship you are saluting does the same. When she starts to rehoist her ensign, you do the same, but slowly so that you finish the job last. If you are saluting at sea, you lower the ensign about two-thirds of the way down from where it is flying, and once again the procedure of waiting for the other fellow to do the same is followed. All this is known as dipping the ensign. If you are being saluted instead of saluting, you begin to lower your ensign when you see the saluting ship lower hers, and follow the same routine of rehoisting yours before the other ship follows suit.

Flags at half-mast

I think that everyone must know that the

ensign being flown at half-mast, which it certainly does, now fly it from the same staff aft that they use in harbour. This has, I understand, been accepted as, if not correct, at least not incorrect.

The club burgee is worn, both in harbour and at sea, at the principal masthead, usually on a cane hoisted so that it extends above the truck, with a wire swivelling arrangement so that the burgee always flies freely without being able to wrap itself round the cane. It is flown only when the owner is on board or close enough in the yacht's vicinity to be in effective charge of her. Like the ensign, it is lowered at sunset in harbour, but most yachts keep it flying day and night at sea where it acts as a useful wind vane.

These are compulsory flags, but it does not mean that you have to keep them hoisted at all the relevant times. Obviously, if your yacht is sailing in sight of the coast or in waters in which there is a lot of shipping, they must be flown, but if you are making an ocean passage you would normally not bother to hoist them unless you sighted another ship approaching or until you were coming within sight of the coast.

In Australia and New Zealand it is not mandatory to carry these flags, although it is common practice. Likewise in the US, no flags are required by law. Most yachts do fly a yacht or US ensign, a burgee if the people belong to a yacht club, and possibly a Power

sign of mourning is a flag flown at half-mast. Every nation at times has days of national mourning when a member of a royal family or a president dies. Days of national mourning are usually decreed and announced in the press and by radio broadcast. It is no more than common courtesy to observe all such days wherever you may be. The proper way to fly a flag at half-mast is to hoist it fully first, and then lower it to the half-mast position. Private mourning, if unhappily you have a death on board or an officer of your yacht club dies, is observed in the same way.

Dressing ship

On a more happy note, there are days of celebration when ships are dressed overall. The birthday of a king, a queen or a president, or the day of a local yacht club's regatta, are such days. This is an occasion when you really need to carry the flags of the International Code of Signals for these are the flags that you string up. The line of flags extends from the stemhead, or from the end of the bowsprit if you have one, to the masthead, or all the mastheads if you have more than one mast, and then down to the taffrail or to the end of the bumkin if one is fitted. You choose the flags for their contrasting colours, inserting triangular ones at regular intervals, and to finish off you hang the pilot jack (which in Britain is the Union flag with a white border round it) vertically downward from the end of the bowsprit. You will find that you need a weight at the bottom of the fly to hold the flag steady; the weight from your leadline will do this for you. In addition to these International Code flags you should fly the ensign and the burgee in their normal positions – never include these in the actual line of flags when your yacht is dressed.

If the occasion for dressing ship is a national one rather than a yacht club regatta, many yachtsmen fly additional ensigns at each masthead, but if you do this you must make sure that your club burgee does not fly above the ensign at the main masthead. If you are abroad on an occasion of dressing ship, it is proper to fly the ensign of the country at the main masthead, and you would certainly get a few dirty looks if you did not do so.

One important aspect of dressing ship is to keep the line of flags really taut between all the support points. Nothing looks so bad as a sagging line of flags when a vessel is dressed overall, and you should keep an eye on it from time to time to make sure that the original tautness is maintained throughout the day. On occasions of dressing ship, you set up your array of flags when the ensign is hoisted in the morning, either 8.0 or 9.0 am according to the date, and the dressing overall lasts until sunset. Ships are never dressed overall in this fashion when they are at sea; instead they wear an ensign at each masthead.

Sailing into foreign ports

There is one final point of flag etiquette that affects all yachtsmen when they take their yachts into a foreign port. It is a recognized courtesy to fly the ensign of the country being visited in addition to that of your own country, and the proper place to fly it is at the starboard crosstrees. So if you are planning a cruise that includes visits to the ports of other nations, make sure you have the ensigns of those countries on board. In some countries it is compulsory to fly their national ensign in this position; and in those that have no such rule, I fancy that any skipper who ignored the custom would risk being looked upon with raised eyebrows. In this connection, you should not forget the occasional change of plan; the sort of thing that may happen, say, when you arrive at a harbour in south-west France and the owner of the yacht next door says, 'You ought to nip round the corner to Spain and try their brandy.' It is always wise to be fully prepared, and not have to put your hand in your pocket to invest in an ensign that you should have already had on board.

Distress signals

You should be able to recognize the international distress signals, not necessarily because you may need to make one yourself but in order also to be able to offer assistance when you see one displayed by another vessel. There are ten of them, and your nautical almanac will list them. Some will hardly apply if it is a yacht that is in distress – I would not expect any yacht to carry a gun on board to be fired once every minute – but there are others which any yacht can use, such as:

1. Red flares.
2. NC in the International Code of Signals.

3. A square flag above or below a round shape resembling a ball.
4. Raising and lowering your arms slowly and repeatedly.
5. MAYDAY by voice signal if you have a radio transmitter on board – you say it three times, then once more followed by the name of your yacht, your position and what your trouble is.
6. SOS by any form of sound or light signal.

A lot of people think that a national ensign hoisted upside down is a distress signal. It is not, but it would be worth having a shot at if you have no other means on board, since so many people still think it indicates that help is required. My own favourite is 'flames as from a burning tar barrel'; it always sounded fine when I could rattle it off in seamanship examinations at naval college many years ago, hoping to impress the examiner with my knowledge. But who carries a tar barrel on board these days?

Buoys and buoyage

You will need to know, too, the systems of buoys and buoyage in the waters of the various countries you are expecting to visit. There used to be a variety of systems, including the principal ones which were the lateral system where the buoys used indicated the port and starboard sides of channels as you enter in the direction of the main flood (tide) stream, and the cardinal system, used in conjunction with the compass to indicate the direction of navigable water. But now a new combined system, known as the IALA Buoyage System (International Association of Lighthouse Authorities), has been introduced which incorporates both lateral and cardinal techniques.

Lateral marks
Basically, the lateral marks being used in the IALA system are:
Port-hand buoys: red can or spar buoys, with (if fitted) a single red can topmark and a red light of any rhythm.
Starboard-hand buoys: green conical or spar buoys, with (if fitted) a single green cone topmark and a green light of any rhythm.
So if you are entering a channel from seaward you keep the green conical buoys on your starboard side and the red can buoys on your port.

Cardinal marks
The following buoys indicate the compass direction in which safe navigable water lies.

North cardinal mark: a black above yellow pillar or spar buoy with a topmark of two black cones one above the other, points upwards. If lighted, a white very quick (VQ) or quick (Q) flash.

East cardinal mark: a black with single yellow broad horizontal band pillar or spar buoy with a topmark of two black cones one above the other, base to base. If lighted, a white VQ flash (three) every five seconds or Q flash (three) every ten seconds.

South cardinal mark: a yellow above black pillar or spar buoy with a topmark of two black cones one above the other, points downward. If lighted, a white VQ flash (six) followed by a long flash every ten seconds or a Q flash (six) followed by a long flash every fifteen seconds.

West cardinal mark: a yellow with a single black horizontal band pillar or spar buoy with a top mark of two black cones one above the other, point to point. If lighted, a white VQ flash (nine) every ten seconds or Q flash (nine) every fifteen seconds.

There are of course other buoys, of different shapes and different colours, marking isolated dangers, middle grounds, spoil grounds, traffic separation channels, and so on. These are illustrated in most nautical almanacs. Until the IALA Buoyage System has reached all areas, it may be necessary to know the colours and shapes of the buoys of both the old and the new system. It sounds a bit complicated but in fact it is fairly straightforward, as all the buoys are very recognizable for what they are. If you have any doubts consult the nautical almanac.

Most buoys and lights are marked on the chart, and so by the time you sight a buoy you have usually already noted its position on the chart and are expecting to see it. The usual sequence is not that you sight a buoy and wonder what on earth its meaning is but that you look for a buoy because you know it ought to be there and what it indicates. And it is a relief to see it, as it proves that your navigation is as good as it ought to be. If a buoy appears to you as a question mark, it is not the buoy's fault (unless it is badly out of position); it is yours.

CHAPTER 15

Postscript on unseamanlike practices

During the last twenty years or so yachting has been one of the biggest of the growth industries. A natural result of this phenomenal growth is a big increase in the number of people who sail for their leisure and pleasure. Not all of them become accomplished yachtsmen; not all of them seem to think it necessary to acquire all those skills that a good yachtsman needs if he is to get the best out of himself and his yacht.

Quite the easiest task in a yacht is to steer it. Any mug can point it in the right direction. But carrying out a manoeuvre such as coming alongside, for example, requires real skill to fend off at the crucial moment, with strength deployed at exactly the right angle and exactly the right second, as opposed to standing feebly mewing at the helm while the crew stagger about under vague instructions and make an inelegant hash of the operation. Seamanship is not the mere ability to get a yacht from A to B with the minimum necessary competence; it is a question of handling her at all times in the best possible way, so that every detail is correct and controlled. And as this chapter hopes to illustrate, it is often as a result of neglecting the smallest details that the most truly unseamanlike disasters will occur.

It should, I think, be obvious even to a beginner that the lines by which you are made fast in harbour should always be ready for instant departure. You cannot foretell an emergency. I know a man who lost a large yacht because he made his lines fast with knots at their shoreside ends. When the wind blew up into the harbour he could not retrieve his lines quickly; one of them parted and went under the propeller, and that was the end. By morning the yacht was holed and sunk. If only the lines had been taken round the shoreside points and secured with

both ends aboard the boat he could have cast off quickly, even in the dark, and perhaps the yacht would be sailing yet.

Leave nothing to chance. I once waved goodbye to a man whose intention was to cross the Atlantic. He never reached the other side. A little research revealed that he probably sank during a storm between Casablanca and the Canaries. He had bought the yacht, an old one, without survey, stating that he was a trained shipwright, and that if anything should prove wrong with her he was quite capable of renewing it himself. She was iron-fastened. At a guess I would think that all the fastenings were good except at the little points you cannot see between plank and frame. During the storm the yacht was probably jarred by a big wave and sprang a plank or two. The end may have been quite agonizingly slow. It was a great and important lesson, that it is always wisest to employ a surveyor when purchasing any type of boat. If that man had employed a surveyor who knew what to look for, he might have survived. But even with his shipwright's training he did not know enough to spot a weakness which was to let him down when he was beyond any help. So how can the rest of us, who probably are not even shipwrights, be expected to spot the weak points?

That leak must have been terrifying for the doomed single-hander. Another one is engraved in my memory. We were crossing the Bay of Biscay and unlikely to come near any land for three days in no matter which direction we steered. The owner and his wife had been pumping a bit. After a while they requested the other two crew members and me to give a hand periodically. I began logging the number of pumps per hour, but when the owner discovered the entries in the log

2

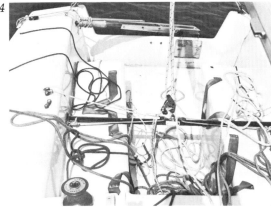

4

5

7

It isn't done . . .

1. . . . to moor outside another craft without putting out your own bow and stern lines.

2. . . . to sit on guardrails and pulpits.

3. . . . to put to sea with fenders dangling.

4. It is dangerous to leave lines uncoiled.

5. . . . especially over the side.

6. . . . and to walk on the low side when the boat is heeled.

7. . . . or overload the dinghy.

he was incensed. What help did I think that was, he asked? It was destroying morale. I said it was a very great help indeed, for the entries showed that we were pumping more and more each hour and that far from going away, as the owner hoped, the leak was actually getting worse and we were failing to keep pace with it. We would soon be pumping the whole time, and it seemed to me doubtful whether we could keep the boat afloat until she reached Spain.

It is difficult to argue with an owner aboard his own boat and so I turned in. At about three in the morning I was awakened by the owner surreptitiously raising the floorboards near my bunk and I joined him in the clandestine search for the point of entry. It involved a lot of pumping, a lot of mopping out from sumps with sponges, a lot of craning about with torches, a lot of unscrewing ceiling that had been lovingly assembled many years before. After a while we established that the flow was from forward to aft. Tracking it down we found it still flowing forward of the forecastle bulkhead and began to fear for the soundness of the stem timber.

Demolishing the lockers round the stem, we could actually hear the splash of water entering the hull. Then we found the leak – a small, feeble, badly designed, fractured plastic pipe supplying the flushing water for a modern lavatory installed recently in the forecastle, many years after the honest craftsman had put together the teak planking and oak frames of the hefty ship. That rotten little fitting nearly brought about the loss of the complete vessel and all her complement as well. It just goes to show that even the most well-found ship depends for its integrity on the weakest component. Never forget that if it should fail, all the plumbing inside the vessel below the waterline can sink the ship as quickly as can a sprung plank. So never hope for the best but always inspect every part with the gravest suspicion. Nothing but the best is good enough.

I know of one occasion when water froze in the cockpit drainpipe of a yacht left in a fresh-water canal over the winter. The ice split the pipe and when it melted the yacht settled quietly down on the bottom. An incident on another vessel happened after a lady had cleaned some nail varnish off in the heads using varnish remover. She left the bottle of solvent unstoppered. It tumbled down into the bilge when the yacht heeled and the chemical ate a hole in the resin of the GRP hull, as a result of which yet another yacht went to the bottom. (The cause of this loss was established by the insurance company.) It all goes to show that small things can be the cause of big disasters, and that attention to the minutest details is the only safeguard.

The real emergency is something that should occupy the mind of even the most confirmed optimist. When a vessel is sinking fast it is too late to begin thinking what to collect together before taking to the liferaft. Water, food, a knife, and fishing gear would come high on my list and, curiously enough, it is also important to have the ship's log, passports, and (sad to say) money. An acquaintance of mine who was run down, rammed and sunk by a French fishing boat at night told me that when he was eventually picked up from the water the fishermen could not be made to believe that they had really sunk the yacht and thought that a confidence trick was being played. None of the survivors had any proof at all with them that the yacht had ever existed. In another accident, three men were sailing a Folkboat at night, two below and one on deck steering. A Spanish fishing boat turned towards them, rammed them and smashed the yacht's planking, leaving them half-sinking. By a curious fluke the young man who had been steering leapt onto the fishing boat as it passed, thinking on the spur of the moment that that was his only hope of survival. He had no identification on him and could not convince the Spaniards that he was from a foreign yacht and that it was sinking. The Spaniards thought he was a stowaway. Fortunately, the young man was extremely tough, and by putting his hands round the fishing captain's neck and threatening to throttle him, he managed to get him to return to the sinking Folkboat and tow it to harbour. But it was a close thing and no compensation was ever paid. This is an extreme example but it proves the point that it is important to have the ship's log and identification to hand when they are needed.

Electricity on board
There are of course many tasks on board that are made considerably easier with the help of electricity, but there are also drawbacks that have to be borne in mind. Electric pumps for the bilges, for example, can be a tremen-

dous boon, but I would say that they should never be the only means of getting water out of the bilges and you should also fit a hand-pump as a back-up. Any electricity in the watery part of a boat can lead to electrolytic action which can wear away a metal skin-fitting in an astonishingly short time, and of course in a metal hull can actually lead to the wasting away and eventual failure of the hull plates themselves.

As for electric pressure pumps in the domestic system, I am afraid I have no patience whatever with people who cannot be bothered to pump the water they need for drinking or washing. I once sailed in an all-electric luxury yacht and we went to sea with the intention of going abroad. After a while the owner's wife went into the washroom of her luxury suite, put the plug in the basin, and turned on the fresh-water tap (faucet). Because the electric refrigerator had depleted the ship's batteries, the water did not run. So she left the plug in and the tap on. The wind was contrary and I managed to start the auxiliary. It immediately began charging, and the lady's tap began to run. Unfortunately she was no longer in her cabin to notice, and before long the fresh water was running merrily from the basin and into the bilge. A little later the wind freshened and I decided to hand the electric roller-furling genoa. Since the electricity there would not work I put the electric automatic pilot on and went forward to lower the sail by hand. While engaged on this task the steering went haywire and gybed the ship, nearly throwing me overboard. The automatic pressure system had pumped the water tank dry and shorted out the electrics. I went aft to take over the steering and a pale-faced husband came up from the saloon saying the ship was sinking and the water was already over the axminster carpet. The whole luxurious bag of tricks was one enormous all-electric rod with which to beat one's own back. We returned to harbour and went home gratefully.

The problem with any kind of sophisticated equipment is that, the more invaluable it is, the greater is the anguish it can cause if it lets you down. Sometimes, when I have met people prevented from going sailing simply because some piece of electronic equipment which they are incapable of mending themselves has gone on the blink, I have thought nostalgically of the sailing I enjoyed most of all – in a small boat with no engine and no instruments and where there was nothing on board that we could not mend ourselves.

I think that two important attributes needed to make a seaman are, first, that he should perform all his actions at the right speed (many people fail through trying to do things too fast) and, second, that he should be the master (rather than the slave) of every piece of equipment on board his yacht. There are many other attributes he cannot do without, of course, but it seems to me that these two are not well enough acknowledged. You hear a lot about courage, about respect for the sea, about versatility, endurance, skill and all the other human virtues which seamen, I am sure, possess in remarkable abundance, but in my opinion the two mentioned at the start of this paragraph are at least of equal importance.

I hope this chapter does not suggest that there is more gloom and disaster in sailing than there is pleasure. Of course the reverse is true, and there is nothing to equal the satisfaction of completing a good passage in the boat you have chosen yourself and with the equipment you have selected to go in her. In a way a voyage is a work of art. True, there is nothing left when it is over as there is when an artist has completed a painting, sculpture or piece of architecture. Nevertheless, the seaman too is an artist in his own right, and if his work is successful it will live on into posterity through the happy memories of all who shared it.

Acknowledgements

The author would like to thank Owen Lawrence-Jones for his overall assistance, and Mrs Roberts for typing the manuscript.

The publishers wish to thank Bill Beavis, Robbie Boutler and Lisa le Guay for taking many of the black-and-white photographs; and gratefully acknowledge the following photographic sources: Ajax News and Features Service (pages 199 and 229), Alistair Black (pages 50, 67, 118 courtesy of Sadler Yachts Ltd, 153 and 224), Bridon Fibres and Plastics Ltd (pages 60 and 61), Camper and Nicholsons Ltd (page 128), Dancer Yachts (page 188 top), Daniel Forster (pages 49, 117, 135, 136, 154, 171, 172 and 223), Goodchilds Ltd (page 18 top), Ambrose Greenway (pages 34, 35, 39 top, 51, 53 top, 83, 92 left, 149, 173, 174, 200, 205, 206, 209, 212 centre, 221, 233 top left, top right and bottom left), James Hall (page 15), International Paints Ltd (pages 13 and 193 both), Colin Jarman (page 75), Latchway Developments Ltd (page 175), League of Venturers (page 134), Maclear and Harris Inc (page 32), Benjamin Mendlowitz (page 68), Mike Peyton (page 23), Mike Rose (page 111), Schermuly Ltd (page 176 bottom), Searfarer Marine Ltd (pages 177, 202, 203 and 207), Westerly Yachts Ltd (page 129), *Yachting Monthly* (pages 14, 21 bottom, 39 bottom, 40, 94 left, 95, 107, 155, 157 top left, 168, 178 top left, 180 both, 181, 188 bottom left, 190, 191, 233 bottom right), *Yachting World* (pages 81 bottom and 82), and Yorkshire Television Ltd (pages 46 right, 71 and 233 below centre right).

Index

Page numbers in *italic* refer to the illustrations.